TUNE IN:

God's Voice. Your Purpose.

Bible Study

Chantel Ray Finch

COPYRIGHT PAGE

TUNE IN: God's Voice. Your Purpose. Bible Study

Disclaimer

This book is intended for spiritual encouragement and educational purposes only. The author is not a licensed counselor, therapist, or clergy member. Readers are encouraged to seek professional guidance for medical, psychological, or legal matters.

Published by

INTRODUCTION

Learning to Trust God's Voice Again

We are so excited that you are joining us on this journey of learning to hear God's voice. Before we dive in, I want to share a little about what this study will look like and how it's designed to help you get the most out of it.

Each chapter will include a few icebreaker questions, a Bible passage, an explanation of what that passage means, and then questions that help you apply it directly to your life. This study is meant to be both reflective and practical, helping you not just understand Scripture, but actually live it.

We strongly encourage you to do this study with a group. There is something powerful about processing God's voice in community, and you will almost always gain more insight when you walk through this with other people. If you'd like to join a group, you can visit the *Tune In: God's Voice* website and click on the tab that says "Join a Bible Study." We would love to help connect you with others who are doing this together.

Groups may be organized by state, by city, or even through Zoom, so no matter where you are, there is an opportunity to be part of a community. We would also love for you to bring this study into your church or small group if that feels like the right next step.

My hope is that this study helps you take your relationship with God to another level. This introduction actually shares something that isn't in the book. It's a bonus section that came to me after I finished writing, centered around the beauty and depth of learning to trust God's voice again. I truly hope you enjoy this journey.

ICEBREAKER QUESTIONS

1. Have you ever sensed God asking you to do something that felt uncomfortable or confusing?

2. When God's direction feels unclear, do you tend to wait, rush ahead, or try to regain control?

3. Has disappointment ever made it harder for you to trust what you think God might be saying?

BIBLE PASSAGE

Genesis 22:1–8 (NIV)

1 Some time later God tested Abraham. He said to him, "Abraham."

"Here I am," he replied.

2 Then God said, "Take your son, your only son, whom you love—Isaac—and go to the region of Moriah. Sacrifice him there as a burnt offering on a mountain I will show you."

3 Early the next morning Abraham got up and loaded his donkey. He took with him two of his servants and his son Isaac. When he had cut enough wood for the burnt offering, he set out for the place God had told him about.

4 On the third day Abraham looked up and saw the place in the distance.

5 He said to his servants, "Stay here with the donkey while I and the boy go over there. We will worship and then we will come back to you."

6 Abraham took the wood for the burnt offering and placed it on his son Isaac, and he himself carried the fire and the knife. As the two of them went on together,

7 Isaac spoke up and said to his father Abraham, "Father."

"Yes, my son?" Abraham replied.

"The fire and wood are here," Isaac said, "but where is the lamb for the burnt offering?"

8 Abraham answered, "God himself will provide the lamb for the burnt offering, my son." And the two of them went on together.

Question

1. How does Abraham's immediate obedience and his statement "we will come back" reveal both trust and expectation even when God's request makes no sense?

_____

_____

2. What does Abraham's response to Isaac "God Himself will provide" teach about speaking faith out loud before provision is visible?

_____

_____

3. What might God be asking you to place on the altar right now, and how would your response change if you truly believed God would provide what you cannot see yet?

_____

_____

Section 1 - When God feels silent, do you draw closer to Him... or pull away?

One day, God used something simple to reveal this to me. Something so every day and ordinary... but it hit me like a revelation. I was calling my son, Kyle... "Kyle!... and he didn't respond. Nothing. Silence. Now imagine Kyle was 500 feet away and couldn't hear me. If he truly wanted to hear my voice, should he walk farther away... or come closer? Obviously... he should move closer.

And then God gently whispered to my heart: **"Chantel, why don't you do the same thing with Me?"** When I can't hear Him... when He feels far away... when answers seem delayed... Instead of leaning in, sometimes I drift. Instead of seeking Him more, I get frustrated. Instead of quieting my soul, I let noise take over. Yet the truth is... when you can't hear someone clearly, the solution is simple: **You move closer.** God isn't pushing you away with His silence. He's pulling you closer.

Observation Questions

1. What everyday example does the story use to explain why someone might not be able to hear a voice clearly?

_____

_____

2. According to the section, what does God's silence actually mean, and what invitation is hidden in it?

_____

_____

Application Questions

1. When God feels quiet in my life, what is my natural tendency… to lean in or to drift away?

    _____

    _____

2. What would "moving closer" to God look like for me right now in a very real, practical way?

    _____

    _____

Section 2 - The White Noise in Our Lives

Every night before bed, I use a white noise machine. Some people use a fan, others the TV, others soft music. We've trained ourselves to fall asleep with noise in the background. But spiritually… many of us live the same way. So let me ask you: **What's the biggest noise in your life that keeps you from hearing God clearly?** Is it mental noise… the constant swirl of thoughts and worries? Emotional noise… stress, fear, anxiety, or busyness? Worldly noise… endless scrolling, people's opinions, comparison, distraction? Noise doesn't mean God isn't speaking. It just means *we can't hear Him through the static.*

Recently, after moving to Florida, I was driving from Bradenton to Sarasota and kept missing turns. Every wrong turn triggered the GPS to say: "Rerouting… rerouting!" And it hit me: **Have you ever felt like God was "rerouting" you?** maybe a door closed, a job fell through, a relationship shifted, plans you thought were perfect suddenly changed.

Sometimes the reroute isn't punishment. It's protection. It's redirection. It's guidance. The Holy Spirit whispers, "I'm rerouting you," and often we get frustrated instead of trusting. But God never loses track of the path… even when we do.

Observation Questions

1. What kinds of "noise" are named in this section that can make it harder to hear God?

    _____

    _____

2. How does the GPS "rerouting" story explain the purpose behind unexpected changes or closed doors? _____

Application Questions

1. What is the loudest source of noise in my life right now that may be drowning out God's voice?

   _____

   _____

2. Is there a recent "reroute" in my life that I've been resisting instead of trusting… and what might God be protecting or redirecting me toward?

   _____

   _____

Section 3 - Speak, Lord… I'm Listening

One of the biggest *aha* moments for me has been realizing how willing God is to speak to us…and that He actually gives us ears to hear Him. As I write this book, I never get over it. Anytime something confirms that I really did hear from God, I'm amazed all over again. The whole process is miraculous.

Communication is the essence of all relationships. My husband and I are so different in personality and in how we express ourselves. Our first seven years of marriage were rough…we even went through counseling just to learn how to communicate. Without communication, there is no real relationship. And it's the same with God. Hearing His voice and responding to Him is one of the most important things you will ever do. That's why I wrote this study…because walking with God always comes back to communication. It's not just about listening, but also about responding. And here's the truth…reading the Bible has always been the hardest way for me to hear Him. I was a math major, and I've always struggled with reading comprehension. Sermons are easier, but they're like "hand-me-down revelation." They're still good and valuable, but they came through with someone else. Reading God's Word directly…that's first-hand revelation. That's next level. It's not easy for me, but it's powerful.

It's like my son Kyle's hand-me-down clothes. We buy him nice things…not luxury brands, but better than average…and my sister's son gets them when Kyle is done. Sermons are like that: hand-me-downs. Still good, but not as powerful as hearing God's voice straight through His Word. That's what I long for more of, even though it's a challenge for me.

Here's the key: when you're discerning God's voice, it can't rest on just one thing. It's like a line of buoys guiding a boat...you want them all to line up. Scripture, godly counsel, circumstances, peace, and the Holy Spirit. If one of those is off, it's a warning sign. For example, if I felt peace about buying a luxury car but it would put me deep in debt, God's Word already says that's not wise. His voice always confirms itself through multiple channels.

Praying for something like a parking spot might seem trivial or unnecessary, but it serves as a powerful reminder that we can bring *all* things to God...big or small. Our doubts, worries, frustrations, and even everyday inconveniences are opportunities to communicate with Him. When we invite Him into even the little details of life, it builds intimacy and strengthens our relationship with our Heavenly Father.

When we moved from Virginia Beach to Sarasota, Florida, it was right in the middle of hurricane season. The very day we moved in, Hurricane Debby hit. The winds were so strong that it took four men to move a dresser that normally two could carry.

Right after Debby came, Hurricane Helene, and then Hurricane Milton. One of those storms knocked out our power for seven days. To make it worse, we had just remodeled our home and installed smart toilets that required electricity...so we couldn't even flush!

We needed a hotel, but of course, every single hotel in town was fully booked. We called everywhere, and every answer was the same: "Sorry, no rooms." Finally, Kyle looked at us and said, *"Mom, did you even pray about it?"* We hadn't.

So right there, we stopped and prayed together as a family. Within minutes, one of the hotels we had just called phoned us back to say a room had opened up.

Kyle was right...God wanted us to pray first, not last. That moment reminded me that prayer is never too small, never too late, and never wasted. I even pray for parking spots at Christmas...and now Kyle does too.

But sometimes, when we pray, it feels like nothing happens. That's when doubt creeps in. James 1:6–7 warns us that those who doubt shouldn't expect to receive anything from the Lord. Doubt is the enemy of hearing. I think of the story in 1 Samuel 3, when the boy Samuel kept hearing his name.

He thought Eli was calling him, but it was the Lord. Finally, Eli told him, *"Go and lie down, and if He calls you, say, 'Speak, Lord, your servant is listening.'"* That simple posture of faith is so powerful.

When I can't hear God, I literally pray that verse: *"Speak, Lord, your servant is listening."* It shifts my heart from doubt to expectation.

That hurricane season taught us more than how to prepare for storms. It taught us how to pray through them. We were completely exhausted from calling hotel after hotel, trying to find a room. Nothing was available anywhere. Then Kyle looked at us and said, "Why don't we just stop and pray?"

The moment we did, everything shifted. God opened a room where there hadn't been one before.

That night reminded us to never underestimate the power of prayer, even in the middle of chaos. It's the same with the small things too. Sometimes God's silence isn't rejection. It's an invitation. He's waiting for us to invite Him in.

When I pray, even for little things like parking spots, it's not because I think God needs my help to make something happen. It's because He wants to remind me that He's close. He cares. And He's listening.

At the end of the day, hearing God's voice is all about alignment. His Word, His Spirit, His peace, godly counsel, and the doors He opens or closes all work together. When everything lines up, you know you're on course.

If something feels off, don't rush. Wait.

That's what this whole journey is really about. Realizing that silence doesn't mean absence. God is always speaking. Sometimes through Scripture, sometimes through people, and sometimes through the gentle nudge of His Spirit.

Observation Questions

1. What does the section teach about the connection between communication and relationship—both with people and with God?

    _____

    _____

2. What factors are described as needing to line up when discerning whether something is truly God's voice?

    _____

    _____

Application Questions

1. Which area of communication with God do I rely on most—and which one might He be inviting me to grow in?

   _____

   _____

2. Where do I need to shift from praying last to praying first, even in the small or everyday moments of my life?

   _____

   _____

HEARING GOD – PERSONAL REFLECTION

Take a few moments to sit in stillness. Do not rush to answer. Let the questions linger. Let them surface what has been quiet beneath the noise.

1. God, where have I been asking for certainty when You have been inviting me into trust instead?
2. God, what part of my life have I been holding tightly because surrender feels costly or risky?
3. God, what have You already been showing me that I have been hesitant to listen to or respond to?

Week 1

Learning to Listen

Before we jump into the chapters, I want to pause for a moment. Because this week matters more than you might realize.

Most people do not struggle because God is silent. They struggle because life is loud. Somewhere along the way, many of us learned to believe that hearing God is rare. That it is for pastors, prophets, or people who seem more spiritual than us. And when life feels confusing or quiet, we start to wonder if God has stopped speaking or if we are doing something wrong.

This week is about unlearning that lie.

God has not stopped speaking. He never has. The question is not whether He is speaking. The question is whether our hearts are quiet enough to hear Him.

Week one is an invitation to slow down. To soften your heart. To stop striving for clarity and start paying attention. It is about shifting from asking Why is God not speaking to asking What might He already be saying.

As you move through these chapters, you will look at Scripture and real life together. You will begin to see how busyness, distraction, and unprepared hearts can drown out God's voice. And you will discover that He speaks in deeply personal and relational ways.

This is not about being perfect. It is not about copying someone else's experience. It is about posture.

Come into this week honest. Bring your questions. Bring your desire to hear Him.

Quiet the noise.

And let's begin.

Chapter 1

God Still Speaks Today

ICEBREAKER QUESTIONS

1. Have you ever felt like other people hear God clearly, but you are stuck second guessing every decision and wondering if you are on the right path?

2. Can you think of a time you felt a nudge deep in your spirit, but you brushed it off because it sounded crazy, inconvenient, or uncomfortable?

3. If I asked you honestly, are you living like God is always speaking, or like God is silent unless you are in church?

BIBLE PASSAGE

1 Samuel 3:1-21 (NIV) The LORD Calls Samuel

3 The boy Samuel ministered before the LORD under Eli. In those days the word of the LORD was rare; there were not many visions.

² One night Eli, whose eyes were becoming so weak that he could barely see, was lying down in his usual place. ³ The lamp of God had not yet gone out, and Samuel was lying down in the house of the LORD, where the ark of God was. ⁴ Then the LORD called Samuel.

Samuel answered, "Here I am." ⁵ And he ran to Eli and said, "Here I am; you called me."

But Eli said, "I did not call; go back and lie down." So he went and lay down.

⁶ Again the LORD called, "Samuel!" And Samuel got up and went to Eli and said, "Here I am; you called me."

"My son," Eli said, "I did not call; go back and lie down."

⁷ Now Samuel did not yet know the LORD: The word of the LORD had not yet been revealed to him.

⁸ A third time the LORD called, "Samuel!" And Samuel got up and went to Eli and said, "Here I am; you called me."

Then Eli realized that the LORD was calling the boy. ⁹ So Eli told Samuel, "Go and lie down, and if he calls you, say, 'Speak, LORD, for your servant is listening.'" So Samuel went and lay down in his place.

¹⁰ The LORD came and stood there, calling as at the other times, "Samuel! Samuel!"

Then Samuel said, "Speak, for your servant is listening."

¹¹ And the LORD said to Samuel: "See, I am about to do something in Israel that will make the ears of everyone who hears about it tingle. ¹² At that time I will carry out against Eli everything I spoke against his family—from beginning to end. ¹³ For I told him that I would judge his family forever because of the sin he knew about; his sons blasphemed God,[a] and he failed to restrain them. ¹⁴ Therefore I swore to the house of Eli, 'The guilt of Eli's house will never be atoned for by sacrifice or offering.'"

¹⁵ Samuel lay down until morning and then opened the doors of the house of the LORD. He was afraid to tell Eli the vision, ¹⁶ but Eli called him and said, "Samuel, my son."

Samuel answered, "Here I am."

¹⁷ "What was it he said to you?" Eli asked. "Do not hide it from me. May God deal with you, be it ever so severely, if you hide from me anything he told you." ¹⁸ So Samuel told him everything, hiding nothing from him. Then Eli said, "He is the LORD; let him do what is good in his eyes."

¹⁹ The LORD was with Samuel as he grew up, and he let none of Samuel's words fall to the ground. ²⁰ And all Israel from Dan to Beersheba recognized that Samuel was attested as a prophet of the LORD. ²¹ The LORD continued to appear at Shiloh, and there he revealed himself to Samuel through his word.

Questions

1. What stands out about Samuel's willingness to respond immediately even before he fully understood it was God speaking, and how does that challenge the way you respond when you sense a nudge you're not sure about?

   _____

   _____

2. Why do you think God chose to speak to Samuel in a season when "the word of the Lord was rare," and how might God be inviting you to listen more closely in a spiritually quiet or confusing season of your own life?

   _____

   _____

3. What would it look like for you to adopt Samuel's posture of "Speak, Lord, your servant is listening," especially when God's message might be uncomfortable, unexpected, or difficult to share with others? _____

Section 1 - Samuel's Call

One of my favorite stories about hearing God's voice is tucked right into the beginning of 1 Samuel. Samuel was just a boy. Not a priest. Not some religious elite. Just a child serving in the temple under Eli.

One night, as he lay down to sleep, he heard it: *"Samuel."*

He jumped up, ran straight to Eli, and said, "Here I am...you called me." But Eli just blinked at him, confused. "I didn't call you. Go back to bed."

So, Samuel went back. But again, he heard it: *"Samuel."* Again, he ran to Eli. Again, Eli said, "I didn't call you. Go back to bed."

The third time, Eli finally realized something bigger was happening. He told Samuel, "The next time you hear the voice, say: *'Speak, Lord, your servant is listening.'*" So, Samuel went back, laid down, and sure enough...he heard it again. *"Samuel, Samuel."* This time, instead of running to Eli, he whispered back, *"Speak, Lord, your servant is listening."*

That single moment shifted Samuel's life forever. From then on, God entrusted him with words that would shape the future of Israel. He became the prophet who anointed Saul, and later David, as kings. One boy's decision to listen changed the course of history.

And here's what wrecks me every time I think about it: God didn't start by speaking to the priest. He didn't pick the most experienced leader in the room. He chose to speak to a child. Just a boy with a heart that was willing.

If He did it then, He'll do it now.

Samuel's story reminds me of this: God's voice is rarely loud or dramatic. It often whispers. And whispers are easy to miss if your life is loud. I'll give you an example. Right now, as I write these words, my house is the quietest it has been in months. My husband and son are away on a trip to Keys. Even our dog is with a sitter. The house feels almost foreign without the constant noise of life...no phones buzzing, no dishes clinking in the sink, no voices echoing down the hallway. Just stillness.

And it's in these rare moments...when the noise dies down...that I can hear God's whisper most clearly.

But here's the reality: most of my life doesn't look like this. Most of the time, it's busy, noisy, and chaotic. Between work, kids, ministry, phone calls, and deadlines, there's hardly a quiet corner left in the day. And if I'm not careful, I can go for days...even weeks...without truly stopping long enough to tune my heart toward His whisper.

That's why the very first step to hearing God is simple but hard: you've got to get quiet.

There's a little poem my pastor shared with me years ago that I never forgot. It goes like this:

"O give me Samuel's ear,

An open ear, O Lord,

Alive and quick to hear

Each whisper of Thy Word;

Like him to answer to Thy call,

And to obey Thee first of all."

Every time I hear those words, my heart says, *yes, Lord...that's my prayer too.* Give me ears like Samuel. Quick to hear Your whisper. Quick to obey. Because let's be honest: it's one thing to hear God's voice, but it's a completely different thing to obey it. I can't even count how many times I've heard Him clearly and then wrestled with actually doing it. Sometimes because it felt inconvenient. Sometimes it makes me uncomfortable. And sometimes...if I'm being really honest...because it scared me to death.

But here's what I've learned: obedience is what tunes your ear. Every single time I obey...even when it feels small, even when it feels crazy...His voice becomes clearer. And every time I delay or argue, it gets harder to hear.

So, this is where we begin. Before we talk about calling or destiny or purpose, we've got to settle this first: God still speaks today. He is speaking to you right now. The real question is this...will you quiet yourself enough to hear Him? And will you trust Him enough to obey?

Observation Questions

1. What happens each time Samuel hears his name, and how does Eli eventually help him understand what is happening?

   _____

   _____

2. According to the section, why is it significant that God chose to speak to Samuel... a child... rather than to a priest or experienced leader?

   _____

   _____

Application Questions

1. What noise or busyness in my life might be keeping me from recognizing God's whisper the first time He speaks?

_____

_____

2. Is there something God may already be asking me to obey that I've been delaying because it feels uncomfortable, inconvenient, or scary?

_____

_____

Section 2 - The Lie That God Is Silent

One of the greatest lies I think the enemy has ever whispered into the church is this: "God doesn't speak anymore."

I can't tell you how many Christians I've met who believe that. They think God only spoke in Bible times, or that He only speaks to pastors, prophets, or "super-spiritual" people. And because they believe that lie, they wander through life without direction, second-guessing every decision, wondering if they're on the right path.

If Satan can convince you that God is silent, you won't even try to listen. And if you're not listening, you'll miss the very thing you were created for...hearing and following the One who loves you most.

But here's the truth I've lived: God still speaks. He's always speaking. The real question is...are we tuned in to hear Him?

Observation Questions

1. What belief about God's voice does the section describe as a lie that many Christians have accepted?

_____

_____

2. According to this section, how does believing that God is silent affect the way people live and make decisions? _____

Application Questions

1. Have I ever assumed, maybe without realizing it... that God isn't speaking to me personally?

_____

_____

2. What would change in my daily life if I truly believed God is always speaking and wants me to hear Him?

_____

_____

Section 3 – The Loudest Noise I've Ever Heard

The loudest I have ever heard God speak to me wasn't in church. It wasn't during worship. It wasn't even while I was praying. It was on an ordinary morning, in an ordinary place, while I was jogging down the boardwalk in Virginia Beach.

It was one of those perfect mornings when everything just feels right. The air was crisp but warm enough that I could wear a light tank top and feel the ocean breeze on my skin. The sun was rising, that kind of soft golden light that makes the water sparkle like diamonds. Seagulls were flying low, surfers were paddling out, and for once, my mind was quiet.

I was jogging with my friend Jen. She's one of my closest friends now, but at the time, she wasn't a believer. She was curious about faith, but she hadn't made a commitment yet. So I definitely wasn't planning on turning our casual morning jog into a "Jesus moment."

We were chatting about normal things...business, family, life...when I noticed a woman sitting on a bench just ahead of us. She looked peaceful, head down, reading a book. I barely glanced at her as we ran by. But as soon as I passed her, I felt it...that unmistakable nudge deep in my spirit. A sudden, clear sentence that wasn't mine. *Pay for that woman to have a hotel room for a week.*

I literally laughed out loud mid-run. *What? God, that's ridiculous. I don't even have my wallet. I'm sweating. I look crazy. My car is a mile away. And what am I supposed to say...Hi, random stranger, God told me to pay for your hotel?*

I brushed it off. There was no way that was God. It didn't make sense. But then, a few seconds later, I heard it again. *Turn around.* It wasn't loud, but it was strong. It carried weight. I ignored it and kept jogging. I tried to distract myself with more conversation. Then I heard it again, louder this time. *Turn around.*

Now my heart started to race...not from running, but from that internal battle that happens when you know it's God speaking, but you really don't want to do what He's saying. I thought, *God, You know Jen isn't even a Christian yet. This is going to be so weird. Can't we do this another time?* Still, I kept running.

But by the fourth time, I could hardly move forward. It wasn't an audible voice, but it felt like the air around me got thick...like I was being pulled backward. It was the loudest, clearest, deepest prompting I've ever experienced.

I finally stopped. Jen stopped beside me, confused. "What's wrong?"

I looked at her and said, "We need to turn around."

She gave me this look like, *Are you serious? We just hit our stride.*

"Why?" she asked.

And I took a deep breath and said the only thing I could: "Because God told me to pay for that woman's hotel room for a week."

Jen blinked at me. "What?"

I nodded. "I know how it sounds, but I can't shake it. I have to go back."

She hesitated, probably wondering if she should follow me or have me committed, but she turned around anyway. We jogged back toward the bench. My heart was pounding harder than it had during the entire run. I was nervous. I didn't even know what I was walking into. When we got close enough, I saw what I hadn't noticed before...the woman wasn't just reading a book. She was reading a Bible.

I stopped in front of her and said, "Hi, I know this is going to sound really strange, but God told me to pay for your hotel room for a week. Do you need one?"

Her eyes widened. She froze. Then, out of nowhere, she burst into tears. Through her sobs, she said, "I just picked up my friend from the hospital this morning. We're both homeless. I literally just opened my Bible a few minutes ago and prayed, 'God, if You're real, send someone to pay for a week in a hotel for us.'"

Now all three of us were crying...me, her, and Jen.

Jen just stood there, completely stunned. I could see it all over her face. She was watching the supernatural unfold right in front of her.

I told the woman, "Okay, wait right here. I'm going to make this happen."

I took off running...but this time, not for exercise. I ran all the way back to my car, grabbed my wallet, and drove to a nearby hotel. I walked straight to the front desk, still sweaty and out of breath, and said, "I need to pay for a room for someone for a week."

The hotel clerk looked at me like I was crazy, but I didn't care. I paid for seven nights up front and explained what was happening. Then I called a local organization called PIN Ministries...they work with the homeless community in Virginia Beach...and got the woman connected with them so she could get long-term help.

When I went back to tell her everything was set, she hugged me and said through tears, "You have no idea what this means. We didn't know where we were going to sleep tonight. I just prayed that prayer out loud before you came back."

That moment changed everything for me.

It was the loudest I've ever heard God speak...not because it was audible, but because it was undeniable. It wasn't subtle. It wasn't symbolic. It was direct, specific, and confirmed instantly.

And you know what's crazy? I almost missed it. If I had dismissed that first whisper as weird or too random or probably not God, I would have missed the miracle entirely. And I can't even take credit for it. Because honestly, I argued with God four times before I obeyed. I wasn't bold; I was hesitant. I wasn't fearless; I was awkward and sweaty and nervous. But that's the beauty of God's voice...it doesn't require perfection. It just requires obedience.

And the best part? That moment didn't just change the woman's life. It changed Jen's.

When we walked back to the car, she was quiet for a long time. Then finally, she said, "Chantel, I can't explain what just happened, but I know God is real." It was the first time she had ever said those words...all because of one moment of obedience.

That day taught me something I will never forget. God's instructions rarely come at convenient times. They often sound crazy. They almost always make you uncomfortable. But when you follow them, you get a front row seat to miracles.

And sometimes, the miracles aren't just for the person you're helping. They're for the people watching too.

That's why I tell people all the time...when God nudges you, don't wait. Don't overthink it. Don't reason it away. You never know. Your obedience might be the answer to someone else's prayer.

And to this day, when I think about that moment on the boardwalk...the sunrise, the bench, the Bible, the tears...I still get chills. Because it reminds me that God's voice isn't just powerful. It's personal.

And sometimes, the loudest thing you'll ever hear from Him won't be in a sermon. It will be a whisper that changes someone's world.

Observation Questions

1. What details in the story show how persistent and specific God's prompting was during the jog on the boardwalk?

_____

_____

2. How does the moment with the woman on the bench confirm that the prompting was truly from God?

_____

_____

Application Questions

1. How do I usually react when God nudges me to do something uncomfortable, inconvenient, or that doesn't make sense?

_____

_____

2. Is there a time I may have almost missed a moment of obedience because I overthought it or talked myself out of it?

_____

_____

Section 4 - God Speaks Differently to Each of Us

When I first decided to write this book, I started by asking one question: "How do you hear from God?"

I asked pastors, friends, leaders, people from my Bible study, even a few strangers sitting next to me at church. And do you know what? Every single person had a different answer.

Some paused and said, "I'm not sure." Others spoke with confidence and described exactly how they recognize His voice. And as I wrote their answers down, I started to notice something powerful: God doesn't speak to everyone the same way...but He does speak to everyone willing to listen.

Top 10 Ways People Hear from God

1. Through a pastor or a trusted friend
2. Through a sermon at church
3. Through open doors...or closed ones
4. Through a podcast
5. Through reading the Bible or a book
6. Through a vision or picture in their mind
7. Through a quiet whisper from God
8. Through the Holy Spirit's prompting
9. Through a deep peace in their heart
10. Through dreams

When I looked at that list, I smiled...because every one of them is real. Every one is biblical. God is endlessly creative in the ways He reaches His children. He can speak through a conversation, a moment of silence, a door that suddenly opens, or even one that slams shut. Sometimes He speaks in a way that feels loud and undeniable. Other times, it's a still, small whisper that you only catch when you quiet the noise around you.

You know, we have a son and a daughter, and the way we talk to each of them is completely different. They're both incredible kids, but they're wired differently. One responds to gentle encouragement; the other needs direct, no-nonsense honesty. What works for one simply doesn't work for the other. So as parents, we adjust.

That's exactly how God works with us. He doesn't use a one-size-fits-all approach. He's a personal God. He knows our hearts, our personalities, our sensitivities...and He speaks in the way we'll understand best. That's why trying to copy how someone else hears from God never works. The goal isn't to imitate someone's method; it's to cultivate your own relationship. Because when you know someone deeply, you recognize their voice instantly...no matter how they speak.

There's a powerful moment in the book of Numbers that reveals something incredible about how personally God speaks to each of us.

Miriam and Aaron had started to question Moses' leadership. They said, "Has the Lord only spoken through Moses? Hasn't He also spoken through us?" You can almost feel the tension in their words. It wasn't just curiosity...it was comparison. They wanted to know why Moses seemed to hear God in ways they didn't.

And God's response was stunning. He said, "If there is a prophet among you, I, the LORD, make Myself known to him in a vision; I speak to him in a dream. But this is not true of My servant Moses; he is faithful in all My house. With him I speak face to face, clearly and not in riddles; he sees the form of the LORD."

Think about that for a second. God was basically saying, *I speak to everyone differently, but Moses is in a category all his own.*

Most prophets got dreams and visions...pictures and symbols that needed interpretation. But Moses didn't just get glimpses; he got conversations. God spoke to him directly, clearly, like a friend talking to a friend.

It shows us something vital about hearing God's voice: it's not one-size-fits-all. Some people hear through Scripture. Others feel His nudges in prayer or dreams or worship. Some sense Him through peace, others through pictures or impressions.

But for all of us, the goal is the same...intimacy.

Moses didn't earn that closeness through perfection. He built it through faithfulness. He showed up, listened, obeyed, and trusted. That's why God spoke to him differently. It wasn't about position. It was about relationship.

And that gives us so much hope. Because the same God who spoke face to face with Moses still speaks today. Maybe not through burning bushes or thunder on mountains, but through quiet moments, steady peace, and whispers that reach the heart.

When you walk closely with Him, you don't just hear His words...you recognize His voice.

Here's what's beautiful: God meets us right where we are. You might start by hearing Him through a sermon, a podcast, or a book. Then, as your relationship deepens, He might begin to speak more personally...in dreams, in whispers, in visions, or through Scripture that suddenly comes alive. And just like with any relationship, the more time you spend together, the easier it becomes to recognize His voice instantly.

Don't compare your experience to someone else's. Don't assume that if God isn't speaking the same way He used to, He's gone silent. He may just be teaching you to hear Him in a new way. He's not changing...you are growing.

Key Thought: The more time you spend with God, the more His voice becomes unmistakable.

Observation Questions:

1. How does the Top 10 list reinforce the truth that God is endlessly creative in how He speaks?

   _____

   _____

2. What does the key thought reveal about the connection between time with God and clarity?

   _____

   _____

Application Questions:

1. What are the Top 3 ways do you think you have experienced most often, even if you did not label it as God at the time?

   _____

   _____

2. What is one practical way you can spend more time with God this week so His voice becomes more unmistakable?

   _____

   _____

Section 5 - Seasons of Hearing, Silence, and Trust

Let me be really raw for a second. There have been seasons when I felt like God was practically shouting at me...so clear, so undeniable, it was like He was sitting right across from me. His voice wasn't vague; it wasn't confusing...I knew that I knew *that I knew* it was Him. And in those moments, it gave me courage, direction, and peace I never could've manufactured on my own.

But there have also been times...maybe even longer seasons...where I've cried out with everything in me, "God, where are You? Why can't I hear You?" And the silence felt deafening.

It really does feel like a roller coaster sometimes. High points where His voice feels closer than the air in my lungs, and then dips where I'm groping in the dark, wondering if I missed Him completely. If you've ever felt like that, let me say this: you're not crazy, and you're not alone. I've been there more times than I can count.

And on top of that, there's skepticism. I know you've heard of it too. People saying, "Well, God told me to divorce my spouse" or "God told me to do this thing that completely contradicts Scripture." And everything in you wants to say, *no, friend...that's not God. That's just your flesh talking.* Then on the other extreme are those who flat-out declare, "God doesn't speak anymore. That was just in Bible times." But I can tell you from my own life...over and over again...that God still speaks. And His voice has carried me through seasons I never would have survived otherwise.

Observation Questions

1. What contrast does Chantel describe between seasons of clear direction and seasons of painful silence?

    _____

    _____

2. How does this section address both extremes… people misusing "God told me" and people denying that God speaks at all?

    _____

    _____

Application Questions

1. What season am I currently in… clarity or silence… and how am I responding to it emotionally and spiritually?

    _____

    _____

2. When God feels quiet, what would it look like for me to trust Him instead of questioning whether He's still there?

    _____

    _____

HEARING GOD - PERSONAL REFLECTION

1. Let me be really raw for a second. Are you in a season where God feels like He is practically shouting, or a season where you have cried out, God, where are You? Why can't I hear You? What do you think God might be doing in you right now through that season?

2. If God nudged you today and it sounded inconvenient and made you uncomfortable, will you quiet yourself enough to hear Him, and trust Him enough to obey?

Chapter 2

Why I Can't Hear God's Voice

ICEBREAKER QUESTIONS

1. Have you ever found yourself thinking, why does it seem like other people hear God so clearly while you are praying and still feel frustrated?

2. Can you describe a season when you were constantly asking God for direction but felt like heaven had gone quiet?

3. If you were honest, would you say your life right now is more quiet and receptive, or busy and loud?

BIBLE PASSAGE

Luke 10:38–42 (NIV) At the Home of Martha and Mary

[38] As Jesus and his disciples were on their way, he came to a village where a woman named Martha opened her home to him. [39] She had a sister called Mary, who sat at the Lord's feet listening to what he said. [40] But Martha was distracted by all the preparations that had to be made. She came to

him and asked, "Lord, don't you care that my sister has left me to do the work by myself? Tell her to help me!"

[41] "Martha, Martha," the Lord answered, "you are worried and upset about many things, [42] but few things are needed—or indeed only one.[a] Mary has chosen what is better, and it will not be taken away from her."

Questions

1. What do you notice about the difference between Mary sitting at Jesus' feet and Martha being distracted by good responsibilities, and how might that reflect the tension between busyness and listening in your own life?

   _____

   _____

2. Where might Jesus be gently inviting you to choose "what is better" by pausing your activity, quieting distractions, and simply sitting with Him instead of trying to do more for Him?

   _____

   _____

Section 1 – God's Rhythm of Direction

One of the most important things I've learned about walking with God is that His direction almost never comes all at once.

He doesn't hand you the full blueprint. He gives you a single step...and waits to see if you'll take it.

He leads us through a rhythm I've come to recognize...a divine pattern that repeats in every season of life:

1. **Discomfort**...when God stirs your heart and makes what once felt comfortable feel too small.
2. **Disruption**...when He removes what can't go with you into the next season.
3. **Direction**...when His whisper gives you the next small step of faith.
4. **Decision**...when obedience requires courage to act before you fully understand.
5. **Deliverance**...when hindsight reveals how every detour was part of His perfect plan.

Once you see this pattern, you stop fearing change...because you realize every shift is just God leading you closer to purpose.

If you've walked with Him long enough, you start to recognize His rhythm. There's a divine pattern to how He leads...not just in your faith, but in your finances, your relationships, your calling, your purpose.

Observation Questions

1. What five stages make up the pattern the author describes for how God typically leads?

   _____

   _____

2. According to this section, why does God often give only one step at a time instead of the full plan?

   _____

   _____

Application Questions

1. Which stage of this rhythm do I recognize most in my life right now… and why does it feel familiar?

   _____

   _____

2. How might my response to change shift if I truly believed God was leading me step by step on purpose?

   _____

   _____

Section 2 - Disruption...The Divine Interruption

Once God has your attention through discomfort, He often allows *disruption*.

This is when something shifts...sometimes suddenly, sometimes painfully.

It could be a door closing you thought would always stay open. A friendship ending. A plan unraveling.

We think disruption means we've failed.

But often, it's God removing the things that can't go with us into our next season.

Sometimes He has to break our rhythm to reset our direction.

When disruption comes, don't cling to what's leaving...ask Him what's coming.

Observation Questions

1. What examples does the section give of what disruption can look like in real life?

   _____

   _____

2. How does the author reframe disruption as something God uses rather than something to fear?

   _____

   _____

Application Questions

1. What disruption am I currently facing that I may have labeled as failure instead of God's redirection?

   _____

   _____

2. Instead of clinging to what's leaving, what question do I need to start asking God about what's coming next?

   _____

   _____

Section 3 - Direction...The Gentle Whisper

After the noise of disruption, comes direction.

It doesn't usually arrive as a neon sign or a thunderclap. It comes as a whisper...a thought, a scripture, a conversation, a peace that doesn't make sense. This is the stage where God speaks most clearly...but only to the hearts quiet enough to listen.

Direction rarely looks like clarity at first. It looks like a single step. He says, *"Start the business."* *"Make the call."* *"Move to the new city."*

And you don't get the next instruction until you act on the first one. God doesn't reveal the map until you start walking.

Observation Questions

1. How is God's direction described in this section, and what forms does it usually take?

   _____

   _____

2. What does the section say about when God reveals the next step after giving direction?

   _____

   _____

Application Questions

1. Is there a small step God may be asking me to take right now that I've been waiting to fully understand first?

   _____

   _____

2. What would it look like for me to quiet my life enough to recognize God's whisper instead of waiting for a sign?

   _____

   _____

Section 4 - Decision...The Step of Faith

Once He gives direction, the next stage is *decision.*

This is where obedience becomes real. This is where faith stops being theoretical and starts becoming visible. And honestly, this is where most people get stuck.

Because obedience almost never feels convenient. It rarely makes sense. It usually costs something.

But if you've ever obeyed when it didn't make sense...and then watched everything align...you know what I mean when I say: *obedience is the key that unlocks peace.*

You don't need to see the whole staircase to take the first step. You just need to trust the voice of the One who built it.

Observation Questions

1. Why does Chantel say this stage is where most people get stuck?

   _____

   _____

2. According to the section, what does obedience often require, and what does it ultimately unlock?

   _____

   _____

Application Questions

1. Where in my life do I feel God has already given direction, but I'm hesitating to decide?

   _____

   _____

2. What would it look like for me to take the first step… even without seeing the full staircase?

   _____

   _____

Section 5 - Deliverance...The Reward of Obedience

Then comes *deliverance*.

This is the moment when everything finally makes sense.

It's when you look back and realize, "That disruption wasn't rejection...it was redirection."

It's when you see the way God used every delay, every detour, every disappointment to position you exactly where you were meant to be.

Deliverance doesn't always look like rescue.

Sometimes it looks like peace.

Sometimes it looks like purpose.

And sometimes it looks like you...standing in the very place you once cried about, now realizing it was all part of His plan.

Observation Questions

1. How does the section describe deliverance differently than just rescue or relief?

_____

_____

2. What perspective does hindsight provide about past disruptions and delays?

_____

_____

Application Questions

1. Can I look back at a past season and now see how God was positioning me, even when it hurt?

_____

_____

2. What would change if I trusted that my current struggle may one day make sense through deliverance?

_____

_____

Section 6 - The Flow of Faith

This five-step pattern repeats itself throughout our lives. It's the rhythm of relationship with God...not a one-time lesson, but a lifelong process.

Discomfort → Disruption → Direction → Decision → Deliverance.

Once you recognize it, you stop panicking when things fall apart. You stop questioning God every time He shifts something in your life. You start saying, "Okay, I know what this is. I'm in the middle of the pattern. I may not see the finish line yet, but I know Who's leading me."

The next chapters will show you how to walk in that rhythm...how to live in alignment with God's voice, how to hear Him not just in moments, but in movements. Because your purpose isn't something you chase...it's something you *become* as you follow His lead, one obedient step at a time.

When you learn the pattern of His direction, you'll stop striving for answers and start walking with confidence. You'll stop asking, *"God, where are You?"* and start declaring, *"God, I trust You, even here."* Because purpose isn't a destination. It's the peace that comes when your heart beats in rhythm with His

Observation Questions

1. How does Chantel describe this pattern as something ongoing rather than a one-time experience?

   _____

   _____

2. What shift in mindset happens once someone recognizes they are "in the middle of the pattern"?

   _____

   _____

Application Questions

1. How can recognizing this rhythm help me respond with trust instead of panic when life feels unstable?

   _____

   _____

2. What would it look like for me to stop striving for answers and start walking confidently with God right where I am?

HEARING GOD PERSONAL REFLECTION

1. Are you in a season where God feels clear and close, or distant and quiet? What might God be forming in you during this season?

2. If God nudged you today and it felt inconvenient or uncomfortable, will you quiet yourself enough to hear Him and trust Him enough to obey?

Chapter 3

The 7 Spiritual Buoys... Stay on Course with God's Voice

ICEBREAKER QUESTIONS

1. Have you ever felt unsure whether something you were sensing was truly from God or just your own thoughts?

2. When life feels turbulent, what do you usually rely on to make decisions clarity peace logic or pressure?

3. Have you ever wished you had clearer markers to know whether you should move forward or pause?

BIBLE PASSAGE
Numbers 12:6–8 (NIV)

⁶ he said, "Listen to my words:

"When there is a prophet among you,

   I, the LORD, reveal myself to them in visions,

   I speak to them in dreams.

⁷ But this is not true of my servant Moses;

he is faithful in all my house.

⁸ With him I speak face to face,

clearly and not in riddles;

he sees the form of the LORD.

Why then were you not afraid

to speak against my servant Moses?"

Questions

1. What does this passage reveal about the way God speaks differently to different people, and how does that free you from comparing how you hear God with how someone else hears Him?

   _____

   _____

2. What might it look like to grow in faithfulness and intimacy with God so that His voice becomes clearer and more personal over time, just as it was with Moses?

   _____

   _____

Section 1 - WIIIDOH: A Framework for Discernment

It's easier to stay aligned when you have clear markers. Imagine a framework of spiritual buoys, each one in its place to show you the direction of God's Word. No matter how turbulent the water might be, as long as you follow the high visibility buoys you will always be guided safely home. I've called it the WIIIDOH framework, and it's one of the simplest and most powerful ways to discern whether something is truly from God. Whenever you're unsure if God wants you to do something, you run it through WIIIDOH.

W stands for the Word of God...does it align with Scripture or contradict it?

I stands for Interruptions…did anything interrupt your normal routine to get your attention?

I stands for Intentional Prayer and Fasting…have you truly prayed and asked God for what He wants you to do? Did you fast so you could hear Him more clearly?

I stands for Images and Visions…did you have any images in your mind, or did you have any visions or dreams about what you're facing?

D stands for Doors Opening and Closing…is this a door that's opening or closing? Pay attention, because sometimes the answer comes through opportunity.

O stands for Other Godly People…has this been confirmed by wise counsel? It's so important to ask, "Have other godly people confirmed this?" And finally,

H stands for the Holy Spirit…what peace or conviction remains after you've prayed?

That is the WIIIDOH framework. It is designed to help you decide whether something is truly from God or not. We can also follow this framework at a deeper level. The original seven steps are markers that test whether you should move forward or pause.

For example, let us say you are asking, "Should I work at Hooters Restaurant as a waitress?"

1. Start with the Word of God. Would that be a place that honors Him with their actions?
2. Then look for interruptions. Has anything been happening that seems to block that path. Maybe every time you go to the interview they keep canceling or rescheduling.
3. Next comes intentional prayer and fasting. Did you pray and fast about it and ask God for direction?
4. Then images and visions. Did you have any dreams or inner pictures about it?
5. Doors opening or closing. Are they hiring you easily, or is it falling through?
6. Other godly counsel. What do spiritually mature people in your life say?
7. And finally the Holy Spirit. Do you have peace, or do you feel uneasy about it?

When all the buoys line up like a ship in calm waters, that is usually a green light. If even one feels off, it is worth stopping to pray again.

Observation Questions

1. What are the seven WIIIDOH markers Chantel lays out to help discern whether something is truly from God?

_____

_____

2. According to this section what does it mean when all the buoys line up and what does Chantel say to do if even one buoy feels off?

_____

_____

Application Questions

1. What decision or situation right now needs to be run through WIIIDOH instead of being guessed through or stressed over?

_____

_____

2. Which buoy is usually skipped or rushed past and what would it look like to slow down and truly test it this time?

_____

_____

Section 2 - W – Wisdom or Word of God

The first way God speaks is through His Word.

The Bible isn't just a book; it's alive. Hebrews 4:12 says, "The Word of God is living and active, sharper than any two-edged sword."

If you think you're hearing God, like something that goes against Scripture...that's not God. He never contradicts Himself. His Word is your anchor.

When I'm unsure about a decision, the first thing I do is ask, "What does the Word of God say about this?" That question alone has saved me from so many wrong turns.

Observation Questions

1. What does this section say is the primary way God speaks and why is Scripture described as an anchor?

_____

_____

2. According to Chantel what does it mean if something believed to be from God contradicts Scripture?

_____

_____

Application Questions

1. Before making a big decision do you start by asking what the Word of God says or do you look for feelings signs or validation first?

_____

_____

2. Is there an area of life where something is being justified even though it does not fully line up with Scripture?

_____

_____

Section 3 - I – Interruptions

Okay, this one hit home for me. Sometimes, God doesn't whisper...He interrupts. He shakes up your plans. He closes doors you thought would open. He reroutes you when you were sure you were headed the right way.

Think of Jonah. God told him to go to Nineveh, and instead, Jonah ran the opposite direction. The Bible says, "The Lord sent the storm." That storm wasn't punishment; it was protection. It was a divine interruption to save Jonah from destroying his own life.

One of the biggest things that I can do to hear God is to turn the radio off, turn Facebook off, turn Instagram off, turn off the notifications on my phone...and sometimes just turn off the phone completely. I know that sounds simple, but one of the most spiritual things you might ever do is just turn off your phone.

My husband did something years ago that I really admire. He turned off all the dings, pings, and buzzes from his social media and text notifications. He said, "Every ding is an invitation for interruption." And that's so true.

I realized one of my biggest struggles is that I'm overly responsive. I like being available, so I'm glued to my phone all the time. But that constant attachment means my spirit is always on high alert for other people's voices...and not God's.

So, on Sundays, we made that rule: phones off, completely.

It's now become a sacred rhythm for us. No text. No notifications. No distractions. And let me tell you...it's powerful. Because when you stop responding to the world, you finally start responding to heaven.

Observation Questions

1. What kinds of interruptions does this section describe as ways God gets attention?

    _____

    _____

2. How does Chantel explain the impact of phones notifications and constant responsiveness on hearing God clearly?

    _____

    _____

Application Questions

1. What interruption or closed door right now might actually be God protecting or rerouting you?

    _____

    _____

2. What is one practical boundary that could be set this week to turn down the noise and make room to hear heaven?

    _____

    _____

Section 4 - I – Intentional Prayer and Fasting

If you truly want to hear from God, you must make space for His voice.

Fasting quiets the noise of the world, your cravings, distractions, and busyness, while prayer tunes your heart to Heaven's frequency. Together, they become one of the most powerful tools for spiritual clarity.

When you intentionally pull back from the world and press into God, you begin to notice His whispers more clearly than ever before. Fasting disciplines your soul to wait patiently and listen, while prayer opens your spirit to God's presence. This combination unlocks a deeper connection where God's voice emerges unmistakably.

Fasting is not about self denial or earning favor. It is about humility, acknowledging your deep need for God above all else. It sharpens your spiritual hunger and sensitivity to the Holy Spirit, making you more receptive to divine guidance and breakthroughs. Scripture teaches the power of this spiritual discipline. Esther fasted to seek God's deliverance, Daniel fasted for wisdom, and Jesus Himself fasted before launching His ministry. Fasting and prayer together invite God's authority and favor to work in extraordinary ways.

Practical fasting can look different for everyone. It might be a meal, a day, or simply stepping away from social media, whatever creates space for your spirit to focus fully on God. Even short intentional fasts can produce breakthroughs, clarity, and renewed faith.

Ask yourself, "What am I willing to lay down so I can tune in."

The answer to that question leads you toward a quieter soul, a sharper spiritual ear, and a heart aligned with God's voice. When combined with prayer, fasting becomes not just a practice but a pathway to intimacy, transformation, and revelation.

Observation Questions

1. What does this section teach about how prayer and fasting work together to bring clarity and help hear God?

   _____

   _____

2. What biblical examples are used in this section to show fasting as a spiritual discipline?

   _____

   _____

Application Questions

1. What is something that could be laid down right now to create space to hear God more clearly?

   _____

   _____

2. Have you been asking God for direction while staying distracted and what would intentional prayer look like this week?

Section 5 - I – Images & Visions

Another way God speaks is through images and visions. And no, this isn't spooky or strange. It's deeply biblical. Sometimes God gives you a picture in your mind or a dream that lingers. It's what I like to call a spiritual snapshot, a glimpse of something God is showing you.

Now this is one that many people overlook, but it's very real. God doesn't just speak in words. He speaks in pictures, symbols, and even dreams. He's been doing it since the beginning of time. Sometimes He speaks through nature, like a sunset that stops you in your tracks, the way the waves crash on the shore, or even a rainbow after a storm. If you want to know where God's voice often whispers loudest, go outside.

For me, the ocean is that place. I live just a few minutes from the water, and when I sit by the waves, I feel like I can finally hear clearly. The ocean preaches without words. It reminds me that God is vast, powerful, and unchanging. If you don't have an ocean nearby, find a lake or a quiet place in nature. Because sometimes being stuck inside, surrounded by to do lists and laundry and clutter, makes it harder to hear.

That's why one of my favorite sayings is this: a change of place plus a change of pace equals a change in perspective. If you feel stuck, go somewhere different. Get outside. Get quiet. Let creation speak.

Visions also come in dreams. A few days before President Trump was shot, I had a dream about it. Three days before it happened. I told four friends about it because I didn't even know what to do with that information. It wasn't like I could call the Secret Service and say, "Hey, I had a dream…" But that dream taught me something important. It wasn't about the event. It was about awareness. God speaks through dreams and visions more often than we realize.

When I wake up from a dream that feels different, I immediately grab my notepad. Because I know I'll forget it in thirty seconds if I don't write it down. I jot down what I saw, what I felt, what emotions lingered. Later, I pray and ask, "God, what are You showing me?"

That's exactly what Joseph did in the Bible. Before Joseph ever stood in Pharaoh's palace, he sat in a prison cell. Forgotten by people but not forgotten by God. In that dark season, God trained

Joseph to recognize His voice in a really unusual way, through dreams. Joseph's ability to interpret the dreams of the cupbearer and the baker wasn't random. It was born out of relationship. Even in confinement, Joseph's spirit stayed in tune with the Holy Spirit.

And I think that's true for us too. Sometimes your prison season, your waiting, your struggle, your isolation, is where God fine tunes your spiritual hearing. When you're stripped of distractions, your spirit becomes sharper. Dreams are divine downloads, one of the quietest and most personal ways God still speaks today.

Jesus' disciples received visions in different ways just like we do. For example, Peter's vision happened while he was awake. Paul's came while he was asleep. That tells us something powerful. God speaks in both ways. Sometimes He gives an open vision, a moment so vivid it feels like seeing with your physical eyes. Other times, He speaks through night dreams, planting images or impressions that carry His truth. We don't need to seek after these visions and images. It's enough to know that He can use them to communicate, and that we should keep our spiritual eyes open.

Observation Questions

1. What does this section explain about how God uses images visions dreams and even nature to communicate?

   _____

   _____

2. In Chantel's story what practical steps are taken when a dream feels different or significant?

   _____

   _____

Application Questions

1. Where do you tend to hear God most clearly when you slow down and what place could you go this week to get quiet?

   _____

   _____

2. If God has been giving repeated pictures impressions or dreams have you been writing them down and praying for clarity?

   _____

   _____

Section 6 - D – Doors Open

God also speaks through open and closed doors. Sometimes He doesn't say "yes" or "no" with words...He does it through timing and opportunity. An open door that lines up with His Word and peace is often His way of saying "Go." A door that slams shut, no matter how much you push, might be His way of saying "Wait."

Over the years, I've learned that when God closes a door, it's not rejection...it's redirection. It's protection. So instead of fighting it, thank Him for it. Because that closed door might be the very thing keeping you from a disaster you can't see yet.

Observation Questions

1. How does this section describe God speaking through open and closed doors without using words? _____

2. According to Chantel what is the difference between rejection and redirection when a door closes? _____

Application Questions

1. What door are you pushing on that keeps staying shut and what might God be protecting you from? _____

2. What open door in front of you lines up with God's Word and peace and could be an invitation to move forward? _____

Section 7 - O – Others

God often confirms His word through other people. He uses pastors, mentors, friends, or even strangers to bring clarity or confirmation. When two or three people say the same thing that's been stirring in your spirit...that's often the Holy Spirit's way of saying, "Pay attention."

When you're uncertain about something you believe God is saying, bring it to godly counsel. Proverbs 11:14 says, "Where there is no guidance, a people falls, but in an abundance of counselors there is safety."

The key word there is godly. Not every voice deserves a vote. You want people who love Jesus, who know His Word, and who want His will more than they want your approval.

Sometimes, someone else will speak a single sentence that unlocks everything you've been praying about. That's the beauty of community...God uses the body to confirm the Head's voice.

Observation Questions

1. What does this section say about how God uses other people to confirm what He is speaking?

   _____

   _____

2. According to Chantel what kind of counsel should be trusted and why does she say not every voice deserves a vote?

   _____

   _____

Application Questions

1. Who is one godly person you trust that you need to bring this decision to for wise counsel?

   _____

   _____

2. Are there voices being listened to that are loud but not godly and what boundary needs to be set around that influence?

   _____

   _____

Section 8 - H – Holy Spirit

And finally, the "H" stands for the Holy Spirit. The Holy Spirit is your internal GPS. He ties everything together...the Word, the interruptions, the fasting, the images, the doors, and the counsel. He is the peace that surpasses understanding. He is the still, small voice that whispers when the world is loud. Whenever I'm unsure, I stop and ask, "Holy Spirit, give me peace or take it away." That's it. If I feel at peace, I move forward. If I feel that check...that inner hesitation...I wait. Because the Holy Spirit is never confusing. He leads with peace, not pressure. He confirms with calm, not chaos. So, if what you're hearing feels frantic, forced, or fear-driven...that's not Him. The Holy Spirit's voice is gentle but powerful. It's the kind of peace that makes no sense to your mind but brings absolute clarity to your heart.

When I was building Canzell, there were moments when opportunities looked incredibly promising...but deep down, I knew they didn't pass the WIIIDOH test. Some doors looked profitable but lacked integrity. Others seemed exciting and full of potential, but when I prayed about them, there was no peace from the Holy Spirit.

For example, there were partnerships that could have brought in quick money. On the outside, they looked like golden opportunities, but something about them felt "off." Wisdom wasn't there, and I knew that if I stepped into them, I might compromise my values. There were other situations where everything lined up logically, but I couldn't get past the uneasiness in my spirit. That lack of peace was the Holy Spirit's way of saying; this isn't from Me.

The more I leaned on WIIIDOH, the more confident I became in discerning God's voice...even in seasons where it felt like silence. I realized God was training me. Not every open door is from Him, and not every closed door is a loss. Sometimes the "no" is actually His protection. Over time, I saw that using WIIIDOH wasn't just about decision-making...it became a way of tuning my ear to His Spirit. It reminded me that God is always speaking. He's guiding, leading, and confirming, often in ways I never would have expected. That's why alignment matters so much. That's why tools like the WIIIDOH framework are essential...they keep us steady when the waves of life try to throw us off course.

Here's the truth: before we can ever discover God's purpose for our life...or even what it means to walk boldly in it...we first have to hear His voice. If you can't recognize His whisper, every decision will feel like guesswork. But when you do learn to hear Him, it changes everything: your peace, your relationships, your choices, your confidence about the future.

Observation Questions

1. How does this section describe the Holy Spirit's voice compared to voices that feel frantic pressured or fear driven?

   _____

   _____

2. In Chantel's Canzell story what signs showed that certain opportunities did not pass the WIIIDOH test?

_____

_____

Application Questions

1. What decision needs to be paused long enough to ask Holy Spirit give peace or take it away?

_____

_____

2. Right now are you being led by pressure or by peace and what would it look like to wait until your spirit feels settled?

_____

_____

Section 9 - Recognizing God's Voice vs. Other Voices

Every believer wrestle with this question at some point in their walk with God: "How do I know if this is God's voice...or just my own thoughts... or even the enemy trying to confuse me?" It's one of the most important lessons we'll ever learn...and one that takes time, sensitivity, and practice.

When our son Kyle was born...and I know he'll roll his eyes when he reads this...I honestly thought he was the most handsome boy on the planet. And he is now! His blue eyes, blonde hair, and that big smile...he's stunning. But when he first came out? Not so much.

I had been in labor for thirty-three hours. Thirty-three! I refused to get a C-section, and my husband, Rhyan, stood beside me saying, "We're not staying in this hospital another night. You've got this. Push!" They tried everything...the forceps, repositioning...that boy did not want to come out. His head was huge, bless his heart, and when they finally pulled him out, he looked like he had been through a battle. So, when friends came to visit, I told them upfront, "Listen, my baby is not cute. Like, at all." They laughed, but I was being honest. I adored him, but let's be real...most newborns don't exactly come out looking like Gerber models.

When I went to the nursery, I looked at the rows of swaddled babies and couldn't even tell which one was mine. I remember thinking, they all look the same. So, I started eliminating options until I finally saw the little name tag that said Finch. And it hit me later...that's exactly what it's like when you're brand new in your faith. When you've just met Jesus, all the "voices" sound the same. You're trying to figure out, was that God speaking to me? Or was that just me? Everything blends together because you don't yet know His tone.

But the longer you walk with Him, the more familiar His voice becomes. Now, years later, I could pick out Kyle's voice in a crowded room. I'd know his laugh, his tone, even his footsteps. Why? Because I've spent time with him. I know his character.

And the same is true with God. The more time you spend in His presence, the easier it becomes to recognize when it's Him speaking...and when it's not.

God speaks differently to each of us. He doesn't use a one-size-fits-all voice. My two incredible kids...Kyle and Shayla...are complete opposites. What motivates one completely frustrates the other. If you're a parent, you know exactly what I mean. You can't use the same tone, the same correction, or the same encouragement with both. They're wired differently. My sister and I are the same way. We love each other dearly, but we couldn't be more different. I'm driven, focused, organized. She? She works one day a week...and you have to beg her to show up that day. Her car is a disaster. One of her doors doesn't even open! I've literally said, "Please, let me pay to fix it," because I can't handle it. But that's just who she is...she's content, relaxed, unbothered.

God knows our wiring. He knows what gets our attention. He knows whether we respond better to a whisper or a wake-up call.

"He said, 'Listen to my words:
When there is a prophet among you,
I, the Lord, reveal myself to them in visions,
I speak to them in dreams.
But this is not true of my servant Moses;
he is faithful in all my house.
With him I speak face to face,
clearly and not in riddles;
he sees the form of the Lord.'"

Isn't that incredible? God literally says, I speak differently to different people. Some hear Him in dreams, some in visions, some through quiet impressions in their spirit, and others through His Word. Moses heard Him face to face. As we walk with God, we learn His rhythms...and we begin to notice when He changes the channel. In one season, He may speak through Scripture. In another, through people or circumstances. The key is staying sensitive enough to notice, and not being distracted by the pushing, rushing noise of the world.

The enemy pushes. The flesh rushes. But God's Spirit leads with peace. So when you are not sure, pause. Ask yourself, does this voice bring peace or pressure? Conviction or condemnation? Rest or fear?

The voice of God always aligns with His nature, calm, patient, and filled with love. And when you learn to tune your ear to that tone, you will never mistake the noise for the truth again.

In Acts 12, Peter gives us one of the most beautiful pictures of what it looks like to truly trust God's voice. The night before he is supposed to stand trial, facing the possibility of death, Peter is sleeping between two soldiers. Sleeping. The angel who comes to rescue him has to strike him on the side to wake him up. Can you imagine having that kind of peace on death row? Peter wasn't pacing. He wasn't overanalyzing. He wasn't praying the same prayer a hundred times. He had learned to trust the voice of God so deeply that even in chaos, he could rest. That is what peace that passes understanding looks like. And sometimes, that peace is the loudest confirmation you will ever get.

Observation Questions

1. What does Chantel's story about newborn Kyle reveal about learning to recognize God's voice over time?

   _____

   _____

2. What contrasts does this section give to help test a voice such as peace versus pressure or conviction versus condemnation?

   _____

   _____

Application Questions

1. Where might God's voice be getting lost in the noise and what would help deepen familiarity with His tone?

   _____

   _____

2. When uncertainty shows up this week what simple question can be asked to test whether a voice reflects God's calm loving leading or feels rushed and pressured?

_____

_____

HEARING GOD – PERSONAL REFLECTION

1. Which of the WIIIDOH buoys do I tend to overlook or rush past when I am making decisions?

2. Where in my life have I mistaken pressure, urgency, or fear for God's voice?

3. What recent decision have I made without fully checking Scripture, peace, or godly counsel?

4. When I pause and listen honestly, do I feel led by calm assurance or driven by internal noise?

Week 2

When God Speaks in the Quiet Places

As we step into week two, we move into a part of hearing God that many people either dismiss or fear. Dreams. Night thoughts. Those moments when your body is asleep but your heart is wide awake.

For some people, dreams feel confusing. For others, they feel unsettling. And for many, they feel easier to ignore than to bring to God. We wake up, shake it off, and move on. Or we overanalyze every detail until we end up more anxious than before.

But Scripture tells us something important. God speaks again and again, even when we do not recognize it. Sometimes He speaks when our defenses are down. When our schedules are quiet. When our minds are no longer managing the message.

This week is not about becoming obsessed with dreams or trying to decode every image. It is about learning discernment. It is about understanding that God is not trying to scare you. He is trying to reach you. Often beneath the surface. Often in places you cannot control.

Dreams can reveal fears we have buried. They can uncover wounds we have ignored. They can expose places where God wants to bring healing, trust, or freedom. And when God is the one speaking, the result is never chaos. It is always peace, clarity, and deeper intimacy with Him.

As you move through this week, resist the urge to rush to conclusions or brush things aside. Bring what unsettles you to God. Ask Him what He is revealing. And then wait without fear.

God does not speak in the night to lead you toward loss. He speaks to draw you closer to life.

Take a breath.

Stay open.

And let's listen together.

Chapter 4

When God Speaks Through Dreams

ICEBREAKER QUESTIONS

1. Have you ever had a dream that stayed with you long after you woke up and made you wonder if it meant something more?

2. Do you tend to ignore unsettling dreams, overanalyze them, or bring them to God in prayer?

3. Have you ever noticed fear or unresolved emotions showing up in your dreams before you fully recognized them while awake?

BIBLE PASSAGE

Job 33:14–18 (NIV)

¹⁴ For God does speak—now one way, now another—

though no one perceives it.

¹⁵ In a dream, in a vision of the night,

when deep sleep falls on people

as they slumber in their beds,

¹⁶ he may speak in their ears

and terrify them with warnings,

¹⁷ to turn them from wrongdoing

and keep them from pride,

¹⁸ to preserve them from the pit,

their lives from perishing by the sword.

Questions

1. What stands out about the ways this passage describes God speaking through dreams and warnings, and how does it challenge the idea that silence always means God is not communicating?

   _____

   _____

2. How might God be using a dream, a nudge, or an inner warning right now to protect you, redirect you, or keep you from something that could harm your future?

   _____

   _____

Section 1 – When Fear Speaks Through Dreams

For quite a while, I started having dreams that my husband was going to die. They didn't happen just once or twice. For years, these dreams would come and go, sometimes so vivid that I'd wake up in tears, my heart racing, whispering, "God, please no." It made no sense. He's healthy. We're close. We're in one of the best seasons of our marriage. We laugh together, pray together, dream together. Honestly, we hardly ever want to be apart. He went away recently on a four-day men's trip and called me during every break just to say he missed me. It was so sweet...and yet, even in the middle of all that love and security, the dreams would still come.

So what was God trying to say?

One of the biggest lessons I've learned about hearing God's voice is that not every message is meant to be taken at face value. Dreams are one of the ways God speaks, but they often speak in symbols, not sentences. When Joseph interpreted Pharaoh's dream in Genesis, the dream wasn't literally about cows or corn...it was about famine and provision. The image was symbolic of something God wanted to reveal. That's what I began to sense about my own dreams. Maybe these dreams weren't about death at all. Maybe they were about fear.

I started to ask myself, "What am I afraid of losing?"

Observation Questions

1. What pattern do Chantel's dreams follow and why do they feel confusing given the reality of her marriage?

   _____

   _____

2. How does this section explain the difference between taking a dream literally versus understanding it symbolically?

   _____

   _____

Application Questions

1. Have you ever had a dream that stirred fear even though nothing in real life supported that fear?

   _____

   _____

2. What fear might God be revealing beneath the surface instead of warning about a literal event?

   _____

   _____

Section 2 – Discerning God's Meaning in the Dream

Sometimes, dreams of death are really dreams about change. They can represent the death of a season, an old version of yourself, or even a fear that something you love is temporary. When I looked closer, I realized that part of me...deep down...still carried this old self-protective belief: Don't get too close. Don't get too attached.

That belief came from old wounds. Growing up, I had learned to survive by staying in control...by keeping my heart guarded. But God had been teaching me to let go of control, to love freely, to trust fully. And the closer I got to my husband emotionally and spiritually,

the more that old part of me panicked. It's almost like my subconscious was saying, "If you love this deeply, you might lose it." So, in my sleep, fear began painting pictures that looked like death...when really, God was revealing where He wanted to bring life.

When it comes to dreams, we can't just jump to conclusions. Some dreams come from God. Some come from fear. And some come from that late-night pizza you probably shouldn't have eaten. That's why the most important step is to bring every dream before the Lord and simply ask, "God, what are You trying to show me through this?"

For me, He began gently showing that the dream wasn't about my husband's literal death...it was about dying to fear. It was about releasing control and trusting God with the people I love most. It was His way of saying, "Chantel, you don't have to brace for loss. You can rest in love."

It's important to neither dismiss your dreams nor obsess over them. When it comes to dreams, there's a balance. If you obsess over every detail, you'll start seeing hidden meanings that were never there. But if you dismiss them altogether, you might miss God's gentle whisper in the night.

Job 33:14–15 says, "For God speaks again and again, though people do not recognize it. He speaks in dreams, in visions of the night, when deep sleep falls on people as they lie in their beds." Dreams can be one of God's languages...but He always speaks in alignment with His Word and His peace. If a dream leads you to fear, shame, or confusion, that's not God's heart. If it leads you to pray, trust, or heal, then He's likely inviting you into deeper revelation.

Observation Questions

1. What does this section explain about dreams of death often representing change rather than loss?

_____

_____

2. How does Chantel connect fear based dreams to old beliefs wounds or a desire for control?

_____

_____

Application Questions

1. Is there an area of life where fear shows up as self protection instead of trust?

_____

_____

2. What would it look like to bring a troubling dream to God and simply ask what He is revealing rather than jumping to conclusions?

_____

_____

Section 3 – Trusting God Through Dreams and Waiting

I'll be honest...even after I prayed about it, I still didn't want to think about those dreams. They made me sad, so I just pushed them down. But even that avoidance was part of God's lesson for me. He was saying, "You don't have to run from what scares you...bring it to Me." So now, when I dream something that unsettles me, I don't panic or push it away. I write it down. I pray over it. And then I wait.

Sometimes, God brings clarity right away. Sometimes, it takes years...like Abraham and Sarah, who waited 25 years for God's promise to come to life. The waiting doesn't mean God is silent. It means He's working in the unseen.

So now when those thoughts come...that little nudge of fear...I pause and ask, "God, are You preparing me for something, or are You simply prompting me to trust You more deeply?" Either way, the answer is peace. Because the truth is: even if my worst fear ever came true, God would still be faithful. But most often, He's not warning me of disaster...He's inviting me to intimacy.

Dreams are one of the ways God helps us see what we're not seeing when we're awake. They can uncover hidden fears, reveal unhealed places, or prepare our hearts for what's ahead. But they're never meant to control us...they're meant to draw us closer to the One who comforts us.

So if you ever have a dream that shakes you, remember: Don't fear it. Don't ignore it. Don't interpret it alone. Bring it before God. Ask, "What are You showing me?" And then wait in faith, not fear. Sometimes, the dream isn't about what's dying...it's about what God is trying to bring to life.

Observation Questions

1. How does this section describe the role of waiting when clarity does not come immediately?

   _____

   _____

2. What examples are given to show that waiting does not mean God is silent or absent?

   _____

   _____

Application Questions

1. When unsettling thoughts or dreams surface do you tend to avoid them or bring them honestly before God?

   _____

   _____

2. What fear could be surrendered by choosing to wait in faith instead of reacting in panic?

   _____

   _____

HEARING GOD – PERSONAL REFLECTION

1. Is there a dream, fear, or recurring thought God may be using to invite you into deeper trust? Sit quietly and ask Him what He wants you to see.

2. How can you create space to listen for God's voice without fear, control, or avoidance?

Chapter 5

How to Spend 15 Minutes a Day in Complete Quiet

ICEBREAKER QUESTIONS

1. Does silence feel refreshing to you, or does it make you uncomfortable and restless?

2. When was the last time you sat quietly with God without an agenda, a list, or a distraction?

3. What noises or habits most often compete for your attention first thing in the morning?

BIBLE PASSAGE

Psalm 46 (NIV)

[1] God is our refuge and strength,

   an ever-present help in trouble.

[2] Therefore we will not fear, though the earth give way

   and the mountains fall into the heart of the sea,

[3] though its waters roar and foam

   and the mountains quake with their surging.

[4] There is a river whose streams make glad the city of God,

   the holy place where the Most High dwells.

[5] God is within her, she will not fall;

   God will help her at break of day.

[6] Nations are in uproar, kingdoms fall;

   he lifts his voice, the earth melts.

[7] The LORD Almighty is with us;

   the God of Jacob is our fortress.

⁸ Come and see what the LORD has done,

    the desolations he has brought on the earth.

⁹ He makes wars cease

    to the ends of the earth.

He breaks the bow and shatters the spear;

    he burns the shields with fire.

¹⁰ He says, "Be still, and know that I am God;

    I will be exalted among the nations,

    I will be exalted in the earth."

¹¹ The LORD Almighty is with us;

    the God of Jacob is our fortress.

Questions

1. What do you notice about the contrast between chaos in the world and the repeated reminder that God is a refuge and fortress, and how does that speak to the fears you may be carrying right now?

2. Why do you think God commands "Be still" in the middle of shaking, noise, and uncertainty, and what might stillness look like in your current season?

3. Where might God be inviting you to stop striving, release control, and trust His presence as your strength rather than trying to hold everything together on your own?

Section 1 – The 15-Minute of Silence Challenge

If you're like me, silence does not come naturally. I have a strong personality, I move fast, and my brain is always working. Even when I'm trying to relax, I'm planning, creating, or thinking about the next thing. I used to think silence was just "doing nothing." But I've learned that silence is one of the most powerful spiritual disciplines in existence.

For years, I wanted to hear God more clearly. I prayed for it. I begged for answers. I read every devotion I could find. But no matter how hard I tried, I still felt like His voice was distant. I didn't realize that the problem wasn't that God wasn't speaking...it was that I wasn't *still* enough to listen.

Think about how we live today. The first thing most people touch in the morning isn't their Bible...it's their phone. Before our feet hit the floor, we'd already scrolled through texts, emails, and social media. We're bombarded with information before we've even said "Good morning" to God.

I was the queen of this. My mornings were chaos. I'd jump straight into my inbox, respond to a few messages, check what was happening at work, maybe glance at Instagram or Facebook...and then suddenly realize I'd lost an hour of my morning to other people's voices.

By the time I actually tried to pray, my mind was already overloaded. I would sit there thinking, "Why can't I focus?" or "Why can't I hear God today?" But looking back, I see that my soul was drowning in noise. And the truth is, that's where most people live...distracted, hurried, constantly stimulated, but spiritually starving. You can't hear a whisper in a hurricane. And that's exactly what silence is meant to fix...it calms the hurricane so you can hear His whisper.

There was a season where I was completely burned out...emotionally, mentally, spiritually. I was running a company, managing people, speaking, recording, and trying to be present for my family. On the outside, everything looked great. On the inside, I was empty.

One morning, I woke up with my heart pounding so hard I thought something was wrong. I wasn't anxious about anything specific...I was just overwhelmed by *everything*. I remember praying, "Lord, I'm exhausted, and I don't even know why."

That day, I called a friend who's a licensed counselor, and she said something I'll never forget: "Chantel, your soul is screaming for stillness. If you don't slow down, your body will eventually force you to."

That hit me. She was right. I was addicted to movement. If I wasn't doing something, I felt unproductive...even guilty. Silence felt like laziness to me. But that's when the Holy Spirit gently nudged me with this thought: "You've been giving everyone else your attention. When will you share it with Me?"

It was like a punch in the gut. I realized I was talking *at* God but rarely being still *with* God. That's when He led me into what I now call the **15-Minute of Silence Challenge.**

I felt prompted to spend fifteen full minutes a day sitting in complete silence before God. No phone, no music, no journaling, no worship playlist, no productive praying. Just silence.

I still remember the first day I tried it. I set a timer for fifteen minutes, sat down, and said, "Okay, God, I'm here." Within two minutes, I was already fidgeting. My brain was jumping everywhere. I thought about laundry, emails, dinner plans, what I was going to post on social media...everything except God. It was honestly embarrassing. But I didn't stop. I kept coming back the next day, and the next. Some days it felt powerful. Other days it felt completely pointless. But slowly, something started to change.

At first, I didn't hear anything new. But I started to feel different. The peace of God began to settle into my mornings like a soft blanket. I wasn't rushing through my quiet time anymore...I actually started craving it. And then, one morning, while I was sitting there in the stillness, I sensed the Holy Spirit whisper in my heart, "Stop trying to fill every gap. I meet you in the gaps."

That one sentence changed everything for me.

That moment reminded me why stillness matters so much. In a world that glorifies noise, silence felt almost rebellious. But it was in that quiet space that I finally began to hear Him clearly...not because He was speaking louder, but because everything else had finally grown quiet enough for me to listen. Here's why silence is so powerful. It's the opposite of everything the world teaches us. The world says, "If you're not doing something, you're falling behind." But God says, "Be still, and know that I am God." (Psalm 46:10). The world teaches us to react, to respond instantly, and to keep up with everyone else. But God teaches us to rest, to wait, to listen.

When you silence the world, you allow God to reorder your soul. You'll find that peace isn't the absence of problems...it's the presence of His voice. Physically, silence even rewires your brain. Studies show that just a few minutes of silence a day can lower your blood pressure, calm your nervous system, and increase focus. But spiritually, it does something even deeper: it makes room for revelation.

When you sit quietly before God, you're saying, "Lord, You don't have to shout to get my attention. I'm already listening."

My 15-minutes of silence soon evolved. After practicing for a while, I developed a rhythm that truly changed my life. I call it the **15-15-15 Method**. It's simple:

- 15 minutes of silence

- 15 minutes in the Word

- 15 minutes in prayer

That's 45 minutes total...and it will completely change your relationship with God if you commit to it.

Observation Questions

1. What does this section reveal about why silence feels so difficult in a fast-paced distracted world?

_____

_____

2. How does Chantel's story explain that the issue was not God being distant but the soul being too noisy to listen?

_____

_____

Application Questions

1. What is usually the very first thing reached for in the morning and how might that be shaping spiritual focus?

_____

_____

2. What would it look like to intentionally create silence before giving attention to everyone else's voices?

_____

_____

Section 2 - Step 1: 15 Minutes of Silence

Find a quiet space...maybe it's your car before work, a chair on your porch, or even your closet. Turn off every distraction. I mean every distraction...phone on airplane mode, no background noise, no multitasking.

Then just sit there. You can close your eyes or keep them open but focus on being fully present.

Start small if you need to. If fifteen minutes feels impossible, start with three. Set a timer so you're not watching the clock. As you sit, take a few deep breaths and invite the Holy Spirit by simply saying, "God, I'm here. I'm listening." Your mind will wander...that's okay. When it does, gently bring it back by repeating, *"Speak, Lord. Your servant is listening."*

Over time, your mind will settle faster. What felt awkward will start to feel holy.

Observation Questions

1. What practical instructions does this section give for creating a true space of silence before God?

   _____

   _____

2. How does this section describe what happens to the mind during silence and how it changes over time?

   _____

   _____

Application Questions

1. What place could realistically become a daily quiet space for silence without distractions?

   _____

   _____

2. If fifteen minutes feels overwhelming what smaller step could be taken consistently to begin?

   _____

   _____

Section 3 - Step 2: 15 Minutes in the Word

Once you finish your silence, open your Bible. Read slowly. Don't rush through chapters. Ask God to highlight what He wants you to see.

Sometimes I'll read just one or two verses and feel the Holy Spirit underline a word or phrase. When that happens, I stop and meditate on it. I'll ask, "God, what are You trying to show me here?"

The key is to approach Scripture not as information, but as conversation. God speaks primarily through His Word, so when you give Him 15 minutes of reading time after 15 minutes of listening time, your spiritual ears are already open and tuned to His frequency.

This is also where fasting ties in beautifully. When you're fasting...especially from food...reading the Word becomes spiritual nourishment. Jesus said in Matthew 4:4, *"Man shall not live by bread alone, but by every word that comes from the mouth of God."*

Observation Questions

1. How does this section describe the difference between reading Scripture for information versus conversation?

_____

_____

2. What connection does this section make between silence before Scripture and hearing God more clearly through His Word?

_____

_____

Application Questions

1. When reading the Bible is the goal usually to finish a passage or to listen for what God is highlighting?

_____

_____

2. What would it look like to slow down and sit with a single verse instead of rushing through multiple chapters?

_____

_____

Section 4 - Step 3: 15 Minutes of Prayer

Now that you've quieted your heart and filled it with His Word, it's time to talk to Him.

Prayer should be a continuation of the conversation God started in silence and Scripture. It's not about performing or checking a box...it's about relationships.

Talk to God like you would talk to your best friend. Tell Him what you're thankful for. Tell Him what's bothering you. Ask for wisdom. Then pause again at the end and give Him space to speak back.

Prayer isn't meant to be a one-way monologue. It's an ongoing dialogue.

And that's it! That's the 15-15-15 method that can completely transform your intimacy with God. Pretty simple. And here's something important: you don't have to follow the exact order every time. Some days you might start with Scripture and then move into silence. On other days, you might pray first and then sit quietly. The goal isn't perfection...it's connection.

Observation Questions

1. How does this section explain prayer as a continuation of silence and Scripture rather than a separate activity?

   _____

   _____

2. What does this section say about prayer being dialogue instead of a one way conversation?

   _____

   _____

Application Questions

1. What would change if prayer sounded more like talking to a trusted friend instead of performing or rushing?

   _____

   _____

2. How often is space given at the end of prayer to listen instead of immediately moving on?

   _____

   _____

Section 5 - Silence: Where God Does His Deepest Work

Let's be honest...silence can feel awkward and even intimidating. We live in a culture that glorifies busyness. If you're not hustling, people assume you're falling behind. But silence forces you to confront what's really happening inside you.

At first, it can feel like all the buried noise in your heart comes rushing to the surface. You'll notice thoughts, emotions, and memories that you didn't realize were sitting there. That's actually the point. God uses silence to bring healing.

There were days I would sit in silence and end up crying for no apparent reason. But it wasn't "no reason"... it was God gently pulling up things I had ignored. Resentment. Fear. Unforgiveness. Pressure. When you finally slow down, He can start cleaning out the clutter. Silence is like detoxing your spirit. It's uncomfortable at first, but the freedom on the other side is worth it.

Try seeing silence as a form of fasting...an *intentional sacrifice*. When you fast, you intentionally give up something physical to gain something spiritual. Silence is the same thing. You're giving up the noise and stimulation that keep your soul distracted, and you're creating sacred space for God to move. So if you're someone who struggles to fast from food because of health reasons, practicing silence can be your starting point. It's fasting from noise.

The enemy knows that if he can't destroy you, he'll distract you. That's why silence is spiritual warfare. Every time you choose quiet over chaos, you're fighting back against a world that's trying to keep you disconnected from God.

Silence and fasting are powerful on their own, but when you combine them, they multiply in impact:

- When you fast, you quiet your body.

- When you sit in silence, you quiet your soul.

- When you read the Word, you fill your spirit.

All three together create a kind of spiritual alignment that opens the channel for God's voice more clearly than anything else I've ever done.

When you're fasting, your physical hunger will remind you to pray. When you're silent, your mental hunger will remind you to listen. Together, they tune your whole being to Heaven's frequency. So, if you're fasting during a particular season, add silence to your daily rhythm. Use the time you'd normally spend eating or scrolling to sit in quiet before God. That's where clarity and breakthroughs happen.

Here's the secret...consistency beats intensity. You don't have to have a life-changing revelation every time you sit in silence. Some days it will feel powerful. On other days, you'll wonder if anything is happening at all. But I promise you...it is.

God honors consistency. Over time, your spiritual ears will sharpen. You'll recognize His nudges faster. You'll catch yourself before reacting in anger or fear because you've learned what peace feels like. You'll start to hear Him not just in those fifteen minutes, but throughout the entire day...in conversations, in opportunities, in random thoughts that suddenly feel "different." That's how intimacy with God develops.

When I started practicing this rhythm, my life began to change in ways I couldn't even explain. My anxiety decreased. My creativity increased. My relationship has improved. And most importantly, I stopped striving for control because I could finally *feel* God leading me instead of guessing.

There will be days when you sit in silence, and nothing happens. You'll feel distracted, bored, or even frustrated. That's okay. It's part of the process. Think of it like a workout. The first time you exercise, you don't see the results. But your muscles are still growing. Silence works the same way. Even when you don't feel it, your spiritual capacity increases. So, on days when it feels dry, don't quit. God is building your discipline. Keep showing up. The reward is always worth it.

If you want to hear God's voice, you have to give Him room to speak. Start with fifteen minutes of silence every day. Then build up to the full 15-15-15 rhythm. Make it part of your life the way eating or sleeping is...non-negotiable.

Turn off your phone. Close the door. Take a deep breath. Say, "Speak, Lord, I'm listening." Do it daily, not just when you need something. And before long, you'll notice something incredible...you won't just hear God in silence. You'll hear Him in conversations, in decisions, in moments of peace throughout your day. Because once you learn to quiet the noise, you'll find out He's been speaking all along.

Observation Questions

1. What does this section reveal about why silence often feels uncomfortable at first?

   _____

   _____

2. How does Chantel explain silence as a form of spiritual detox and fasting from noise?

   _____

   _____

Application Questions

1. What emotions thoughts or distractions tend to surface when life slows down and silence begins?

   _____

   _____

2. What would consistency in silence look like even on days when nothing seems to happen?

   _____

   _____

HEARING GOD PERSONAL REFLECTION

1. When you picture sitting in complete silence before God, what emotions come up for you right now, resistance, fear, discomfort, or longing, and what might God be gently revealing about your heart through that response?

2. If God were to meet you in the gaps of your day instead of the noise, what would you need to surrender in order to truly listen and trust Him in that quiet place?

Chapter 6

Fasting...The Forgotten Key to Hearing God

ICEBREAKER QUESTIONS

1. Have you ever gone through a season where you were praying and reading the Bible, but still felt distant from God's voice? What did that season feel like for you emotionally or spiritually?

2. What is your first reaction when you hear the word fasting? Be honest. Does it stir curiosity, resistance, fear, confusion, or past experiences?

3. When life feels overwhelming or noisy, what do you usually turn to for comfort or distraction instead of stillness with God?

BIBLE PASSAGE

Matthew 6:16–18 (NIV)

16 "When you fast, do not look somber as the hypocrites do, for they disfigure their faces to show others they are fasting. Truly I tell you, they have received their reward in full. 17 But when you fast, put oil on your head and wash your face,18 so that it will not be obvious to others that you are fasting, but only to your Father, who is unseen; and your Father, who sees what is done in secret, will reward you.

Questions

1. What does Jesus' instruction about fasting in secret reveal about God's desire for intimacy rather than performance, and how does that challenge the way spiritual disciplines are sometimes practiced today?

   _____

   _____

2. How might approaching fasting as a private act of surrender and trust position your heart to hear God more clearly instead of seeking validation from others?

   _____

   _____

Section 1 - Rediscovering God's Voice Through Biblical Fasting

There was a time when I could pray, read my Bible, attend church faithfully, and still feel distant from God's voice. It wasn't that He had stopped speaking...I just couldn't hear Him clearly anymore.

Some days, I'd pray and feel like my words were bouncing off the ceiling. Other days, I'd open my Bible but couldn't concentrate long enough to absorb a single verse. I was spiritually full of noise...full of opinions, tasks, and distractions...but not full of God. Then I discovered something that changed my entire relationship with Him: **fasting**. When I say fasting, I'm not talking about a trendy "cleanse" or skipping social media. I'm talking about the kind of fasting that appears over and over in the Bible...**abstaining from food for a spiritual purpose**.

The word "fast" in Hebrew is *tsum,* which literally means *"to cover the mouth."* In Greek, it's *nēstis,* formed from *nē* ("not") and *esthiō* ("to eat"). Biblical fasting simply means not eating...period. It's not metaphorical. It's not symbolic. It's physical hunger that opens a spiritual door.

Now, I know what you're thinking: *"Wait... no food?"* Yes. That's exactly it. We're not fasting television, social media, or shopping. We're fasting in the true Biblical sense...abstaining from food in order to grow closer to God.

For years, I believed fasting was optional...something reserved for overly spiritual people or ancient prophets. But once I saw it in Scripture, I realized that fasting isn't *extra credit* in the Christian life; it's a command. Fasting is mentioned more than seventy times in the Bible. And in Matthew 6, Jesus didn't say *if* you fast...He said *when* you fast.

"When you give…" (Matthew 6:2)

"When you pray…" (Matthew 6:5)

"When you fast…" (Matthew 6:16)

Giving, praying, and fasting are the three pillars of a Christian's walk with God. We do all three not because we *have* to, but because Jesus expected we *would.* And yet, in today's church, fasting is the least discussed and least practiced of them all. I went the first twenty years of my Christian life without hearing a single sermon about fasting. Not one. We talk about prayer. We talked about generosity. But fasting? Crickets. That silence cost me years of dullness in my faith. Because fasting is the discipline that quiets everything else so that the voice of God can finally be heard.

Observation Questions

1. What does this section explain about why it is possible to pray read Scripture and attend church yet still feel distant from God's voice?

_____

_____

2. What does this section teach about the biblical meaning of fasting and how it differs from modern ideas of fasting?

_____

_____

Application Questions

1. Have spiritual distractions or constant noise been filling life more than the presence of God?

_____

_____

2. What would change if fasting was viewed as a biblical expectation instead of an optional spiritual extra?

_____

_____

Section 2 - Fasting as Obedience, Surrender, and Spiritual Power

There's something sacred about hunger. When your stomach growls, it's your body saying, *"I need something."* But when you fast, it's your spirit saying, *"I need Someone."*

I've seen fasting change lives, heal bodies, and bring peace in chaos. Through fasting, I've broken strongholds of addiction to food, overcome emotional eating, found physical healing, and gained supernatural clarity in moments of confusion. Fasting is not about losing weight...it's about losing **whatever stands between you and God.** Jesus expected you to fast, in Matthew 6:16–18, Jesus gives one of the clearest teachings on fasting:

"When you fast, do not look somber as the hypocrites do, for they disfigure their faces to show others they are fasting. Truly I tell you, they have received their reward in full. But when you fast, put oil on your head and wash your face, so that it will not be obvious to others that you are fasting, but only to your Father, who is unseen; and your Father, who sees what is done in secret, will reward you."

Notice the assumption: **"When you fast."** Not *if*.

Jesus didn't treat fasting as optional. He didn't limit it to prophets or monks. He expected it from His followers. And that makes sense, because fasting is not about showing off your spirituality...it's about emptying yourself so that God can fill you.

While fasting is deeply personal, it doesn't have to be lonely. Jesus said to keep your fasting private, but He didn't forbid fasting with others. In fact, I believe fasting with a friend or small group brings strength and accountability. When one of you feels weak, the other can lift you up in prayer. There's power in unity...especially when two or three agree on a fast.

Let's be honest: food is one of the greatest pleasures in life. And there's nothing wrong with that...God created us to enjoy His provision. But when food becomes our comfort instead of God, it becomes a chain.

When we fast, we're not punishing ourselves...we're practicing surrender. Fasting says, *"God, I'm not driven by my cravings. I'm driven by Your Spirit."* It's a physical act of obedience that produces spiritual power. When I finally realized this, everything changed. I stopped seeing fasting as deprivation and started seeing it as **invitation**...an invitation to hear God more clearly.

If we're called to follow Jesus, then we must ask: *Did Jesus fast?* absolutely.

"Then Jesus was led by the Spirit into the wilderness to be tempted by the devil. After fasting forty days and forty nights, He was hungry." ...Matthew 4:1–2

Jesus fasted at the beginning of His ministry...before His first miracle, before His first sermon, before His first public moment. That should tell us everything. He didn't fast because He was distant from God...He fasted because He wanted to remain fully dependent on Him. Fasting doesn't make God love you more. It doesn't make your prayers more valuable or your faith more visible. Fasting doesn't change God. It changes **you.** It quiets your flesh so your spirit can finally hear what God has been saying all along.

I don't believe God moves closer to us when we fast...I believe *we* move closer to Him. When you fast, you're saying, "Lord, I want Your voice more than I want this meal." That's not a punishment. That's positioning.

Observation Questions

1. How does this section describe fasting as an act of obedience rather than deprivation?

   _____

   _____

2. What examples from Scripture does this section use to show that Jesus expected His followers to fast?

_____

_____

Application Questions

1. What comfort habit or reliance might be standing between deeper intimacy with God right now?

   _____

   _____

2. What might it look like to fast with the heart posture of surrender rather than obligation?

   _____

   _____

Section 3 - Why Christians Don't Fast

Here are some of the most common reasons people tell me they can't fast...and how God's truth dismantles each one:

1. "I have low blood sugar."

So, do I. And yet, fasting has actually helped regulate it. The more I fasted, the more stable my body became.

2. "I can't function without food."

I run a company with hundreds of employees. I used to believe I needed food to stay productive. Now I know the opposite is true. While fasting, my mind is clearer and my spirit is sharper.

3. "No one else is fasting."

Then you are an example. When my friends saw what fasting was doing in my life, they wanted to.

4. "I'll be too hungry to focus on God."

You might at first. But hunger becomes holy when you give it a purpose.

5. "I'm too busy."

If you're too busy to fast, you're too busy to hear God clearly.

6. "It's just too hard."

Yes. It is. But so is everything worth doing...marriage, parenting, obedience. Growth requires resistance. Every excuse against fasting is really just fear...fear of discomfort, fear of discipline, fear of missing out. But fasting is an antidote to all of it. When you fast, you're not just skipping meals...you're clearing spiritual clutter. You become more aware of what really drives you...comfort, control, or fear...and you learn to let God lead instead.

In those moments of physical weakness, spiritual strength is born. Paul said it best: "When I am weak, then I am strong." That's what fasting teaches...dependence.

If I asked you to pray for five minutes, you'd probably say yes. If I asked you to go to church for an hour, you'd show up. But if I asked you to skip a meal...that's when the real battle begins. Fasting stretches faith like nothing else. It forces you to decide who's in charge...your stomach or your spirit. It's the purest form of self-denial and one of the clearest ways to silence distractions and tune in to the voice of God.

There will be moments when fasting feels impossible...when every bite of food seems to whisper your name. That's when you remind yourself: fasting is not about food...it's about freedom. It's about loosening the grip of the physical world and awakening the spiritual one. That moment when your stomach growls the loudest might be the very moment your spirit hears God the clearest.

Jesus warned against fasting for show. He said not to disfigure your face or act miserable for attention. In today's culture, that might look like posting about your fast on social media or telling everyone how "disciplined" you are. Fasting is meant to be sacred, not performative. It's not about proving holiness...it's about pursuing closeness.

If prayer is the way we talk to God, then fasting is the way we quiet everything else so we can hear His reply. In the noise of life, fasting is silence. In the chaos of the flesh, fasting is surrender. In the wilderness of confusion, fasting is clarity. When you fast, heaven doesn't just hear you...you start hearing heaven.

If you've been longing to hear God clearly, start with hunger. Push away the plate. Set aside the excuses. And tell God, "I want You more." Because fasting isn't just about denying yourself food...it's about desiring His voice above all else. That's when the fog lifts. That's when the static clears. That's when your spirit whispers back, *"Speak, Lord...I'm listening."*

Observation Questions

1. What common reasons are listed in this section for why believers avoid fasting?

_____

_____

2. How does this section explain fasting as a way to expose fear control or misplaced dependence?

_____

_____

Application Questions

1. Which excuse listed in this section feels most familiar and why?

_____

_____

2. What step of faith could be taken to begin fasting in a way that builds dependence on God instead of fear?

_____

_____

HEARING GOD – PERSONAL REFLECTION

1. Where in your life do you sense God inviting you to let go of comfort so you can hear Him more clearly? Take a moment to sit with that question without rushing to an answer, and notice what rises to the surface when you imagine saying yes.

2. When hunger, discomfort, or silence exposes restlessness in your heart, what do you usually turn to for relief? What might it look like to bring that discomfort directly to God instead of numbing it?

Week 3

When God's Yes Feels Confusing

By week three, most of us have experienced this tension. You pray. You listen. You feel confident God is leading you somewhere. And then instead of things opening up, they fall apart.

A door closes.

The plan stalls.

What felt clear suddenly feels confusing.

This is often the moment people start questioning everything. Did I really hear God. Did I miss something. Did I move too fast. Or worse, was I wrong the whole time.

This week is about that space.

The space where obedience is followed by disappointment. Where God's yes does not look like progress. Where trust is tested not by silence, but by outcomes that do not make sense yet.

Scripture reminds us that God's ways are higher than ours. Not just morally, but strategically. He sees timing we cannot see. He sees protection where we feel rejection. He sees preparation where we feel delay.

This week is not about forcing clarity or rushing resolution. It is about learning how to stay close to God when you do not understand what He is doing. It is about resisting the urge to pull back when things feel confusing. It is about trusting that a closed door does not mean God changed His mind.

Sometimes God says yes to the destination, but no to the timing. Sometimes He uses detours to protect you. Sometimes His yes is hidden inside a season that feels like loss.

As you walk through this week, hold space for both faith and disappointment. Bring your questions to God instead of away from Him. And remember this. A delayed answer is not a denied promise.

Stay close.

Keep listening.

And trust that God is still leading, even here.

Chapter 7

When God's Yes Looks Like a No

ICEBREAKER QUESTIONS

1. Have you ever been confident God was leading you somewhere, only to watch the situation fall apart afterward?

2. How do you usually interpret closed doors — as protection, punishment, or personal failure?

3. Do delays make you question God's voice, or do they make you pull back from listening altogether?

BIBLE PASSAGE

Isaiah 55:8–11 (NIV)

8 "For My thoughts are not your thoughts, nor are your ways of My ways," says the Lord. 9 "For as the heavens are higher than the earth, So are My ways higher than your ways, And My thoughts than your thoughts 10 "For as the rain comes down, and the snow from heaven, And do not return there, but water the earth, and make it bring forth and bud, that it may give seed to the sower and bread to the eater 11 So shall My word be that goes forth from My mouth; It shall not return to Me void, but it shall accomplish what I please, and it shall prosper in the thing for which I sent it."

Questions

1. What does this passage reveal about the gap between God's thinking and human understanding, and how does that change the way you interpret delays, detours, or unanswered prayers?

    _____

    _____

2. Where might God be asking you to trust that His Word is still at work beneath the surface, even when you cannot yet see the outcome or understand His process?

    _____

    _____

Section 1 - When God Shows You Something Before Everyone Else Can See It

One of the hardest parts about hearing God's voice is when you're *sure* He said yes...then everything falls apart. You pray, you listen, you step out in faith, and then the whole thing crashes. The doors slam shut. The deal dies. The person walks away. And in that moment, you start spiraling: *Maybe I didn't hear God at all. Maybe that was just me. Maybe I'm terrible at this whole hearing-God thing.*

I've been there. More than once. And let me tell you, it can shake your confidence to the core. But over time, I've learned something beautiful: sometimes God's "yes" comes wrapped in what looks like a "no."

When I moved to Sarasota, Florida from Virginia Beach, it was one of the best decisions I've ever made in my life. I've always been a sunshine girl to my core. I love warmth. I love being outside. I love the beach, the palm trees, the salt in the air, and that golden glow that just makes everything feel alive.

Virginia Beach had started to feel heavy. Don't get me wrong...it's a beautiful place, and it holds so many memories for me. But the winters felt longer every year. I'd look out the window in February, see gray skies, and think, *there has to be more*. And when you've lived in that environment for a while, you start to adapt to it. You forget what it feels like to wake up excited about the day. You settle into the rhythm of routine. You stop realizing how much the weather, the environment, and even the atmosphere of a place can affect your soul.

Then I came to Sarasota...and it was like my entire body was exhaled.

I remember stepping off the plane for the first time, feeling the humidity hit me, and instead of thinking, *Ugh, it's hot,* my spirit said, *yes*. The palm trees were swaying, the sky was this piercing blue, and I remember thinking, *this is where I'm supposed to be*.

I didn't know it yet, but God was about to completely rewrite my chapter here.

After I moved, I started to notice this transformation inside me. I wasn't just happier...I was *lighter*. I felt more connected to God, more peaceful, more aware of His presence in the everyday. I started walking to the beach in the mornings, praying out loud as I watched the sunrise. I would say, "Lord, thank You. Thank You for bringing me here."

After a while, my mom started visiting more and more. And every time she came, she'd light up. She'd walk the beach barefoot, collect shells, and sit with me at restaurants under string lights saying, "I get it now. I see why you love it here."

She lived in Jonesboro, Arkansas at the time. It's a sweet town, and she loved her community there, but let's be honest...the "nicest" restaurant in town was Longhorn Steakhouse. That was where people went to celebrate birthdays. There wasn't much variety. No beaches. No ocean breeze. No Trader Joe's or cute boutiques or places where you could just sit outside year-round.

So, every time she came here, it was like her eyes opened wider. She'd say, "Chantel, I can feel something different here. There's just a peace in the air."

Eventually, after months of praying and visiting, she said, "You know what, I'm moving to Sarasota too."

Observation Questions

3. What emotions and doubts does this section describe when God seems to say yes but circumstances fall apart afterward?

   _____

   _____

4. How does Chantel's Sarasota story illustrate that God's yes can sometimes look like a no at first?

   _____

   _____

Application Questions

1. Have you ever stepped out in faith only to watch everything collapse and then questioned whether God really spoke?

   _____

   _____

2. What might it look like to trust that God could still be right even when the outcome feels disappointing or confusing?

   _____

   _____

Section 2 - The House I Thought Was "It"… Until It Wasn't

Now, if you know me, you know I can be a little high-maintenance sometimes. I like things in a certain way. I like clean, pretty spaces. But let me tell you…I got it from my mother. The apple didn't just fall close to the tree; it hit the trunk and rolled back underneath it. She had a *list*. Not just a general list, but a detailed, typed-out list of what she wanted in her Florida home. Ranch-style. Private backyard. Open floor plan. Pool. Big windows. Tons of natural light. High ceilings. The kind of home that felt like vacation every day.

Her budget was around a million dollars. And if you've ever shopped for real estate in Sarasota, you know that sounds like a lot...until you start looking. A million dollars here is not the same as a million dollars in Arkansas. What gets you a mansion there might get you a nice three-bedroom with an older roof here.

But we were determined. We started house-hunting. When I say we looked...I mean *we looked*. I showed her about thirty houses. I'm not exaggerating. Thirty houses.

And she didn't like a single one.

We'd walk into a home, and before I could even finish the first sentence, she'd whisper, "Ugh. This is awful." We'd spend hours driving around in the Florida heat, getting in and out of the car, checking listings, and every single time, she'd find something wrong:

"This kitchen is too small."

"These ceilings feel low."

"The pool's too close to the neighbors."

"The house feels dark."

At one point, I just laughed and said, "Mom, I think you're looking for heaven."

She flew down twice...*twice*...for dedicated house-hunting trips, and after days of looking, we had nothing.

Finally, I said, "Okay, Mom, I'll start previewing houses for you. I'll FaceTime you from the showings so you can see them live."

One morning, before I left to start my showings, I prayed. I remember this prayer vividly: "Lord, I'm frustrated. We've looked at so many houses. She hates everything. Please, help me find the right one. Show me the house You want for her."

That same day, I walked into a house on Grassland Court...and the moment I stepped inside, I felt it.

It wasn't just that it was beautiful...though it was. The air felt different. It had peace. It checked every single box on her list. Ranch-style, open floor plan, light pouring in through big windows, a screened-in pool with privacy. It was perfect.

I FaceTimed her from the kitchen, walking her through the house. Her eyes got big. "Oh my goodness," she said. "That's it. That's the one. Let's write a contract." So, we did. I was thrilled. After thirty houses, I finally felt like I had found what God was trying to show us.

Two days later, she flew in to see it in person. She walked through the door, looked around for about sixty seconds, and said flatly, "Ugh. I hate it."

I blinked at her. "What do you mean you hate it? You just said this was *the one!* We already have a contract!"

Mom crossed her arms and said, "No. I don't like the layout. I don't want it. I'm one-hundred percent sure."

I just stood there, completely stunned.

So, we canceled the contract.

And I'll be honest...I was confused. I had prayed. I had felt the Holy Spirit say, *This is the house.* Everything had lined up. I thought, *Did I miss it? Did I imagine that?*

We went back to looking...twenty more houses. And she didn't like any of them.

A few weeks later, she called me one morning and said, "You know what? I think you were right. That house on Grassland was the one. I think we need to go back and write on it again."

And that's when it clicked for me. God had shown me the right house...but my mom needed to see it for herself. She had to go through the process of eliminating everything else before she could recognize what God had already revealed.

Sometimes, God will show us something early, but we're not ready to see it. We have to walk through confusion, delay, or even frustration before we can discern that what we saw the first time really *was* Him. That experience taught me one of the most valuable lessons about hearing God's voice: sometimes His "yes" doesn't come immediately. Sometimes He'll let you go in circles, not because He's silent, but because He's waiting for you to *catch up* to what He already spoke.

When my mom finally closed on that Grassland house, she loved it. She decorated it beautifully, and it became her happy place...her home base, her refuge. Every time I walk in now, I think, *This is what obedience looks like.*

Sometimes you just have to trust that even when other people can't see what you see...even when it doesn't make sense or takes longer than you expected...God's voice is still right. And when it all comes together, you realize He wasn't withholding the blessing. He was preparing your heart to receive it.

Observation Questions

1. What details in Chantel's story show how clearly the Grassland house appeared to be the right answer at first?

2. How does this section explain why her mom needed to walk through the process before fully seeing what God had already revealed?

_____

_____

Application Questions

1. Is there something God may have shown you early that has required patience frustration or repeated confirmation?

_____

_____

2. How could waiting and revisiting what God already showed you strengthen trust instead of weakening it?

_____

_____

Section 3 – The Detour I Didn't Want but Actually Needed

That wasn't even my first "yes that looked like a no" moment, I had experienced this years earlier back in Virginia. I'll never forget this story because it's one of those times when I thought I had everything figured out...I was sure I'd heard God's voice...and then everything fell apart.

We'd been praying about finding a new house. I wanted a home that felt like peace. You know that feeling when you walk in and just *know*? I wanted that.

Then one day, I found it.

It was a beautiful house...not on the water like I had dreamed, but close enough that you could almost smell the salt in the air. It had character, light, and the kind of charm that made me want to start decorating it in my head before I even left the showing.

I remember walking through it and feeling this deep knowing in my spirit: *This is the one.*

I went home that night and prayed, "God, is this really it?" And I felt His peace wash over me. Not fireworks or goosebumps, just that quiet confidence that says, "Yes."

So, we wrote a contract.

Now, my husband wasn't as convinced. He looked at me and said, "I don't know, Chantel… something about it doesn't feel right."

And, of course, I said what every confident, spiritually tuned-in wife says when her husband disagrees: "Maybe you're just not hearing what I'm hearing."

Looking back, I can laugh about it. But at the time, I really did believe I had heard God clearly. I thought, *He'll come around.*

It was a bank-owned foreclosure, which meant lots of waiting and uncertainty. It wasn't the kind of deal where you get an answer in a few days. We were tied up in that contract for six long months.

Six months of waiting. Six months of hoping. Six months of me telling myself, *This delay must be part of God's plan.*

I'd drive by the house sometimes, just to look at it. I'd imagine the furniture, the family gatherings, the holidays. I was emotionally moved in before we ever closed.

And then…just when it felt like we were finally getting close…the whole thing fell apart.

The inspection came back with termite damage. The bank refused to fix anything. The deal completely collapsed overnight.

It was gone.

I remember sitting on the couch in shock. My chest literally hurt. I felt like someone had punched me in the stomach.

"God," I said out loud, "what happened? I thought I heard You. I prayed. I felt peace. How could I have missed it?"

If you've ever had one of those moments…where you were so sure you heard from God, and then everything seems to crumble…you know how confusing it feels. You start questioning everything. *Was that even God? Was that just my own desire? Did I get it wrong?*

For days, I wrestled with it. I kept replaying the whole thing in my mind. I didn't understand.

Then, one night…and I remember this so clearly…I was lying in bed, completely exhausted. It was around ten p.m., which for me is basically the middle of the night because I'm usually asleep by nine.

I suddenly felt this strong nudge in my spirit: *Get up. Open your laptop.*

I thought, *That's ridiculous. It's late. I'll look tomorrow.*

But the prompting came again: *Get up. Open your laptop.*

So I sighed, got out of bed, and sat down at the kitchen table. I opened my computer and went to one of the real estate sites I used to scroll through during the day.

The very first listing that popped up made me stop in my tracks.

It was a foreclosure...newly listed...and it was *perfect*. I mean, it had everything we wanted. The layout. The neighborhood. The details that felt like they were handpicked just for us.

My jaw literally dropped.

I called the listing agent immediately, even though it was late. He actually answered the phone, which was another miracle in itself.

He said, "Just so you know, there are already ten offers."

Ten.

I remember hanging up the phone and thinking, *there's no way we're getting this house.* But deep down, I felt this strange peace again...that same quiet knowing.

So, I prayed, "God, if this is the house You have for us, I'm not going to manipulate anything. I'm not going to stress. You'll have to make it happen."

The next morning, things started moving fast. A friend of ours heard about ituateion and offered to help. He literally stepped in and offered to strengthen our offer with cash so we'd have a better chance.

And through a chain of events that could only be described as God's hand at work...we beat out all ten other buyers.

We got the house.

And not only did we get it...it turned out to be better than the first one in *every single way*. The location, the layout, the light, the price...everything.

When we finally moved in, I remember standing in the kitchen one morning, looking around and saying, "Okay, Lord. I see it now."

And right then, I heard Him whisper so clearly to my heart: *I told you to write on the first house on purpose.*

It stopped me.

At first, I didn't understand. But then He continued to show me...I needed that first contract. It wasn't the *destination,* it was the *detour.*

That house had been God's way of *stalling us* while He prepared the real one. If we hadn't been tied up in that first deal for six months, we would have jumped into something else too early and missed His perfect timing.

The waiting wasn't wasted...it was divine delay.

And that's something I've seen over and over again in my life: sometimes God will say "yes" to something that doesn't end up working out, not because He's playing games, but because He's positioning you for the real blessing that's coming later.

Observation Questions

3. What similarities exist between the first house experience and the later foreclosure story in Virginia?

_____

_____

4. How does this section explain divine delay as positioning rather than denial?

_____

_____

Application Questions

1. Is there a past disappointment that still feels confusing because it once felt like a clear yes from God?

_____

_____

2. What would change if detours were seen as preparation instead of failure?

_____

_____

Section 4 – Trusting God When the Yes Takes the Long Way Around

In the moment, it felt like God had pulled the rug out from under me. But looking back, I see His fingerprints all over it. That experience taught me something so important: When God gives you a "no" after you were sure it was a "yes," don't assume you missed Him. Sometimes His "yes" just takes a different route than you expected.

If He's making you wait, it's not punishment…it's protection.

He's not being silent…He's being strategic.

He's aligning the timing, the details, and even the people involved so that when it finally happens, you'll know it's Him and not you.

When I think back on that story now, I can see how perfectly He orchestrated it all. Every delay, every frustration, every "no" that felt like a heartbreak was just part of His bigger "yes." And that's what I love about God…He doesn't waste anything. Not your tears, not your waiting, not even your confusion. He's always working behind the scenes, setting things up that you can't see yet. And when the timing finally clicks into place, it's so much better than anything you could have arranged yourself.

Both of those experiences taught me something priceless: hearing from God doesn't guarantee the path will be straight or smooth. Sometimes His yes will look like a no. Sometimes it'll feel like the door slammed shut, when He's really just rerouting you to something better.

The trick is to stay close…to keep listening even when you're disappointed, even when you're confused, even when you don't understand. Because when you stick with Him through the detours, you eventually see what He was doing all along: weaving every delay, every dead end, every heartbreak into a plan that was *always* for your good. So the next time it feels like God's "yes" turned into a "no," don't panic. Don't assume you missed Him. You might just be standing in the middle of His yes…you just haven't seen the full picture yet.

Observation Questions

1. How does this section reframe waiting and delay as part of God's strategy rather than His silence?

   _____

   _____

2. What does this section teach about God using confusion heartbreak and timing to accomplish a greater plan?

   _____

   _____

Application Questions

1. When something takes longer than expected does trust tend to grow or does panic begin to take over?

   _____

   _____

2. What would it look like to stay close to God and keep listening even when the path feels unclear?

   _____

   _____

HEARING GOD – PERSONAL REFLECTION

1. Is there a time when you thought God said "yes," but it ended in disappointment? Looking back now, can you see how God may have been working behind the scenes?

2. Are you willing to trust God's voice even when His path feels slower, harder, or more confusing than expected?

Chapter 8

When God Changes the Message

ICEBREAKER QUESTIONS

1. Have you ever been confident in your plan, only to feel God interrupt it at the last minute?

2. How do you usually respond when God's direction feels inconvenient or poorly timed?

3. Do you trust God more in quiet preparation moments, or under pressure when everything is on the line?

BIBLE PASSAGE

Proverbs 16:9 (NIV)

"In their hearts humans plan their course,

but the Lord establishes their steps."

Question

1. How does this verse show the difference between making plans and trusting God with the outcome, and where might God be redirecting your steps right now even if it wasn't part of your original plan?

_____

_____

Section 1 - When God Changes the Plan at the Last Minute

One of the hardest parts about following God's voice is that sometimes He completely interrupts your plans. You prepare, you strategize, you map it all out in your mind...how it's supposed to go, what you're supposed to say, what the outcome should be...and then, right when everything's ready, the Holy Spirit whispers, *"Nope. We're going in a different direction."*

It's unsettling. Sometimes it's downright terrifying. Because you're standing there thinking, *God, You could've mentioned this a little earlier!* But what I've found is that those moments...the inconvenient ones, the ones that throw your plans out the window...are often the very moments God shows up the most.

Not long ago, I was invited to speak at one of the biggest real estate conferences I had ever been part of. We're talking six thousand people in the audience. A massive stage. Spotlights. Cameras everywhere. The kind of event where you feel the weight of it the second you walk into the building.

I remember arriving that morning, feeling a mix of excitement and nerves. I had prepared for weeks...maybe even months...for that moment. I had my notes, my stories, my slides, everything neatly organized and perfectly timed down to the second. I had rehearsed my opening line so many times I could say it in my sleep.

I'd worked hard on this message because I wanted to deliver something powerful. Something polished. Something that would make people take notes and think, *Wow, that was inspiring.*

Backstage, it was all energy. Staff running around with headsets. Production crew testing lights and sound. The music was loud. There was this hum of anticipation in the air. The makeup team had just finished with me. I had my microphone clipped on, my cue sheet in hand, and my slides loaded onto the big screen. Everything was ready. Everything was perfect.

And then...about twenty-five minutes before I was supposed to walk out...I felt that unmistakable whisper of the Holy Spirit.

"Chantel, that's not the message I want you to give today."

I froze. I didn't even move.

For a second, I thought, *Did I just imagine that?*

So, I brushed it off and tried to refocus. I thought, *Maybe I'm just nervous.* But then it came again.

"This isn't the message I want you to give."

Observation Questions

2. What does this section describe about how God sometimes interrupts carefully prepared plans right before the moment of execution?

    _____

    _____

3. How does Chantel's conference story show the contrast between human preparation and the Holy Spirit's prompting?

    _____

    _____

Application Questions

1. How do last minute changes typically feel when plans are already set and expectations are high?

    _____

    _____

2. What would it look like to trust that God's interruption might actually be an invitation instead of an inconvenience?

    _____

    _____

Section 2 - Choosing Obedience When Everything Is on the Line

My heart started pounding. I looked at my perfectly typed notes sitting there on the table, and I thought, *God, what do You mean? This is the one I've practiced! This is what the organizers approved! This is what the CEO expects!*

But the whisper didn't go away. In fact, it got stronger. It was like this quiet weight that settled in my chest, firm but gentle, saying, *Change the message.*

My stomach dropped.

I glanced at the countdown clock...24 minutes until I was supposed to walk on stage. Thousands of people waiting. And I could feel the internal tug-of-war starting:

Was that really God, or was that just me overthinking?

What if I mess this up?

What if people think I'm unprepared?

then another thought hit me: *What if it really is God, and I ignore Him?*

So, I took a deep breath and whispered, "Okay, Lord. I'm listening."

I turned to one of the event coordinators and asked, "Hey, is there a quiet room I can use for a few minutes?" They led me to this small backstage room...just a plain folding table, a chair, and a water bottle. I sat down, pulled out a notepad, and my hand was literally shaking. I could hear the muffled sound of the music from the main room and the emcee warming up the crowd.

Twenty minutes.

I whispered, "Okay, Holy Spirit, I need You. What do You want me to say?"

And suddenly, it was like a flood. Thoughts, ideas, phrases...they started coming faster than I could write. My hand could barely keep up. Whole new stories, new scriptures, new points I hadn't planned at all. It was raw, unpolished, but it was alive.

I remember sitting there thinking, *this doesn't even sound like me. This sounds like You.*

The event assistant poked her head in and said, "You're up in five."

I looked at my notes...a mess of scribbles...and felt the panic rise for just a moment. My heart was racing. Everything in my human brain wanted to cling to my original plan. The safe one. The practiced one. The one I knew would go smoothly. But the whisper came again, so gently: *Trust Me.*

So, I grabbed my notepad, said a quick prayer..."Okay, Lord, if this is You, You're going to have to speak through me"...and walked toward the stage.

I could feel the bright lights hit my face as I stepped up to the podium. I looked out at six thousand faces staring back at me, waiting. My hands were shaking, but I smiled and said, "Before I start, I need to be honest. I had a completely different message prepared for today. But twenty minutes ago, the Holy Spirit told me to change it. So, if this is for you...just know God stopped an entire message to speak directly into your life."

You could have heard a pin drop.

And then, as I began to speak, it was like something took over. The nerves disappeared. The words flowed. It didn't feel like I was preaching *to* the audience...it felt like God was speaking *through* me.

Observation Questions

1. What internal conflict is described when the Holy Spirit asks for obedience under pressure and limited time?

     _____

     _____

2. How does this section show the difference between a safe prepared plan and a surrendered response to God's voice?

     _____

     _____

Application Questions

1. When pressure is high do you tend to cling to what feels safe or pause to listen for God's direction?

     _____

     _____

2. What fear tends to surface most when obedience could risk reputation comfort or control?

     _____

     _____

Section 3 - The Peace That Only Comes From Obedience

I shared stories I hadn't planned to tell. I talked about obedience, about trusting God's redirection, about the difference between *good* ideas and *God* ideas. I remember saying, "Sometimes, what looks like a last-minute detour is actually divine direction."

People were crying. I could see it from the stage...grown men wiping their eyes, women nodding, hands being raised. And when I finished, the room stood in complete silence for a second...and then everyone started clapping. But it wasn't that loud, hyped-up kind of applause. It was slow, deep, reverent. You could feel God's presence in the room.

Afterward, person after person came up to me, tears in their eyes, sharing from their hearts:

"That message was exactly what I needed."

"I was going to quit real estate after this conference, but now I know God's not done with me."

"I've been praying for confirmation, and you said the exact words I asked God to show me."

I stood there, completely undone. Because I knew...this wasn't me.

What I had prepared was good...professional, polished, and safe. But what God gave me in those twenty minutes was *anointed*.

That day changed how I viewed obedience forever.

I realized that hearing from God isn't just for early mornings in your prayer chair. It's not just for quiet moments with worship music playing softly in the background. It's also for the moments when everything is on the line. When you're under pressure. When saying "yes" might cost you something.

And here's what I've learned:

When God speaks, obedience is the only right response...even when it makes no sense.

That day, I learned that I never want to be so polished that I miss His presence. I never want to be so prepared that I leave no room for His prompting. The Holy Spirit isn't interested in perfect presentations...He's after surrendered vessels. And I'll tell you what...the peace I felt after that talk wasn't the peace of a job well done. It was the peace of knowing I had done what He asked me to do, no matter what. That's the kind of peace you can't earn, plan, or fake. That's the kind of peace that only comes when you choose obedience over comfort. And that moment...standing on that stage, with my messy handwritten notes...became one of the most powerful "God moments" of my life.

That moment changed me forever. Because it showed me that when God interrupts your life, it's never to inconvenience you...it's to partner with you in a miracle. Sometimes He changes your message at a conference. Sometimes He reroutes your morning jog. Sometimes He wrecks your plans just to let you witness His power. And every single time...it's better than what you had planned.

The key is this: when you hear His voice, obey. Even if it feels crazy. Even if it doesn't make sense. Even if everyone around you thinks you've lost it. Because on the other side of your obedience might be someone else's answered prayer.

Today, I can honestly say I'm grateful for those lessons...as costly as they were. Because without them, I wouldn't have learned that the peace of God is not a soft feeling; it's a strong boundary. It's how He keeps His children safe from the deals that glitter but aren't gold.

That's why Proverbs 10:22 has become one of my anchor verses:

"The blessing of the Lord brings wealth, and He adds no sorrow to it."

If there's sorrow attached, if there's striving, if there's confusion...it's not from Him. God's blessings don't come with fine print. So now, before I say yes to anything...whether it's a business deal, a move, or even a friendship...I don't just ask, "Does it look good?"

I ask, "Does it feel peaceful?" Because peace is the currency of the Kingdom...and I never want to go bankrupt again.

Observation Questions

1. What fruit followed obedience in this story and how did it differ from a typical successful outcome?

   _____

   _____

2. How does this section define peace as something deeper than relief or accomplishment?

   _____

   _____

Application Questions

1. Have you ever experienced peace after obedience even when the choice felt risky or uncomfortable?

   _____

   _____

2. What decision right now needs to be filtered through the question does this bring peace or pressure?

_____

_____

HEARING GOD – PERSONAL REFLECTION

1. When was the last time God interrupted your plans, and how did you respond?

2. Are you willing to obey God even when it costs comfort, control, or reputation?

Chapter 9

Radical Encounters and Reluctant Obedience

ICEBREAKER QUESTIONS

1. Have you ever felt God ask you to do something that immediately made you uncomfortable or afraid?

2. When God interrupts your routine, do you tend to resist first or respond quickly?

3. Is there an area of obedience you have delayed because it feels too costly or inconvenient?

BIBLE PASSAGE

Acts 9:1–19 (NIV)

1 Meanwhile Saul was still breathing out murderous threats against the Lord's disciples. He went to the high priest

2 and asked him for letters to the synagogues in Damascus, so that if he found any there who belonged to the Way, whether men or women, he might take them as prisoners to Jerusalem.

3 As he neared Damascus on his journey, suddenly a light from heaven flashed around him.

4 He fell to the ground and heard a voice say to him, "Saul, Saul, why do you persecute me?"

5 "Who are you, Lord?" Saul asked.

"I am Jesus, whom you are persecuting," he replied.

6 "Now get up and go into the city, and you will be told what you must do."

7 The men traveling with Saul stood there speechless; they heard the sound but did not see anyone.

8 Saul got up from the ground, but when he opened his eyes he could see nothing. So they led him by the hand into Damascus.

9 For three days he was blind, and did not eat or drink anything.

10 In Damascus there was a disciple named Ananias. The Lord called to him in a vision, "Ananias!" "Yes, Lord," he answered.

11 The Lord told him, "Go to the house of Judas on Straight Street and ask for a man from Tarsus named Saul, for he is praying.

12 In a vision he has seen a man named Ananias come and place his hands on him to restore his sight."

13 "Lord," Ananias answered, "I have heard many reports about this man and all the harm he has done to your holy people in Jerusalem.

14 And he has come here with authority from the chief priests to arrest all who call on your name."

15 But the Lord said to Ananias, "Go! This man is my chosen instrument to proclaim my name to the Gentiles and their kings and to the people of Israel.

16 I will show him how much he must suffer for my name.

17 Then Ananias went to the house and entered it. Placing his hands on Saul, he said, "Brother Saul, the Lord—Jesus, who appeared to you on the road as you were coming here—has sent me so that you may see again and be filled with the Holy Spirit."

18 Immediately, something like scales fell from Saul's eyes, and he could see again. He got up and was baptized,

19 and after taking some food, he regained his strength.

Questions

1. What do you notice about how God interrupts Saul's life and speaks to Ananias at the same time, and where might God be working in ways you cannot yet see or fully understand?

_____

_____

2. How does this passage show that obedience often requires action before clarity, and what step might God be asking you to take even though it feels uncomfortable or risky?

_____

_____

3. What does Saul's season of blindness, waiting, and dependence reveal about how God prepares hearts for transformation, and how might God be using a waiting or humbling season in your own life right now?

_____

_____

Section 1 - When Obedience Feels Risky but Changes Everything

If you really want to hear God's voice, you have to be ready for two things:

1. He may speak in ways that radically interrupt your life.
2. He may ask you to do something you don't want to do.

One of my favorite Bible stories is about Saul, who absolutely hated Christians. Not dislike..._hate_. He hunted them, dragged them from their homes, watched them beaten and even killed. And one day, he set out for Damascus to do more damage.

But on that road, heaven broke through. A blinding light hit him so hard it knocked him straight off his horse. Face-down in the dirt, he heard a voice:

"Saul, Saul, why do you persecute Me?"

Shaking, covered in dust, he stammered, "Who are You, Lord?"

And the voice answered, "I am Jesus, the One you are persecuting."

When Saul got up, he couldn't see a thing. For three long days he sat in darkness...blind, broken, and unsure what just happened.

Meanwhile, miles away, God spoke to a man named Ananias. "Go lay hands on Saul so he can see again."

Ananias instantly pushed back. "Lord… that guy kills Christians! You can't be serious."

But God was clear: "Go. He's My chosen instrument."

So Ananias went. Heart pounding, palms sweating, he went. He walked right up to the man who had terrified the church, placed his hands on him, and said, "Brother Saul, the Lord Jesus...who appeared to you on the road...has sent me so that you may see again and be filled with the Holy Spirit."

Immediately, scales fell from Saul's eyes. Sight returned. His heart transformed. The man who once destroyed believers became the apostle who wrote much of the New Testament.

I love that story because it's full of reluctant obedience on *both* sides. Saul never planned to meet Jesus that day. And Ananias definitely didn't want to meet Saul. Yet both of them obeyed...and that one act of courage changed history.

Observation Questions

1. What does this section show about how God's voice can interrupt life suddenly and ask for obedience that feels uncomfortable or frightening?

   _____

   _____

2. How does the story of Saul and Ananias demonstrate that God often speaks to more than one person to accomplish His plan?

   _____

   _____

Application Questions

1. Has there ever been a moment when obedience felt risky because it involved people or situations that felt unsafe or undeserved?

   _____

   _____

2. What might change if obedience was viewed as participation in God's plan rather than personal risk?

   _____

   _____

Section 2 - Small Yeses That Build Big Trust

That story hits home for me because I've had my share of "Are You sure, God?" moments. There was the time I was in line at a grocery store behind a young mom with two toddlers. She swiped her card...declined. Tried again...declined. I could feel the panic rising in her. I had already finished paying, and I heard that gentle nudge: *"Go back. Pay for her groceries."*

Everything in me resisted. *God, that's awkward. Everyone's watching. She'll be embarrassed. I don't even know if she wants help.* But the whisper came again, firmer this time.

So I turned around, smiled at the cashier, and quietly said, "Add her total to mine."

The mom burst into tears. Between sniffles she said, "I just told my kids, 'We'll have to come back another day when I get paid.'"

It was such a small thing...a few bags of groceries...but the presence of God was so strong in that checkout line, I could hardly hold it together. Moments like that taught me that obedience doesn't have to be grand. It just has to be *yes*.

One of the biggest areas where God has stretched my obedience is in giving. Years ago, He spoke clearly to my heart: *"You're going to live on 10% and give 90% away."*

I laughed out loud.

"God, I can barely tithe 10%. You want 90%? That's not giving...that's bankruptcy!"

But the whisper wouldn't leave. So I took small steps. I started increasing what I gave bit by bit. Each time, God showed up in ways that made no earthly sense...refund checks arriving in the mail, debts erased, surprise opportunities I could never have orchestrated. Every act of obedience built another layer of trust. And with each yes, His voice grew clearer.

Obedience isn't easy. It stretches you. It humbles you. It forces you to rely on God when nothing adds up. But it's also where the relationship gets real...where your faith stops being theory and becomes breath-by-breath dependence.

The story of Paul and Ananias reminds me of this: God's voice often leads us into places we'd never choose ourselves. Sometimes it's a grocery store line. Sometimes it's a giant financial leap. Sometimes it's forgiving someone you swore you never would. But that's where the miracles happen. If you want to hear God's voice more clearly, prepare your heart for obedience that might scare you. Because every time you say yes...even when it's uncomfortable...you open the door for transformation: in you, and in the lives He touches through your surrender.

Observation Questions

1. What examples does this section give to show that obedience does not have to be dramatic to be powerful?

    _____

    _____

2. How does Chantel's story illustrate that repeated small acts of obedience build deeper trust over time?

    _____

    _____

Application Questions

1. What small nudge or quiet prompting might God be asking you to respond to right now?

    _____

    _____

2. How could saying yes in a small way today prepare your heart for bigger acts of obedience later?

    _____

    _____

HEARING GOD – PERSONAL REFLECTION

1. Is there something God has asked you to do that you've delayed because it feels uncomfortable or risky?

2. Are you willing to obey God even when the outcome is unclear or inconvenient?

Week 4

Trusting God With What You Can See

Week 4 brings faith out of theory and into real life.

Because few things test trust like money, provision, and security.

It is easy to say we trust God when things feel stable. It is much harder when resources feel tight, answers feel delayed, and the numbers do not add up. This week invites you to examine what happens in your heart when provision feels uncertain. Do you lean into trust, or do you tighten your grip and try to control the outcome?

Throughout these chapters, you will see that God often uses financial pressure to reveal deeper spiritual truths. Not to shame. Not to punish. But to realign trust. Provision is rarely just about money. It is about dependence, surrender, and learning to recognize God as the true source.

You will explore what it means to obey before evidence appears. To give when logic resists. To seek peace rather than opportunity. To learn the difference between confirmation and control. And to recognize that God's voice often becomes clearer when trust replaces fear.

This week is not about reckless faith or ignoring wisdom. It is about learning to trust God beyond what you can calculate, predict, or guarantee. It is about discovering that peace is often the loudest confirmation God gives.

As you move through Week 4, pay attention to where fear rises and where peace settles. Notice where God may be inviting you to loosen your grip and trust Him more deeply.

Because when God becomes your source, everything else begins to fall into its proper place.

Chapter 10

From $9 an Hour to God's Overflow

ICEBREAKER QUESTIONS

1. Have you ever faced a financial situation where trusting God felt harder than trying to control the outcome?

2. How do financial pressures tend to affect your faith and decision-making?

3. What comes to mind when you hear the word overflow in a biblical context?

BIBLE PASSAGE

Proverbs 3:5–6 (NIV)

5 Trust in the Lord with all your heart

and lean not on your own understanding;

6 in all your ways submit to Him,

and He will make your paths straight.

Question

1. What does this passage teach about the difference between trusting God and relying on your own understanding, and where might God be asking you to surrender control so He can straighten your path?

_____

_____

Section 1 – When Rock Bottom Meets a Quiet Whisper

I can still see it as if it happened yesterday...the grocery store line, the beeping of the scanner, the bags piling up at the end of the counter. And then the moment that felt like someone had ripped the floor right out from under me.

"Your card was declined."

Those three words shattered me.

I can still feel my cheeks burning. I can hear the people behind me sighing, shifting their weight, probably thinking, *Come on, lady, hurry up.* I wanted to crawl into the linoleum floor and disappear. The cashier didn't look mean...she was just doing her job...but in that moment it felt like the whole world was looking at me, whispering, *You're a failure. You can't even buy food.*

That wasn't the first time I had felt it, but it was the loudest wake-up call.

Back then, I was working an entry-level job. Nine bucks an hour. Twenty hours a week. I don't even know if you can technically call that a job...it was more like an allowance. By the time I got my paycheck, it was already gone.

Rent was late more than it was on time. Gas went on a credit card. Groceries went on a credit card. And every month I made the minimum payment, just enough to keep the collectors off my back, while the balance climbed higher and higher until I was staring at a mountain of $10,000 in debt.

And here's the worst part: I was still swiping that card, knowing full well there was no money behind it. It's one thing to be broke. It's another to feel trapped by the very choices that got you there.

My definition of "success" at the time was embarrassingly small: if I could just buy groceries without praying the card would clear, if I could just pay rent without juggling late fees, that would feel like a win. Forget about vacations or new clothes. Forget about eating out at restaurants. At that stage of my life, *a full tank of gas* felt like luxury.

One Sunday, I sat in church...exhausted, numb, and desperate for something to change. The pastor started preaching on tithing.

"The Bible says, *'Test Me in this,'*" he read. "Bring the whole tithe into the storehouse, and see if I won't throw open the floodgates of heaven."

I wanted to roll my eyes. *Test God? With what?* I didn't even have enough money for groceries. The idea of giving away any of it felt impossible. But I couldn't shake it. Something deep inside me was stirring. It wasn't a booming voice or lightning from heaven...it was just this quiet whisper: *Trust Me.*

That whisper wouldn't leave me alone. I wrestled all week. By the next Sunday, I was still broke...completely broke. I didn't even have enough in my account to cover a tithe, but I grabbed my checkbook anyway. With trembling hands, I wrote a check for $30. I remember staring at it, knowing full well that I didn't have that much in my account.

It was reckless by every logical standard. I literally whispered, "God, please let this go through." It wasn't a faith moment filled with confidence...it was a faith moment filled with desperation. I was testing Him, just like the verse said: *"Test Me in this."* That night, I went to bed with my stomach empty but my heart strangely peaceful.

The next day, I went to the mailbox and saw an envelope from Dominion Power...my old utility company. My first thought was, *Great, another bill.*

I tore it open, and inside was a check.

Three hundred dollars.

I just stood there, frozen, then burst into tears.

Three hundred dollars...exactly ten times what I had given the day before. It was as if God Himself whispered, *See? You can trust Me. I've got you.* That moment changed everything. I didn't just believe God could provide...I *knew* He would.

That moment gave me a glimpse of God's faithfulness, but He wasn't done yet. Not long after, my aunt called me. Totally out of the blue. I wasn't expecting it. I wasn't asking. She just said, "I've decided I want to pay off your credit card debt."

I almost dropped the phone. "Wait, what? Are you serious?"

She wired the money and just like that, $10,000 of debt...gone. I hung up the phone and literally bounced up and down in my tiny little apartment. I couldn't believe it. I went from standing in a grocery store with a declined card to having my entire debt wiped clean. And in that moment, I knew it wasn't luck. It wasn't coincidence. It was God. He was showing me, *If you trust Me with the little you have, I will take care of you in ways you can't even imagine.*

That would've been enough. But God wasn't just trying to pay off my debt. He was trying to change my whole perspective on money.

Observation Questions

2. What does this section reveal about how God often speaks most clearly during moments of humiliation or desperation?

   _____

   _____

3. How does the quiet whisper of trust contrast with the loud fear and shame experienced in the grocery store moment? _____

Application Questions

1. Have you ever experienced a moment where fear was loud but God's voice felt quiet yet persistent?

   _____

   _____

2. What would it look like to trust God with obedience even when logic and circumstances say it makes no sense?

   _____

   _____

Section 2 - Learning to Trust God With More Than Makes Sense

One day I was listening to Rick Warren share his story about giving. He explained that he and his wife lived on 10% of their income and gave 90% away. I nearly laughed out loud. "God, are You kidding me? I just started giving 10%, and that feels like a stretch. Now You want me to give away 90%?!"

But deep inside, I knew it was Him. It wasn't just a passing thought. It was that same quiet but firm whisper: *That's what I want you to do.*

So I made a decision. I didn't flip the switch overnight, but I committed that every year I would increase my giving by 3%. By the time I turn 54, I want to be giving away 90% of my income. It wasn't about math. It wasn't about the exact percentage. It was about obedience. Every time I stretched, every time I gave when it didn't make sense, God showed up again and again.

My Giving Progression Chart (Age 27–54)

AGE	Giving %
27	10%
28	13%
29	16%
30	19%
31	22%
32	25%
33	28%
34	31%
35	34%
36	37%
37	40%
38	43%
39	46%
40	49%
41	52%
42	55%
43	58%
44	61%
45	64%
46	67%
47	70%

48	73%
49	76%
50	79%
51	82%
52	85%
53	88%
54	90%

Observation Questions

1. What pattern of obedience and trust is demonstrated through the gradual increase in giving over time?

   _____

   _____

2. How does this section show that God often invites obedience before providing visible security?

   _____

   _____

Application Questions

1. What area of life might God be asking you to trust Him with more than feels reasonable right now?

   _____

   _____

2. How could small, consistent steps of obedience build long term confidence in God's faithfulness?

   _____

   _____

Section 3 - From Obedience to Overflow

Two years later, God opened a door I never could have seen coming: real estate. I didn't have the connections. I didn't have the money. I didn't even have the confidence. But I had one thing: obedience.

In my very first year, I sold 54 houses. *Fifty-four.* To put that in perspective, the average real estate agent sells maybe three a year. Some don't sell any. I was named Rookie of the Year, and my business exploded almost overnight. From there, God kept multiplying. Before long, I wasn't just surviving anymore. I was leading a multimillion-dollar company with over 130 employees, multiple offices, and growth rates that averaged 40% year after year.

I went from not being able to buy groceries to running a business I never even dreamed was possible. And through it all, I knew one thing: it wasn't me. It was Him.

Now one of my greatest joys is teaching my son Kyle the same principles that saved my life. When he gets his $10 allowance, I remind him:

"One dollar goes back to God. One dollar goes into savings. The rest...you can choose. Save it. Spend it. Or give more."

And do you know what he said one day that made me cry?

"I like giving my allowance because then I can help other people."

That's it. That's the whole point. That's the legacy I want to pass on. Not just money. Not just success. But a heart of obedience that says, *God, I trust You. Whatever I have, it's Yours.*

Observation Questions

1. How does this section illustrate the connection between obedience and unexpected provision?

   _____

   _____

2. What role does faithfulness with small things play in the growth and multiplication described here?

   _____

   _____

Application Questions

1. Where might God be inviting you to step into obedience before feeling fully qualified or prepared?

   _____

   _____

2. How could teaching generosity and trust to the next generation shape a lasting spiritual legacy?

Section 4 - Remembering Who the Fries Belong To

One day, I was at the grocery store with my two kids...Shayla, who was about 12 at the time, and my son Kyle, who was just a little guy. Now, anyone who knows me knows I'm passionate about eating healthy. So when we went grocery shopping, I usually kept the cart full of fruits, veggies, and clean foods. But I also tried to be balanced, so I told the kids, "You each get to pick one junk-food item." It was their little treat for coming with me.

That day, Shayla picked a can of sour cream and onion Pringles. As we were at the register paying, she popped open the can, and that familiar smell hit me. I said, "Oh, those smell good, Shayla...let me have one." Without hesitation, she pulled the can back and said, "No, they're my Pringles!" I didn't say a word. I just quietly took the Pringles from her, turned around, and dropped the entire can right into the trash can behind the register.

The air went completely still. Nobody said a word...Shayla didn't, Kyle didn't...but everyone felt what I was saying. They weren't her Pringles. I had bought the Pringles. I drove them to the store, chose to let her pick them, paid for them, and could buy her ten more cans if I wanted to. But I could also take them away in an instant.

That moment stayed with me...not just as a parenting lesson, but as a spiritual one. A few years later, I had a similar moment with my son Kyle. He was about five years old, and we stopped at McDonald's to get him some fries. I didn't order any for myself because I was trying to be "good." But when that smell of hot, salty fries filled the car, I couldn't resist. I reached over and grabbed one. Kyle immediately shouted, "You can't have any! They're mine!"

In that instant, God spoke to me. Kyle forgot three things:

1. I was the source of all his fries. I drove him there, I ordered them, I paid for them. Without me, there would be no fries.

2. I controlled how many fries he got. I could take them away, or I could have bought him an entire truckload.

3. I didn't need his fries. I could've bought my own...or ten more if I wanted. But I wanted him to learn something deeper: the joy of sharing.

And that's exactly what God teaches us. He is the source of all our "fries" ...our money, our gifts, our opportunities. Proverbs 21:26 says, "Some people are always greedy for more, but the godly love to give."

We all know John 3:16... "For God so loved the world that He gave His only Son." You can give without loving, but you cannot love without giving. Generosity is how we reflect God's heart. It's how we tune our ears to His frequency. Every time we give, we make room for Him to speak. For years, I practiced giving quietly because Matthew 6:3 says, "Don't let your left hand know what your right hand is doing." But one day, God spoke to me clearly: "You're allowed to share your story...not to boast, but to inspire others to give." That's when I began to tell people what I had learned about giving...and how my goal became to give away 90% and live on 10%.

It wasn't easy at first. I had to fight fear, control, and the old belief that giving meant losing. But the more I gave, the more I realized: you can't outgive God. He keeps giving back...not just money, but peace, purpose, and provision. He multiplies generosity like a ripple in water.

Every time you give, you open a new channel for God to flow through your life. So the next time you feel that nudge to give, remember: God is the source of your fries. He gave you the car that got you there, the job that paid for the meal, and the breath in your lungs to enjoy it all. The fries were never really yours to begin with...they were always His. Generosity isn't about losing. It's about aligning your heart with the Giver Himself. And when you live that way...hands open, heart willing...you'll start to hear His voice more clearly than ever before.

When I look back at that girl in the grocery store, standing there humiliated with her declined credit card, I want to hug her and say, "Hold on. You have no idea what God is about to do."

I went from $9 an hour to multimillion-dollar overflow. Not because I was smart enough or lucky enough or worked hard enough...though I worked plenty hard. It happened because I trusted God with the little I had, and He proved Himself faithful with the much I never imagined.

"Trust in the Lord with all your heart, and lean not on your own understanding. In all your ways acknowledge Him, and He will direct your paths." (Proverbs 3:5–6)

I wrote a $30 check I wasn't sure would clear. And from that one act of obedience, God started a cycle of blessing that has carried me every step of the way.

So if you're standing in your own "grocery store line" moment right now...if you feel humiliated, overwhelmed, and unsure of how you'll even make it to next week...hear me: God sees you. He is faithful. And He's not finished yet.

Observation Questions

1. What lesson about ownership and stewardship is revealed through the Pringles and fries stories?

   _____

   _____

2. How does this section connect generosity with recognizing God as the true source of everything?

   _____

   _____

Application Questions

1. What "fries" might you be holding onto too tightly instead of trusting God with open hands?

   _____

   _____

2. How could generosity become a practical way to tune your heart more closely to God's voice?

   _____

   _____

HEARING GOD – PERSONAL REFLECTION

1. Where is God inviting you to trust Him more fully in your finances or resources?
2. How might obedience and generosity help you hear God's voice more clearly?

Chapter 11

Giving When It Doesn't Make Sense

ICEBREAKER QUESTION

1. Have you ever sensed God asking you to give at a time when your finances felt stretched?

2. How do you usually decide between saving for the future and trusting God through generosity?

3. Do you believe obedience in giving is a one-time decision or an ongoing practice?

BIBLE PASSAGE

Malachi 3:1 (NIV)

"I will send my messenger, who will prepare the way before me. Then suddenly the Lord you are seeking will come to his temple; the messenger of the covenant, whom you desire, will come," says the Lord Almighty.

2 But who can endure the day of his coming? Who can stand when he appears? For he will be like a refiner's fire or a launderer's soap. 3 He will sit as a refiner and purifier of silver; he will purify the Levites and refine them like gold and silver. Then the Lord will have men who will bring offerings in righteousness, 4 and the offerings of Judah and Jerusalem will be acceptable to the Lord, as in days gone by, as in former years.

5 "So I will come to put you on trial. I will be quick to testify against sorcerers, adulterers and perjurers, against those who defraud laborers of their wages, who oppress the widows and the fatherless, and deprive the foreigners among you of justice, but do not fear me," says the Lord Almighty.

Breaking Covenant by Withholding Tithes

6 "I the Lord do not change. So you, the descendants of Jacob, are not destroyed. 7 Ever since the time of your ancestors you have turned away from my decrees and have not kept them. Return to me, and I will return to you," says the Lord Almighty.

"But you ask, 'How are we to return?'

8 "Will a mere mortal rob God? Yet you rob me.

"But you ask, 'How are we robbing you?'

"In tithes and offerings. 9 You are under a curse—your whole nation—because you are robbing me. 10 Bring the whole tithe into the storehouse, that there may be food in my house. Test me in this," says the Lord Almighty, "and see if I will not throw open the floodgates of heaven and pour out so much blessing that there will not be room enough to store it.

Questions

1. What does this passage reveal about God's purpose in refining and purifying His people, and how might a difficult or uncomfortable season in your life actually be preparation rather than punishment?

   _____

   _____

2. How does God connect returning to Him with obedience in tithes and offerings in this passage, and what might returning to Him look like practically in your own life right now?

   _____

   _____

3. What stands out about God inviting His people to "test" Him in this area, and how might fear, control, or trust be influencing the way you handle what God has entrusted to you?

   _____

   _____

Section 1 - When Giving Stops Feeling Easy

By the time you finish reading my story from the last chapter, you might be thinking, *Wow, God really showed up for you. If I had miracle refund checks and debt paid off, I'd give too.*

But here's the thing...obedience in giving doesn't just happen once. It's not a one-time $30 test. It's a lifestyle of saying yes to God, even when the math doesn't make sense. And let me tell you...there have been plenty of times when I stared at my bank account, stared at my giving goals, and thought, *Lord, this is impossible. I can't keep this up.*

Yet every single time I wrestled with fear, God reminded me: *I am your source. Your business is not your source. Your paycheck is not your source. I Am.*

This story definitely belongs in the section about **giving**...because it's one of those moments where God made His message so clear, it almost took my breath away.

Lately, I'd been wrestling in my heart about giving. I love giving...it's one of the ways I feel closest to God...but if I'm being totally transparent, I'd started to feel stretched. Our expenses were high, the business wasn't bringing in as much as it had in the past, and I found myself worrying more about saving than sowing.

I told myself, *"Giving is good, but saving is important too."* And I meant that...but deep down, I knew something wasn't sitting right. So one night, I started praying about it.

I said, "Okay, Lord, I'm just being honest. I feel like I've been giving too much and not saving enough. Maybe I need to scale back for a while. Unless You show me...like really show me...that You want me to keep giving at the same level or more, I'm going to start lowering my giving this Friday." That was my honest prayer.

Observation Questions

1. What tension do you see in this section between trusting God as the source and the pressure to rely on saving, income, or business stability?

    _____

    _____

2. What patterns emerge in how fear and honesty show up when giving begins to feel unsustainable or uncomfortable?

    _____

    _____

Application Questions

1. Where are you currently feeling stretched or hesitant in your own giving, and what thoughts are influencing that hesitation?

    _____

    _____

2. What would it look like for you to honestly bring your fear, limits, or confusion about giving before God instead of quietly adjusting on your own?

Section 2 – My Fleece Moment in the Mailbox

And then...I kid you not...**the very next day**, I got a check in the mail. Not a small check. Not a refund I was expecting. But a **check for $17,000.**

When I opened it, I literally had to sit down. The memo line said it was for an *"adjustment in membership rewards."* Apparently, there had been an accounting error with our rewards account, and they owed us the cash value back. Not points. Not store credit. Actual money...a check made out for $17,000.

Who even gets a check for "membership rewards" in cash? No one. That's not how those programs work! I actually took a photo of the check because even as I held it, it felt unreal. I thought, *If I tell this story without showing people, no one will believe me.*

But there it was...$17,000, completely unexpected, sitting in my mailbox right after I'd prayed about lowering my giving.

At that moment, I just laughed and cried at the same time. It was like God was saying, *I see you. I hear your heart. Keep trusting Me. I've got you."*

And it's not just this one check. Over the years, I've had multiple random checks show up out of nowhere...things like overpayments, insurance refunds, or adjustments I didn't even know existed. It happens so often now that I started taking screenshots because people literally didn't believe me.

But this one...this $17,000 check...was different. It wasn't just provision; it was **confirmation**. It was God's way of saying, "Don't stop giving just because things feel tight. I'm still your source."

When I think about that story, I'm reminded of one of my favorite stories in the Bible...the story of **Gideon's fleece** in *Judges 6.*

Gideon was struggling with doubt, just like I was. God had told him to do something big...something that required faith...but Gideon wasn't sure if he was really hearing God correctly. So he asked for a sign.

He said: "If this is really You, Lord, make the fleece on the ground wet with dew while everything else stays dry."

And the next morning, that's exactly what happened. The fleece was soaked, but the ground was dry. Still, Gideon wanted to be absolutely certain, so he asked again...only this time he flipped it.

He said: "Okay Lord, this time make the fleece dry, and the ground around it wet."

And once again, God did it.

That's where we get the phrase *"putting out a fleece before God."* It means asking God for a specific confirmation...not because we don't believe, but because we want to make sure we're walking in alignment with His will.

That $17,000 check? That was my fleece moment. I had asked God, "If You really want me to keep giving, show me." And He didn't just whisper...He shouted through that mailbox.

Observation Questions

1. How does the timing and specificity of the $17,000 check function as confirmation rather than coincidence in this story?

   _____

   _____

2. What similarities do you notice between Chantel's experience and Gideon's use of a fleece in asking God for clarity?

   _____

   _____

Application Questions

1. Have you ever asked God for confirmation in a moment of uncertainty, and how did you respond when He answered clearly or unexpectedly?

   _____

   _____

2. Where might God be inviting you to trust His confirmation instead of continuing to doubt or delay obedience?

   _____

   _____

Section 3 – Kingdom Math and a Life of Yes

Sometimes God doesn't confirm His word through a sermon, a song, or even another person. Sometimes He sends it through something so practical...so specific...that there's no doubt it's Him.

That's what this moment was for me. It wasn't just about the money; it was about God's timing and His care. It was Him saying, *"You can't outgive Me. When you obey, I'll always provide."*

And He did...right on time, in the most unmistakable way possible.

Logic and faith rarely agree. Here's what I've learned: giving hardly ever makes sense on paper. If you sit down with a financial advisor and say, "Hey, I want to give away 90% of my income," they'll look at you like you've lost your mind. It doesn't compute in the world's system. But we're not living by the world's system...we're living by Kingdom math. And Kingdom math is different. With God, 90% surrendered always goes further than 100% hoarded. With God, $30 can multiply into $300. With God, a $17,000 check can show up in your mailbox from nowhere.

Faith doesn't ask, *Does this make sense?* Faith asks, *Am I being obedient?*

And it's not just about me. Over the years, I've had countless moments where giving positioned me to be part of someone else's miracle. Like the time I was jogging in Virginia Beach and felt God whisper, *Turn around and pay for that woman's hotel room for a week.* I didn't want to do it. It felt awkward, inconvenient, even a little crazy. But when I obeyed, I discovered she had literally just prayed, *"God, if You're real, send someone to pay for a week in a hotel for us."* Or the countless times I've been in a grocery store line and God nudged me, *Pay for their groceries.* Every time I obeyed, I got to see the tears, the relief, the whispered, *Thank You, Jesus,* from someone who thought they were forgotten. Giving isn't just about money. It's about being willing to be God's hands and feet in someone else's story.

I wish I could tell you that giving gets easier, that once you hit a certain level, it's smooth sailing. But that's not true. Every new season comes with a new stretch. I remember when I first started giving beyond the tithe. Adding 3% here, 5% there. Every increase felt like jumping off a cliff without a parachute.

But here's the secret: the more I obeyed, the clearer God's voice became. The more I trusted Him, the louder His confirmations grew. Obedience in giving isn't just about finances...it's about intimacy with God. It's about saying, *Lord, I trust You more than I trust this dollar amount.*

And with every act of obedience, I heard Him more clearly. Today, I'm still doing my best to live by the 90/10 principle God called me to. My goal is still to live on 10% and give away 90%. I'm not fully there yet, but I'm closer every year. And here's the crazy part: I've never lacked. Never. Oh, there have been tight seasons. There have been moments where I panicked, where I thought, *God, are You sure about this?* But He always came through. Always.

Malachi 3:10 says, *"Test Me in this… and see if I will not throw open the floodgates of heaven."* I've tested Him. Over and over again. And every single time, He's been faithful.

Observation Questions

1. What contrasts are presented between worldly logic and Kingdom math throughout this section?

   _____

   _____

2. How does repeated obedience connect to increased clarity in hearing God's voice according to this section?

   _____

   _____

Application Questions

1. Where are you currently trying to make decisions based on logic alone instead of obedience to God's prompting?

   _____

   _____

2. How might trusting God with a step that feels illogical deepen your intimacy with Him rather than just impact your finances?

   _____

   _____

Section 4 - The Lesson

So here's the bottom line: if you want to hear God more clearly, start obeying Him in the area of giving. It doesn't have to be 90% tomorrow. Maybe it's a $30 step of faith. Maybe it's buying groceries for the person behind you in line. Maybe it's giving to a missionary, or sowing into your church, or blessing a stranger because God nudged you to.

Giving isn't about the size of the gift. It's about the size of your trust. And if He can take a broke, $9-an-hour girl who couldn't buy groceries and turn her into a business owner giving away more than she ever thought possible…He can do the same for you.

So let me challenge you: take the next step. Write the check. Swipe the card. Obey the whisper. You might feel scared. You might feel crazy. But on the other side of that obedience, you'll discover what I discovered: God is faithful. Always.

Observation Questions

1. What core principle about giving and hearing God's voice is reinforced through the summary of this section?

_____

_____

2. How does the story emphasize trust over amount when it comes to obedience in giving?

_____

_____

Application Questions

1. What is one specific step of obedience in giving that feels challenging but possible for you right now?

_____

_____

2. How might obeying God in this area change not just your finances, but your confidence in hearing and trusting His voice?

_____

_____

HEARING GOD – PERSONAL REFLECTION

1. Looking across this week, where do you see a clear pattern of how God has been leading you through discomfort, change, and growth?

2. How has your understanding of God's purpose shifted from something you must figure out to something you are invited to walk out with Him?

Chapter 12

Putting Out a Fleece

ICEBREAKER QUESTIONS

1. Have you ever faced a decision where Scripture didn't give you a clear yes or no?

2. How do you usually seek confirmation when you're unsure of God's will?

3. Do you tend to trust signs more easily than peace?

BIBLE PASSAGE

Genesis 24 (NIV)

Abraham was now very old, and the Lord had blessed him in every way. 2 He said to the senior servant in his household, the one in charge of all that he had, "Put your hand under my thigh. 3 I want you to swear by the Lord, the God of heaven and the God of earth, that you will not get a wife for my son from the daughters of the Canaanites, among whom I am living, 4 but will go to my country and my own relatives and get a wife for my son Isaac."

5 The servant asked him, "What if the woman is unwilling to come back with me to this land? Shall I then take your son back to the country you came from?"

6 "Make sure that you do not take my son back there," Abraham said. 7 "The Lord, the God of heaven, who brought me out of my father's household and my native land and who spoke to me and promised me on oath, saying, 'To your offspring I will give this land'—he will send his angel before you so that you can get a wife for my son from there. 8 If the woman is unwilling to come back with you, then you will be released from this oath of mine. Only do not take my son back there." 9 So the servant put his hand under the thigh of his master Abraham and swore an oath to him concerning this matter.

10 Then the servant left, taking with him ten of his master's camels loaded with all kinds of good things from his master. He set out for Aram Naharaim and made his way to the town of Nahor. 11

He had the camels kneel down near the well outside the town; it was toward evening, the time the women go out to draw water.

12 Then he prayed, "Lord, God of my master Abraham, make me successful today, and show kindness to my master Abraham. 13 See, I am standing beside this spring, and the daughters of the townspeople are coming out to draw water. 14 May it be that when I say to a young woman, 'Please let down your jar that I may have a drink,' and she says, 'Drink, and I'll water your camels too'—let her be the one you have chosen for your servant Isaac. By this I will know that you have shown kindness to my master."

15 Before he had finished praying, Rebekah came out with her jar on her shoulder. She was the daughter of Bethuel son of Milkah, who was the wife of Abraham's brother Nahor. 16 The woman was very beautiful, a virgin; no man had ever slept with her. She went down to the spring, filled her jar and came up again.

17 The servant hurried to meet her and said, "Please give me a little water from your jar."

18 "Drink, my lord," she said, and quickly lowered the jar to her hands and gave him a drink.

19 After she had given him a drink, she said, "I'll draw water for your camels too, until they have had enough to drink." 20 So she quickly emptied her jar into the trough, ran back to the well to draw more water, and drew enough for all his camels. 21 Without saying a word, the man watched her closely to learn whether or not the Lord had made his journey successful.

22 When the camels had finished drinking, the man took out a gold nose ring weighing a beka and two gold bracelets weighing ten shekels. 23 Then he asked, "Whose daughter are you? Please tell me, is there room in your father's house for us to spend the night?"

24 She answered him, "I am the daughter of Bethuel, the son that Milkah bore to Nahor."

Questions

1. What do you notice about the servant's posture of prayer, obedience, and patience in this passage, and how does that shape the way God reveals direction step by step?

   _____

   _____

2. How does this story show God working through ordinary actions and character traits rather than dramatic signs, and where might you be overlooking God's guidance in the everyday moments of your life?

_____

_____

3. What stands out about Abraham's trust that God would go ahead of the servant, and how might believing that God is already at work ahead of you change the way you approach a decision you're facing right now?

_____

_____

_____

Section 1 - When Scripture Doesn't Spell It Out

There are times in life when the Bible doesn't give us a black-and-white answer. You won't find a verse that says, "Move to Sarasota," "Take this job," or "Marry that person." And when you're facing those decisions, it's easy to wonder, *How do I know if this is God's will?*

Remember that fleece? It's one of the tools God has given us to help us discern His will. It's not about testing Him with a bad attitude...it's about saying, *Lord, I want what You want. Please make Your will clear to me.*

Some people don't know this, but I'm Jewish on my mom's side. My dad grew up Muslim, but my mom's whole family is Jewish, and she gave her life to Christ when she was twelve. In Jewish culture, there's a word...*Yenta*...that means "matchmaker."
People used to joke that I was the "Millionaire Matchmaker" back in Virginia, because I introduced so many couples who ended up getting married. So it makes me laugh that one of the clearest biblical stories about fleeces comes from a matchmaking moment.

Observation Questions

1. What tension does this section highlight between wanting clear biblical instructions and facing modern decisions that Scripture does not directly name?

_____

_____

2. How is the purpose of a fleece described, and what attitude toward God is emphasized when using one?

_____

_____

Application Questions

1. What current decision in your life feels unclear because Scripture doesn't give a direct answer, and how does that uncertainty affect your faith?

   _____

   _____

2. How might using a fleece help you pursue God's will with humility rather than control in that situation?

   _____

   _____

Section 2 - A Matchmaking Fleece and the Kind of Character God Highlights

In Genesis 24, Abraham wanted a wife for his son Isaac. His servant prayed for a very specific sign...a fleece. He asked God: *"Let the right woman not only offer me a drink but also offer to water my camels."*

Now, watering ten camels was no small task. Camels can drink gallons and gallons of water. This wasn't just about hospitality...it was about character. And God answered. Rebekah showed up, offered the servant a drink, and then watered all his camels. She proved herself compassionate, hardworking, and generous.

From her story, we learn the qualities worth looking for in any partner:

☐ Genuine faith in God (not just church attendance, but a real love for Him).

☐ Consideration and compassion.

☐ A generous, serving heart.

☐ Hard work and perseverance.

☐ Willingness to walk by faith, even into the unknown.

Rebekah didn't know Isaac, but she trusted God's plan. That's the heart of faith.

Observation Questions

1. What specific qualities does Rebekah demonstrate through her actions at the well, and why are those qualities significant in the story?

_____

_____

2. How does God's response to the servant's prayer reveal what He values beyond outward signs?

_____

_____

Application Questions

1. What character traits are most evident in your daily choices, especially when no one is watching?

_____

_____

2. How might this story challenge you to value character and obedience over convenience or appearance in relationships or major decisions?

_____

_____

Section 3 - Gideon's Fleece and What It's Actually For

The phrase "putting out a fleece" comes directly from Judges 6. Gideon needed confirmation that God was truly calling him to lead Israel. He prayed for a sign: first that the fleece would be wet and the ground dry, and then the opposite. God graciously answered both times.

The point is not that we should constantly demand signs from God, but that He's willing to confirm His will when our hearts are humble and surrendered.

I've used fleeces in my own life. When my husband wanted to move from Virginia to Florida, I wasn't sure if it was God's will. So I prayed: *"Lord, if You want us to move, let our house sell within 30 days."*

Now, this wasn't a small house...it was 10,000 square feet. Normally, a property like that would take nine months to sell. But in just 25 days, we had a ratified contract. That was God's confirmation. Without that fleece, I don't think I would have had the courage to make the move.

One of my close friends was at her breaking point. Her husband had switched jobs so many times that they had moved almost every year and a half. She called me and said, *"Chantel, I can't do it again. I can't pick up and move one more time."*

So we prayed together and asked God for a fleece: if their house sold in one week, it would mean this move was from Him. The very next day, within thirty minutes of the listing going live, someone came to see the house. By the following day, they had a full-price offer.

That was God making it undeniable. Without that fleece, she never would have agreed to move. But because God confirmed it so clearly, she had peace.

Observation Questions

1. What similarities do you see between Gideon's request for confirmation and the modern examples shared in this section?

   _____

   _____

2. How does God respond to Gideon's doubt, and what does that reveal about His character?

   _____

   _____

Application Questions

1. When have you needed reassurance from God before stepping into something difficult, and what did that reassurance look like?

   _____

   _____

2. How can you seek confirmation from God while still maintaining a posture of trust rather than fear?

   _____

   _____

Section 4 - When the Fleece Is Silence and the Closed Door Is Protection

Not every fleece ends with a yes. Sometimes the answer is silence or closed doors...and that's just as much an answer from God.

We once considered moving into another house. I prayed, *"Lord, if this is from You, let it sell in 30 days."* But nothing happened. Not a single showing, not one phone call.

At first I was disappointed. But later I realized...God's "no" was His protection. The house we already had was exactly where He wanted us. Just minutes from the beach, with everything we needed. His no was His way of saying, *Stay put. This is where I want you.*

Here's what matters: the heart behind the fleece. A fleece isn't about saying, *"God, prove Yourself to me."* It's about saying, *"God, I want what You want. Please make Your will clear because I don't trust my own judgment without You."*

If you've already lined things up with Scripture, godly counsel, prayer, and peace...and you're still unsure...a fleece can be the final confirmation.

God loves to lead His children. He's not trying to hide His will. Sometimes He uses open doors. Sometimes He uses silence. And sometimes He uses a fleece.

If your heart is surrendered and you truly want His will above your own, don't be afraid to ask for confirmation. He is a good Father, and He delights to make His path clear.

Observation Questions

1. How does this section redefine silence or closed doors as a form of God's guidance?

   _____

   _____

2. What criteria are listed for discerning God's will before using a fleece as final confirmation?

   _____

   _____

Application Questions

1. Where in your life might God be saying "no" or "wait," and how are you responding to that silence?

   _____

   _____

2. How could viewing closed doors as protection change the way you process disappointment or delay?

   _____

   _____

Section 5 - You Can Have a Fleece Without Having Peace

Let me tell you about a time when the fleece felt right but the peace felt wrong. You know those dreams you talk about for years...the ones that sit quietly in the back of your heart, waiting for the right season to unfold? For Rhyan and me, that dream was Florida. Sunshine, palm trees, beaches... it just felt like home every time we visited. But we always said, *"Someday."* Someday, when Kyle graduates. Someday, when the timing feels right. Someday, when it makes sense. But *"someday"* has a funny way of sneaking up on you.

One night, Rhyan sat us down...me and Kyle...and said, *"I really feel like God is leading us to move now."* I remember blinking at him, thinking, *Now? As in, right now?* We had deep roots in Virginia Beach. Kyle had a solid group of friends, a school he loved, and we had built our life there. Moving wasn't just a decision; it was a disruption. And yet... something about the idea stirred my spirit.

Every time the weather would dip below 60 degrees, Rhyan would joke, *"That's it, pack your bags...I'm done with the cold!"* And before long, our "jokes" turned into spontaneous weekend getaways. A quick trip to Sarasota here, a week in Clearwater there. We found ourselves scrolling Zillow listings *"just for fun."* You know how that goes...you say it's hypothetical, but deep down you're already house shopping. Our hearts were migrating before our bodies ever did.

Then one random day, Kyle...who had been the most resistant of all...casually said, *"I'd be okay moving to Florida."* Rhyan and I froze. It was like the air shifted in the room. I looked at him, he looked at me, and we both knew...*that was our green light.* Within days, we had a *"For Sale"* sign in the yard. But even in the excitement, I wanted to make sure we weren't running on emotion. I've always believed in hearing clearly from God, not just following open doors or good ideas. So I decided to do what Gideon did...I prayed a fleece.

I said, *"Lord, if this house sells within 30 days, I'll know this is Your will."* That felt *safe. Simple. Measurable.* By day twenty, we had a full-price offer. It checked every box: great price, fast timeline, solid buyers. Everyone around us was celebrating... *"See, Chantel, it's confirmation! God's all over this!"* But something in my spirit hesitated. The buyers wanted to turn our home into a retreat center, which sounded wonderful at first, but their financing came with one strange condition...they needed us to personally carry a second mortgage for $1 million. My heart sank.

Rhyan, ever the visionary and man of faith, reminded me, *"You prayed, you set the fleece, and God answered."* And he was right… at least on paper. But peace doesn't live on paper. We went through with it. Everything looked great for the first few months. They put $500,000 down and promised the rest would come through their loan soon after. But a year later, everything fell apart.

They defaulted on their payments. Calls stopped being returned. Promises dissolved. Before we knew it, we weren't just out that money…we were tangled in another *"business opportunity"* with those same people that ended up costing us almost another million dollars. I can't even describe the weight of that season. It wasn't just financial loss; it was emotional exhaustion, the kind that leaves you staring at the ceiling at 2 a.m. wondering, How did we miss it? I replayed every decision, every prayer, every supposed *"sign."* I remember walking outside one night, looking up at the Florida sky…the same sky we had dreamed under for years…and saying, *"God, I thought I was following You. Why does obedience feel like loss?"*

And that's when I heard that still, small whisper deep in my spirit: *"You can have a fleece without having peace."* It hit me like a lightning bolt. Just because God allows something to happen doesn't mean he authored it., sometimes He lets us walk through lessons that recalibrate how we hear Him. That move wasn't punishment…it was preparation.

Looking back now, I realize I had been more focused on signs than stillness. I wanted clear evidence instead of quiet assurance. The fleece gave me confirmation, but it didn't give me peace. And here's what I learned:

God's will isn't always proven by the doors that open…sometimes it's proven by the peace that stays.

It's easy to confuse opportunity with direction. It's easy to assume that just because something works out, it's what God wants. But true obedience is not about chasing signs…it's about cultivating sensitivity. And above all is this: peace is your permission slip. It's the umpire of your spirit…calling "safe" or "out" even when everything else looks logical. You can line up every spreadsheet, every prayer fleece, every wise counsel, and still feel that nudge of unrest. Don't ignore it. That nudge is the Holy Spirit. And peace…not success, not speed, not signs…is the ultimate confirmation.

Even after all that financial loss, God still showed His faithfulness. We eventually did settle in Florida. It wasn't easy, and it didn't happen the way I planned, but it did happen the way He intended. That painful detour taught me to stop trying to make God fit my timeline and start trusting His tone.

And now, when I look back on that fleece...that open door that cost us so much...I don't see failure. I see formation. Because sometimes, God uses the wrong door to train your ear for the right one.

"Let the peace of Christ rule in your hearts."...Colossians 3:15

Let it rule. Let it decide. Let it overrule your logic, your deadlines, and even your fleeces. Because when peace says no, even a miracle-sized "yes" isn't worth the cost.

Observation Questions

1. What warning does this section give about relying on signs without paying attention to peace?

   _____

   _____

2. How is peace described as a spiritual authority in decision-making?

   _____

   _____

Application Questions

1. Have you ever moved forward with an opportunity that looked right externally but felt unsettled internally, and what did you learn from it?

   _____

   _____

2. How can you begin allowing the peace of Christ to rule your decisions more than timing, pressure, or apparent success?

   _____

   _____

HEARING GOD – PERSONAL REFLECTION

1. How do you currently seek confirmation when you are unsure of God's direction?
2. Are you more focused on signs and outcomes, or on peace and alignment with God's will?

Week 5

Clarity Without Pressure

By week five, a lot of us are tired of overthinking. We want to hear God clearly, but the pressure to get it right can quietly take over. We worry that one wrong decision could send everything off course. We pray harder. We analyze more. And instead of peace, we feel stress.

This week is about releasing that pressure.

Many people believe God's will is fragile. Like if you make the wrong choice, you miss Him completely. But God is not that small, and His will is not that narrow. Scripture shows us that God's will is not a maze meant to confuse you. It is a foundation meant to steady you.

Before God gives specific direction, He always starts with alignment. Loving Him. Obeying Him. Staying rooted in His Word. Walking with integrity. Those things are not optional and they are not hidden. They are clear. And when your life is grounded there, the fear of missing God begins to lose its grip.

This week will help you see the difference between God's general will and His specific will. One brings stability. The other brings direction. And when you understand how they work together, decision making becomes less stressful and more relational.

You will also see how God speaks through doors. The ones He opens and the ones He closes. And how silence is not abandonment, but an invitation to trust Him deeper. Obedience does not always come with explanation, but it always leads somewhere purposeful.

As you move through this week, let go of the need to rush clarity. Let go of the fear of getting it wrong. God is not asking you to decode His will perfectly. He is inviting you to walk with Him closely.

Stay aligned.

Stay obedient.

And trust that the God who calls you knows exactly where He is leading you.

Chapter 13

God's General Will vs. Specific Will

ICEBREAKER QUESTIONS

1. Have you ever felt pressure to figure out God's will quickly because you were afraid of making the wrong decision?

2. When you think about God's will for your life, does it feel comforting or stressful, and why?

3. Do you tend to look for specific direction from God before checking whether you are already walking in obedience?

BIBLE PASSAGE

Before discussing, read the following passage in its entirety. This Scripture anchors the idea of God's general will and shows how obedience to what God has already spoken brings clarity, confidence, and direction for what comes next.

Joshua 1:1–9 (NIV) Joshua Installed as Leader

1 After the death of Moses the servant of the LORD, the LORD said to Joshua son of Nun, Moses' aide: 2 "Moses my servant is dead. Now then, you and all these people, get ready to cross the Jordan River into the land I am about to give to them—to the Israelites. 3 I will give you every place where you set your foot, as I promised Moses. 4 Your territory will extend from the desert to Lebanon, and from the great river, the Euphrates—all the Hittite country—to the Mediterranean Sea in the west. 5 No one will be able to stand against you all the days of your life. As I was with Moses, so I will be with you; I will never leave you nor forsake you. 6 Be strong and courageous, because you will lead these people to inherit the land I swore to their ancestors to give them.

7 "Be strong and very courageous. Be careful to obey all the law my servant Moses gave you; do not turn from it to the right or to the left, that you may be successful wherever you go. 8 Keep this Book of the Law always on your lips; meditate on it day and night, so that you may be careful to do everything written in it. Then you will be prosperous and successful. 9 Have I not commanded you?

Be strong and courageous. Do not be afraid; do not be discouraged, for the LORD your God will be with you wherever you go."

Questions:

1. What do you notice about God's promises to Joshua compared to God's commands, and how does this passage show the connection between obedience and experiencing God's provision and presence?

   _____

   _____

2. According to this passage, what role does meditating on God's Word play in courage, confidence, and success, and how might neglecting that discipline affect your ability to move forward in faith?

   _____

   _____

3. Where might God be asking you to "be strong and courageous" right now, not by waiting for new direction, but by obeying what He has already clearly spoken?

   _____

   _____

Section 1 - God's Will Isn't a Secret Code

One of the biggest questions I get asked is, *"How do I know God's will for my life?"* And honestly, I've asked that same question more times than I can count.

Do I take this job?

Do I marry this person?

Do I move to this city?

Do I say yes to this opportunity...or wait?

For years, I thought God's will was this mysterious map I had to decode, like one wrong move would ruin everything. But here's what I've learned: God's will actually comes in *two parts*...His *general will* and His *specific will*. Understanding the difference changed everything for me.

That's exactly what we see in Joshua 1.

Joshua is stepping into leadership after Moses dies. The responsibility is overwhelming, and the future feels uncertain. If anyone needed clear direction, it was him. But notice how God speaks. Before giving Joshua battle plans or detailed strategies, God anchors him in what has already been spoken.

"I will be with you."

"I will never leave you nor forsake you."

"Be strong and courageous."

"Obey My Word."

That's God's **general will**—truths that don't change based on location, season, or decision. Stay in the Word. Walk in obedience. Don't let fear lead. Trust God's presence.

Here's the key: **clarity about God's specific will flows out of faithfulness to His general will.**

Joshua wasn't told to wait until he understood everything. He was told to obey what he already knew, and God would guide him as he moved forward. That's how God leads us too.

When we chase specific answers without anchoring ourselves in Scripture, peace, and obedience, we stay confused. But when we commit to God's general will first, the next step becomes clearer.

God's will isn't a trap—it's a path.

And just like He promised Joshua, He promises us this: **"The LORD your God will be with you wherever you go."**

Observation Questions

1. What do you observe about how God speaks to Joshua in Joshua 1, particularly the order in which He gives promises, commands, and direction?

   _____

   _____

2. How does this section describe the difference between God's general will and His specific will, and why is that distinction important for understanding how God leads?

   _____

   _____

Application Questions

1. Where might you be seeking a specific answer from God while neglecting obedience to something He has already clearly revealed in His Word?

_____

_____

2. What would it look like for you to anchor yourself more fully in God's general will,.. Scripture, obedience, courage, and trust—before asking Him to reveal your next specific step?

_____

_____

Section 2 – God's General Will

God's general will is the same for all of us. It's not hidden, it's not complicated...it's right there in His Word:

He wants us to love Him with all our heart, soul, mind, and strength. He wants us to love our neighbor as ourselves. He wants us to live with integrity, pursue holiness, forgive quickly, and walk in obedience. He wants us to share the good news of Jesus wherever we go.

These are not suggestions; they're clear commands. When we live inside that general will...when we're walking closely with Him and living in alignment with His Word...it becomes a whole lot easier to hear His specific direction for our individual lives. Scripture makes that promise over and over again: _"This Book of the Law shall not depart from your mouth, but you shall meditate on it day and night, so that you may be careful to do according to all that is written in it. For then you will make your way prosperous, and then you will have good success."...Joshua 1:8_

"Now if you obey Me fully and keep My covenant, then out of all nations you will be My treasured possession."...Exodus 19:5

Those verses aren't about rules...they're about relationship. They remind me that when I keep God at the center, I stop chasing answers and start walking in confidence.

Observation Questions

1. What stands out to you about how clearly God's general will is described?

_____

_____

2. According to this section, what connection is made between obedience and clarity?

_____

_____

Application Questions

1. Which part of God's general will do you feel most consistent in right now?

   _____

   _____

2. Is there an area where obedience feels harder — and what might taking one step look like?

   _____

   _____

Section 3 - God's Specific Will

Then there's God's specific will...the unique details of what He's calling _you_ to do. These are the things the Bible doesn't spell out word-for-word. There's no verse that says, _"Chantel, move to Sarasota."_ Or _"Take this job."_ Or _"Hire this person."_

But as you walk in obedience to His general will, you become more sensitive to His whispers about the specifics. And here's what I've learned about those whispers: they often come through peace. Even when something doesn't make sense logically, you'll feel a deep sense of _rightness_...a settled assurance in your spirit that says, _This is it_. And the opposite is true, too. Sometimes you'll feel unsettled, restless, or uneasy even if everything looks perfect on paper. That's often God saying, _"This isn't it."_

Let me give you a small, everyday example. For years, I wrestled with the question: What time of day should I spend my quiet time with God? I'd hear preachers say, "If you're not praying in the morning, you're missing it. Give God your first fruits!" And then I'd hear others say, "It doesn't matter when...just spend time with Him." So I did what I do best: I overthought it. "Lord, what's Your will? Morning or night?"

And what He gently showed me was this: His **general will** is that I spend time with Him. The **specifics**...morning, night, during lunch break...don't matter as much as the consistency of the relationship.

That realization set me free. I stopped feeling guilty for not being a 5 a.m. prayer warrior. I stopped treating quiet time like a spiritual performance. I realized that God just wanted time with me...whenever I'd give Him my full attention.

Another example: journaling. When I read my Bible, I hear God's voice most clearly when I journal. There's something about slowing down, putting pen to paper, and processing what He's saying that makes His words sink deep. But journaling isn't a command in Scripture...it's a *tool*. It's part of God's **specific will** for me. For you, it might look totally different. Maybe you hear God best on long walks. Maybe it's during worship in your car. Maybe it's sitting in silence before bed.

The way He speaks to you might not look like how He speaks to anyone else. And that's beautiful. God is personal. His general will connect us as believers...but His specific will meet us in the details of our own lives.

Observation Questions

1. How does this section describe the way God often communicates His specific will?

   _____

   _____

2. What example is used to show the difference between general and specific will?

   _____

   _____

Application Questions

1. Have you ever felt peace or uneasiness about a decision before you could explain why?

   _____

   _____

2. How might releasing "performance" change the way you spend time with God?

   _____

   _____

Section 4 - The Lesson

Here's the bottom line: Let God's **general will** be the foundation. Love Him. Obey Him. Stay in His Word. Walk in integrity. Keep your heart soft. And let God's **specific will** build on that foundation. It's the individual direction He gives you...the assignments, the places, the timing, the relationships. The mistake most of us make is trying to skip straight to the specifics while ignoring the basics. We want to know, *"God, what's next?"* And He's saying, *"Let's start with what I've already said."*

So, if you're seeking His specific will today...if you're praying for clarity about that job, that move, that next step...start here: Ask yourself, *Am I walking in His general will?* Am I obeying what I already know to be true? When you do that, you won't have to chase after His will...it'll start chasing after you. Because once your heart is aligned with His, the specifics will always follow.

Observation Questions

1. What warning does this section give about focusing only on specifics?

   _____

   _____

2. What order does this chapter emphasize basics first or details first?

   _____

   _____

Application Questions

1. What is one "basic" area God may be asking you to focus on right now?

   _____

   _____

2. How might alignment change the way you seek direction moving forward?

   _____

   _____

HEARING GOD – PERSONAL REFLECTION

1. Where in your life are you currently seeking God's specific will?
2. Are there any areas where you know what God has already said but haven't fully obeyed yet?
3. What would change if you trusted that clarity follows obedience, not the other way around?

Chapter 14

Doors God Opens and Closes

ICEBREAKER QUESTIONS

1. Have you ever had a door close in your life that felt painful or confusing at the time but later made sense?

2. How do you usually respond emotionally when something you want does not work out?

3. Do you find it easier to trust God with open doors or closed ones, and why?

BIBLE PASSAGE

Before discussing, read the following passage in its entirety. This Scripture anchors the truth that God is actively involved in opening and closing doors, not randomly, not harshly, but with intention, authority, and love.

Revelation 3:7–8 (NIV)

"To the angel of the church in Philadelphia write:

These are the words of him who is holy and true, who holds the key of David. What he opens no one can shut, and what he shuts no one can open. I know your deeds. See, I have placed before you an open door that no one can shut. I know that you have little strength, yet you have kept my word and have not denied my name."

Questions

1. What does this verse reveal about who ultimately has control over open and closed doors?

_____

_____

2. How might trusting God's authority over doors change the way you respond to delays or disappointments?

_____

_____

Section 1: God Speaks Through Open and Closed Doors

One of the clearest ways I've seen God speak is through doors...some He swings wide open, and others He shuts so hard they rattle. I used to think closed doors meant I'd done something wrong, that I'd misheard Him or made a bad move. But I've learned that the God who opens doors also closes them out of love. Sometimes He protects you from what you can't see. Sometimes He redirects you to what you never would've found on your own. And sometimes, He just needs to test whether you trust His hand on the handle more than your own.

Observation Questions

1. What are some reasons this section gives for why God might close a door?

_____

_____

2. How does this section reframe the meaning of closed doors?

_____

_____

Application Questions

1. Is there a closed door in your life you've been viewing as failure instead of protection?

_____

_____

2. What would it look like to trust God's hand more than your own effort right now?

_____

_____

Section 2: When a Closed Door Is Divine Protection

When I merged my real estate company into eXp...a $2 billion organization...I had one simple request. I wanted all my commission checks deposited into a particular account, let's call it Company A. It made perfect sense financially and logistically. But for some reason, no matter how many times I asked...ten emails, countless follow-ups...the answer was always no. They insisted everything had to go into Company B. I was frustrated beyond words. *"Lord, this makes no sense. They're breaking their own rules! Why won't You just let this work?"*

I felt ignored, stuck, and honestly a little embarrassed that I couldn't get a basic request approved.

Months later, it all clicked. Someone committed fraud against Company B. They took money. At first I was furious...heart-sick that someone could do that. But then, as the dust settled, my accountant looked at me and said, *"You realize this is a write-off, right? This actually saves you money."*

It hit me like a wave. If the funds had gone into Company A...the one I begged for...it would have been a disaster. But because God closed that door and forced me into Company B, what felt like an irritation ended up being divine protection. That's when I finally understood the verse that says, *"He opens doors no one can shut, and shuts doors no one can open."* Sometimes the "no" isn't punishment...it's strategy.

Observation Questions

1. What emotions stand out in this story before the reason for the closed door became clear?

   _____

   _____

2. How did hindsight completely change the meaning of the closed door?

   _____

   _____

Application Questions

1. Can you think of a situation where frustration later turned into gratitude?

   _____

   _____

2. How might trusting God's strategy help you handle current disappointments differently?

   _____

   _____

Section 3: When God Opens a Door You Don't Want to Walk Through

Another time, God didn't just close a door...He opened one I didn't even *want* to walk through. After years in Virginia Beach, I felt a stirring that my season there was ending. Everything in me fought it. I loved my team, my church, my house. Florida sounded exciting in theory, but the idea of uprooting everything terrified me. Still, I couldn't shake it. Every prayer, every sermon, every random conversation seemed to point south. Meanwhile, door after door in Virginia started closing. Business deals fell through. Opportunities dried up. Even relationships that had felt solid began to shift. It felt like God was slowly dismantling everything that made me comfortable. Then one morning, during prayer, I heard that unmistakable whisper: *"Go where I'm sending you."* So I did. And that step of obedience led to Sarasota...to a city that's become my home, my ministry, my place of peace. If those doors in Virginia had stayed open, I never would've walked into the one that led me here.

Observation Questions

1. What signs showed that God was closing doors in one season while opening another?

   _____

   _____

2. What role did obedience play in stepping into the next chapter?

   _____

   _____

Application Questions

1. Is there a door God may be opening that feels uncomfortable or scary to you?

   _____

   _____

2. What might obedience look like if you trusted where He's leading?

   _____

   _____

Section 4: Redirection, Not Rejection

I've learned that God speaks through closed doors just as clearly as He does through open ones. A closed door isn't rejection. It's redirection. It's His hand saying, *"Not this one...there's something better waiting."* The problem is, we usually only see the purpose in hindsight. In the moment, it feels like failure. It feels like silence. But if you'll trust Him in the waiting, you'll look back and see His fingerprints all over every delay, every disappointment, every detour. Because the God who opens doors is also the God who closes them...and both are for your good.

Observation Questions

1. How does this section redefine what a closed door really means?

   _____

   _____

2. Why do you think clarity often comes only in hindsight?

   _____

   _____

Application Questions

1. Where do you need to shift your perspective from rejection to redirection?

   _____

   _____

2. How can trusting God in the waiting change how you handle uncertainty?

   _____

   _____

HEARING GOD – PERSONAL REFLECTION

1. What door in your life feels closed right now and how are you responding to it?
2. Looking back, can you identify a closed door that was actually God's protection?
3. What would trusting God's plan look like for you in this season, even without full clarity?

Chapter 15

Obedience in the Silence

ICEBREAKER QUESTIONS

1. Have you ever been in a season where God felt silent and it made you question what to do next?

2. When you do not hear clear direction from God, do you tend to wait, push forward, or pull back?

3. How do you usually respond when obedience feels hard and answers feel delayed?

BIBLE PASSAGE

Before discussing, read the following passage in its entirety. This Scripture anchors the theme of obedience that does not depend on explanation, clarity, or immediate reassurance.

Genesis 12:1–9 (NIV) The Call of Abram

12 The LORD had said to Abram, "Go from your country, your people and your father's household to the land I will show you.

2 "I will make you into a great nation, and I will bless you;

I will make your name great, and you will be a blessing

3 I will bless those who bless you,

and whoever curses you I will curse; and all peoples on earth will be blessed through you."

4 So Abram went, as the Lord had told him; and Lot went with him. Abram was seventy-five years old when he set out from Harran. 5 He took his wife Sarai, his nephew Lot, all the possessions they had accumulated and the people they had acquired in Harran, and they set out for the land of Canaan, and they arrived there.

6 Abram traveled through the land as far as the site of the great tree of Moreh at Shechem. At that time the Canaanites were in the land. 7 The Lord appeared to Abram and said, "To your offspring[c] I will give this land." So he built an altar there to the Lord, who had appeared to him.

8 From there he went on toward the hills east of Bethel and pitched his tent, with Bethel on the west and Ai on the east. There he built an altar to the Lord and called on the name of the Lord.

9 Then Abram set out and continued toward the Negev.

Questions

1. What stands out to you about Abram's response to God's command, especially considering how little information God gave him at the start?

   _____

   _____

2. How do you see obedience and worship woven together in Abram's journey throughout this passage?

   _____

   _____

Section 1 - Obedience Before the Explanation

If you've ever been in a season where God felt quiet, you know how tempting it is to stop obeying. You start thinking, *Well, if He's not speaking, maybe I'm on my own now. Maybe I can just take a break, coast a little.*

But here's what I've learned over and over again: **silence is often God's way of testing whether we'll keep obeying what He already told us.**

When God goes quiet, He's not punishing you...He's proving you. He's asking, *Will you still trust Me when you can't trace Me? Will you still obey when you can't hear Me?*

One of my favorite examples of this is Abraham. When God told Abraham, *"Go,"* he didn't hesitate. He didn't ask for a sign. He didn't demand a five-year plan, a GPS location, or a guaranteed salary on the other side. Scripture simply says: "So Abram went, as the Lord had told him."...*Genesis 12:4*... No delay. No excuses. Just obedience.

Later, when God told him to do the unthinkable...to offer up Isaac, the very son God had promised him...Abraham obeyed again. No hesitation, no bargaining, no second-guessing. Can you imagine that? Taking the thing you love most, the promise you waited years for, and laying it on the altar, not knowing how it's going to end?

That's radical trust.

Observation Questions

1. What words or phrases stand out to you in how Abraham responded to God?

   _____

   _____

2. How is obedience described in this section before or after understanding?

   _____

   _____

Application Questions

1. Is there something God has already told you to do that you've been waiting to understand first?

   _____

   _____

2. What would obedience look like if you chose trust over control?

   _____

   _____

Section 2 - Faith in Motion

It challenges me every time I read it. Because if I'm honest, there have been plenty of times I've hesitated. I've wrestled, negotiated, delayed. I've said, "God, I'll obey once I understand." But that's not obedience...that's control. Abraham's story reminds me that the most powerful obedience happens before the explanation.

When my son Kyle was little, he went to a Christian preschool. They taught him this simple, sweet little song that I still hear in my head all these years later:

♪ *"I will obey right away*

I will obey right away

Never asking why,

Never with a sigh

I will obey right away." ♪

Even now, I'll catch myself humming that tune when I don't feel like doing what God's asking me to do. Because that's really the heart of it. Obedience *is* how we show we believe. It's not about feelings...it's about faith in motion. It's saying, "God, I trust You enough to do it now, even before I understand why."

Observation Questions

1. How does this section describe the difference between obedience and control?

   _____

   _____

2. What does "faith in motion" mean based on this section?

   _____

   _____

Application Questions

1. Where might God be asking you to act, not just feel?

   _____

   _____

2. How could immediate obedience change the outcome of something you're facing right now?

   _____

   _____

Section 3 - Seasons of Silence

I've had more than a few seasons where it felt like God went completely silent.

When my dad went to jail, I begged God for answers. Nothing. When I faced financial struggles, I cried out for breakthrough. Silence. When I got sick and couldn't find relief, I pleaded for healing...and heaven still felt quiet.

And in those moments, I'd sit there and wonder, *God, where are You? What did I do wrong?* But looking back, I can see it so clearly now: the silence wasn't punishment. It was preparation. God had already spoken. He had already given me promises in His Word...truths to stand on when everything else went dark.

He was showing me that I'd keep obeying even when I didn't feel anything. This is the real test of faith...not how loudly you worship when you can hear Him, but how steady you walk when you can't.

Silence is not rejection. Silence is not abandonment. It's an invitation to deeper faith. It's God saying, *"Will you trust Me when the lights go out? Will you obey Me even when I'm quiet?"*

So when you find yourself in that silent season...keep going. Keep obeying what He's already told you. Keep doing what you know is right. Silence means He's doing something bigger than your ears can hear. His silence is never empty. It's always pregnant with purpose. And if you'll stay faithful through it, you'll find that on the other side of the quiet… is glory.

Observation Questions

1. What patterns do you notice about what God was doing during these silent seasons?

   _____

   _____

2. How does this section redefine what silence really means?

   _____

   _____

Application Questions

1. Are you currently in a season of silence and how are you responding?

   _____

   _____

2. What truth from God's Word can you stand on when emotions go quiet?

   _____

   _____

HEARING GOD – PERSONAL REFLECTION

1. Where might God be asking you to obey without giving you more information right now?

2. How do you usually respond when silence lasts longer than you expect?

3. What would it look like to trust that God's silence is purposeful, not absent?

Week 6

Hearing God Through Humility and Hunger

By week six, something subtle usually begins to surface. We are hearing God more clearly. We are slowing down. We are becoming more aware of His voice. And that is often when another challenge quietly appears. Pride. Self reliance. Comfort.

Not loud arrogance. Not obvious rebellion. Just a slow shift where we start trusting ourselves a little more than we trust Him.

This week is about humility and hunger. Two postures that keep our hearts soft and our ears open.

Humility is not about thinking less of yourself. It is about making room for God. It is recognizing that clarity does not come from confidence in our ability, but from dependence on His. When humility is present, God's voice is not crowded out by ego, control, or performance. It flows freely.

Fasting builds on that posture. It strips away comfort and reveals what has been quietly ruling us. It brings hunger back to the surface, not just physical hunger, but spiritual hunger. And hunger has a way of sharpening awareness. When we stop filling ourselves with everything else, we begin to recognize how much God has been speaking all along.

This week will challenge you gently. It will invite you to examine where pride may have crept in unnoticed. Where routine has replaced reverence. Where comfort has dulled hunger. Not with shame, but with honesty.

You will see that humility clears the static. Fasting tunes the signal. Together, they restore sensitivity, strength, and faith.

As you move through this week, resist the urge to perform. Do not rush outcomes. Do not measure progress by feelings. Simply stay humble. Stay hungry. Stay open.

God speaks clearly to hearts that are yielded.

And He always meets hunger with more of Himself.

Chapter 16

Being Humble

ICEBREAKER QUESTIONS

1. Have you ever looked back on a season of success and realized pride quietly crept in without you noticing at the time?

2. Do you find it harder to stay dependent on God when things are going well than when life feels difficult?

3. When someone challenges you or slows you down, what usually rises up first in you… patience or irritation?

BIBLE PASSAGE

Before discussing, read the following passages in their entirety. These Scriptures anchor this chapter and reveal how humility positions us to hear God clearly.

Matthew 18:1–5 (NIV) The Greatest in the Kingdom of Heaven

18 At that time the disciples came to Jesus and asked, "Who, then, is the greatest in the kingdom of heaven?"

[2] He called a little child to him, and placed the child among them. [3] And he said: "Truly I tell you, unless you change and become like little children, you will never enter the kingdom of heaven. [4] Therefore, whoever takes the lowly position of this child is the greatest in the kingdom of heaven. [5] And whoever welcomes one such child in my name welcomes me.

Question

1. What would it look like for you to pursue greatness the way Jesus defines it—through humility, trust, and childlike dependence rather than recognition or position?

   _____

   _____

Section 1 – Humility Clears the Line

Humility is one of the greatest keys to hearing from God. Pride clogs our spiritual ears; humility clears the line. When I'm full of myself, there's no space left for God's whisper. But when I choose to bow low...when I admit, *"God, I can't do this without You"*...suddenly His voice cuts through the noise.

And let me tell you...I didn't learn this from reading about it in a book. I learned it the hard way: through success, through failure, and through my own stubborn pride.

Observation Questions

1. How does this section describe the relationship between pride and hearing God?

   _____

   _____

2. What experiences are mentioned as teachers of humility?

   _____

   _____

Application Questions

1. Where might pride be "clogging the line" in your life right now?

_____

_____

2. What would it look like to intentionally make more room for God today?

_____

_____

Section 2 - When Success Turns Sneaky

When I first got into real estate, I came in like a firecracker. I was hungry to prove myself. Those fifty-four homes I sold were a big deal. I was named _Rookie of the Year_ in all of Hampton Roads, and everyone around me was celebrating. And if I'm honest, so was I.

But success can be sneaky. What started as excitement slowly morphed into pride. I started craving recognition...the applause, the awards, the pat on the back. And the more I wanted people to notice _me,_ the less I cared about pleasing _Him._

Looking back, I see how dangerous that season was. Pride is so quiet; it creeps in through compliments and clings to accomplishments. That's why humility is vital if you want to hear God's voice. When you chase human approval more than divine direction, your heart goes dull. But when you surrender your success back to Him, the static clears, and suddenly His whisper is unmistakable again.

Observation Questions

1. How is pride described as entering someone's life?

_____

_____

2. What effect does chasing human approval have on spiritual sensitivity?

_____

_____

Application Questions

1. Are there areas where success might be competing with surrender in your life?

_____

_____

2. How can you intentionally give your accomplishments back to God?

_____

_____

Section 3 - Pride Even Touched the Disciples

Even the disciples...men who walked beside Jesus Himself...struggled with pride. Think about it: they watched Him heal the sick, raise the dead, and calm storms with a word... yet they still argued about which one of them was the greatest.

In Matthew 18:3, Jesus said, "Unless you change and become like little children, you will never enter the kingdom of heaven." In other words, *the way up in God's Kingdom is down*. Humility is the doorway.

Later, in Matthew 20, James and John even had their mom ask Jesus if her sons could sit next to Him in heaven. Can you imagine? You're walking with the Son of God and still jockeying for position! But Jesus didn't shame them. He gently reminded them that greatness in His kingdom isn't about power...it's about serving. Even His closest friends had to be reminded: pride closes your ears; humility opens them.

Observation Questions

1. What does this section reveal about how common pride is... even among faithful people?

_____

_____

2. How does Jesus redefine greatness in God's Kingdom?

_____

_____

Application Questions

1. Where might competition or comparison be sneaking into your walk with God?

_____

_____

2. What would choosing the "way down" look like in your current season?

_____

_____

Section 4 - The Fine Line Between Confidence and Pride

Not long ago, my husband and I were at a Bible study. Everyone was supposed to share one thing they appreciated about their spouse. When it was his turn, he said, "One of the things I appreciate most about my wife is that she is extremely confident. I've never seen anyone so confident."

I smiled...and laughed a little inside. Because I know myself. Confidence is good, but only when it's rooted in *who God is*, not in *who I am*.

There's a fine line between confidence and pride. Pride wears the same outfit...it just forgets where the strength comes from. James 4:6 says, "God opposes the proud but shows favor to the humble." That verse humbles me every time. Because if I'm walking in pride, I'm actually positioning myself against God. But if I walk in humility, I'm walking right beside Him. Real confidence isn't puffed-up self-assurance. It's quiet trust in a mighty God.

Observation Questions

1. How does this section distinguish confidence from pride?

   _____

   _____

2. Why is the verse from James described as humbling?

   _____

   _____

Application Questions

1. How can you check where your confidence is rooted?

   _____

   _____

2. What would quiet trust in God look like for you right now?

   _____

   _____

Section 5 - Humility Through Compassion and Suffering

Pride doesn't only make us self-centered...it can also make us blind to other people's pain. I'll never forget the day my mom sprained her foot. We were at the mall, and she was walking so slowly that I could feel myself getting irritated. I kept thinking, *Come on, Mom, let's move!*

A week later, I was in high heels, rushing through a parking lot, when I twisted my ankle. Suddenly I was hobbling at her exact pace. She looked at me, grinned, and said, "Now who's walking slow?"

That moment humbled me to my core. God used a twisted ankle to teach me compassion. The same has been true with my health. Living with psoriatic arthritis has given me a tenderness I didn't have before. On good days, I feel strong and capable. But on flare-up days...when every joint aches and I can barely move...I'm reminded of my humanity.

Those moments don't make me weak; they make me aware. They make me gentler with others who carry invisible pain. Sometimes humility comes dressed as suffering. God doesn't waste it...He uses it to soften our hearts so we can love people the way He does.

Observation Questions

1. How did personal experience lead to greater compassion in this section?

   _____

   _____

2. What role does suffering play in developing humility?

   _____

   _____

Application Questions

1. How might God be using discomfort to grow compassion in you?

   _____

   _____

2. Who around you may be carrying invisible pain that needs gentleness?

   _____

   _____

Section 6 - Choosing Humility Before God Chooses It for You

Being humble doesn't mean you think less of yourself...it means you think of yourself less. It's not denying your gifts or minimizing your calling. It's using what God gave you for *His* glory instead of your own.

Jesus said in Luke 14:11, "For all those who exalt themselves will be humbled, and those who humble themselves will be exalted." This verse is both a promise and a warning. If we don't humble ourselves, God will do it for us...and believe me, it's always easier to bow willingly than to be knocked flat by circumstance.

The more I humble myself before the Lord, the clearer His voice becomes. Humility tunes your heart to heaven's frequency.

My first year of success taught me something I'll never forget: even good things can derail you if pride is driving. Humility is like adjusting the dial on a radio...it removes the static and brings God's voice into focus. If you want to hear Him more clearly, start here:

Ask Him to give you a humble heart. Ask Him to strip away self-reliance, comparison, and the need to be seen. When you make room for Him, He fills the space. And when He fills the space, His voice becomes unmistakable.

Observation Questions

1. How is humility described as both protection and alignment?

   _____

   _____

2. What imagery is used to explain how humility affects hearing God?

   _____

   _____

Application Questions

1. What is one area where you can choose humility instead of waiting for it to be forced?

   _____

   _____

2. What might God be asking you to release so He can fill the space?

   _____

   _____

HEARING GOD – PERSONAL REFLECTION

1. Where might pride be subtly influencing your thoughts, decisions, or reactions?

2. How has God used success, struggle, or suffering to shape humility in you?

3. What is one intentional step you can take this week to walk more humbly with God?

Chapter 17

Fasting for HOPE...Healing, Overcoming, Provision, and Freedom

ICEBREAKER QUESTIONS

1. When you hear the word fasting, what emotions or assumptions immediately come to mind?

2. Have you ever experienced a season where life felt cloudy or confusing and you longed for clarity from God?

3. What is one area of your life right now where you are hoping God will bring breakthrough, healing, or direction?

BIBLE PASSAGE

Isaiah 58:5–12 (NIV)

Read this passage in its entirety before discussing. This Scripture is the foundation for everything explored in this chapter. It reveals God's heart behind fasting and shows what happens when fasting is done with humility, obedience, and surrender.

5 Is this the kind of fast I have chosen,
   only a day for people to humble themselves?
Is it only for bowing one's head like a reed
   and for lying in sackcloth and ashes?
Is that what you call a fast,
   a day acceptable to the LORD?
6 "Is not this the kind of fasting I have chosen:
to loose the chains of injustice
   and untie the cords of the yoke,
to set the oppressed free
   and break every yoke?
7 Is it not to share your food with the hungry
   and to provide the poor wanderer with shelter—

when you see the naked, to clothe them,

and not to turn away from your own flesh and blood?

[8] Then your light will break forth like the dawn,

and your healing will quickly appear;

then your righteousness[a] will go before you,

and the glory of the LORD will be your rear guard.

[9] Then you will call, and the LORD will answer;

you will cry for help, and he will say: Here am I.

"If you do away with the yoke of oppression,

with the pointing finger and malicious talk,

[10] and if you spend yourselves in behalf of the hungry

and satisfy the needs of the oppressed,

then your light will rise in the darkness,

and your night will become like the noonday.

[11] The LORD will guide you always;

he will satisfy your needs in a sun-scorched land

and will strengthen your frame.

You will be like a well-watered garden,

like a spring whose waters never fail.

[12] Your people will rebuild the ancient ruins

and will raise up the age-old foundations;

you will be called Repairer of Broken Walls,

Restorer of Streets with Dwellings.

Proverbs 16:26 (NIV)

26 The appetite of laborers works for them;

their hunger drives them on.

Psalm 109:24 (NIV)

24 My knees give way from fasting;

my body is thin and gaunt.

Questions

1. What themes do you notice repeated across these passages about fasting?

_____

_____

2. How do these Scriptures connect fasting with freedom, guidance, and renewal?

_____

_____

Section 1: Fasting Brings HOPE

Fasting changed my life...not just physically, but spiritually, emotionally, and even mentally. I used to think fasting was something that only people in Bible times did. I thought it was extreme. Unnecessary. Outdated. But when I began to experience God through fasting, I realized it's not an ancient ritual...it's an *eternal principle*.

Through fasting, I found healing. Through fasting, I learned to overcome temptation and discouragement. Through fasting, I experienced God's provision and protection in ways that left me speechless. Through fasting, I found freedom from sins and strongholds that had controlled me for years.

I like to say that fasting brings HOPE...and that word perfectly captures what it's all about.

H – Heal and Hear

O – Overcome Difficult Times

P – Provision and Protection

E – Enslaving Sins

These four words describe what fasting does in your life when it's done with a pure heart before God. And they come straight out of Isaiah 58...one of the most powerful passages in all of Scripture.

Observation Questions

1. What areas of life does fasting impact according to this section?

_____

_____

2. How is the acronym HOPE used to explain fasting?

Application Questions

1. Which part of HOPE feels most relevant to your life right now?

   _____

   _____

2. How does this section challenge your previous view of fasting?

   _____

   _____

Section 2 - Fasting… Diving Beneath the Surface to Hear God's Voice

Before I ever experienced the kind of breakthrough that fasting brings, I didn't really understand it. I used to think fasting was something only ancient prophets did … something extreme or outdated. But now I see it as one of the most beautiful ways to draw close to God… and one of the clearest ways to hear His voice.

When I lived in Virginia Beach, I used to stand on the shore and look out at the water. From the surface, it looked brownish-black... murky... hard to see through. You couldn't really tell what was beneath it. But now that I live in Sarasota, Florida, it's completely different. The water here is crystal clear. You can stand at the shoreline and see straight down... fish swimming, shells glistening, sunlight bouncing off the sand. It's beautiful.

And I started realizing... fasting is a lot like that. When you're living on the surface, everything feels cloudy and confusing. You can't see what's really going on beneath … what God's doing in your heart, what He's saying, what He's showing you. But when you fast, it's like diving beneath the surface… everything becomes clear.

Observation Questions

1. What comparison is made between fasting and water clarity?

   _____

   _____

2. How does "living on the surface" affect spiritual understanding?

_____

_____

Application Questions

1. Where does your life currently feel cloudy or unclear?

_____

_____

2. What might fasting help you see beneath the surface?

_____

_____

Section 3 - Snuba Diving for the Soul

I'll be honest... I've never been full-on scuba diving. But I've been snuba diving ... it's kind of like a mix between snorkeling and scuba diving. You don't wear a big tank on your back. Instead, the air tank floats on the surface, and you breathe through a 20-foot hose that follows you wherever you go. You're underwater, exploring, breathing freely... but you're still connected to the surface by that air line.

And every single time I've gone snuba diving, I've seen things I could never see from above. Hidden treasures. Bright tropical fish. Coral reefs so colorful they don't even look real. It's like the whole underwater world comes alive... and I always joke that I feel like the fish whisperer, because they'll swim right up to me. And it hit me one day... that's exactly what fasting does for your spirit.

Observation Questions

1. What does snuba diving symbolize in this section?

_____

_____

2. Why is staying connected to the surface still important?

_____

_____

Application Questions

1. What "hidden treasures" might God want to show you spiritually?

    _____

    _____

2. How does fasting help you go deeper without disconnecting from God?

    _____

    _____

Section 4 - Fasting Is Spiritual Snuba Diving

When you fast, your physical body gets hungry... but your spirit gets sharp. You stop living at surface level. You start to see things you couldn't see before... clarity, revelation, hidden beauty, and God's quiet voice beneath the noise of everyday life.

When you fast, everything comes into focus. It's like the murky brown water of life suddenly turns clear. You begin to see what's really happening beneath the surface... what's driving your emotions... where your fears are hiding... and how God's hand has been guiding you all along.

Observation Questions

1. What changes when the spirit becomes sharper?

    _____

    _____

2. What kinds of clarity are mentioned here?

    _____

    _____

Application Questions

1. What emotions or fears might fasting bring into focus for you?

    _____

    _____

2. How could clarity change the way you move forward?

    _____

    _____

Section 5 - Fasting Tunes You Back to God's Station

There's another picture I think about whenever I fast. Back when I lived in Virginia Beach, I used to listen to a Christian radio station called K-LOVE. It was on 90.7, and I'd play it every morning while driving. But when I'd drive to Richmond to visit my sister, somewhere along the way the music would start getting fuzzy. Static would creep in, the songs would fade out, and before long, all I could hear was noise.

It wasn't that K-LOVE stopped broadcasting... the signal was still there. I had just driven too far from the source. Isn't that what happens to us sometimes? We get busy, distracted, overwhelmed. We move away from that spiritual "frequency" where we used to hear God clearly.

Fasting is how we tune back in. It's like putting spiritual antennas on your heart. It clears out the static so you can hear His voice again... strong, clear, and full of peace.

Observation Questions

1. What causes the "static" in this illustration?

    _____

    _____

2. How is fasting described as a tuning tool?

    _____

    _____

Application Questions

1. What distractions may be pulling you off God's frequency?

    _____

    _____

2. How could fasting help you tune back in?

    _____

    _____

Section 6 - The Power Beneath the Surface

The truth is, fasting isn't about starving your body... it's about feeding your spirit. It's an invitation to go deeper. Just like snuba diving lets you see the hidden beauty beneath the waves, fasting lets you see the hidden beauty of God's presence beneath the surface of your life.

It's there all along... you just have to dive in. When you fast, your soul becomes sensitive again. You recognize God's whisper where before you only heard noise. You start to sense His direction... His comfort... His conviction... and everything that once felt cloudy becomes clear.

Fasting pulls you out of the shallow end and takes you into the deep… the place where the treasures are.

When you fast, you're not trying to earn God's voice... you're tuning your heart to hear it. You're saying, "Lord, I want to go deeper. I don't want to just stand on the shore anymore. I want to dive beneath the surface."

So the next time life feels cloudy or confusing... fast. Take a breath. Go beneath the surface. And let God show you what's been waiting there all along.

That's why I believe fasting is one of the most powerful spiritual tools we've been given. It takes you beneath the surface of your busy life so you can hear God's voice again... and that's what this next section is all about.

Observation Questions

1. How is fasting reframed in this section?

_____

_____

2. What shifts when noise is replaced by sensitivity?

_____

_____

Application Questions

1. Where might God be inviting you to go deeper?

_____

_____

2. What clarity are you hoping fasting might bring?

_____

_____

Section 7 - The Kind of Fast God Has Chosen

Isaiah 58:5–12 (NIV) says: "Is not this the kind of fasting I have chosen: to loose the chains of injustice and untie the cords of the yoke, to set the oppressed free and break every yoke?

Is it not to share your food with the hungry and to provide the poor wanderer with shelter... when you see the naked, to clothe them, and not to turn away from your own flesh and blood?

Then your light will break forth like the dawn, and your healing will quickly appear; then your righteousness will go before you, and the glory of the Lord will be your rear guard.

Then you will call, and the Lord will answer; you will cry for help, and He will say: *Here am I.* If you do away with the yoke of oppression, with the pointing finger and malicious talk, and if you spend yourselves on behalf of the hungry and satisfy the needs of the oppressed, then your light will rise in the darkness, and your night will become like the noonday.

The Lord will guide you always; He will satisfy your needs in a sun-scorched land and will strengthen your frame. You will be like a well-watered garden, like a spring whose waters never fail."

Isn't that breathtaking? This passage isn't just poetic...it's prophetic. It tells us exactly what happens when we fast the way God intended.

Observation Questions

1. What actions does Isaiah 58 describe as part of the fast God chooses, and how do they go beyond abstaining from food?

   _____

   _____

2. What promises does God attach to this kind of fasting in terms of guidance, healing, and His presence?

   _____

   _____

Application Questions

1. In what ways might your current understanding of fasting need to expand from personal discipline to outward compassion and justice?

   _____

   _____

2. How could you practically "spend yourself on behalf of the hungry or oppressed" during your next fast?

_____

_____

Section 8 - H – Heal and Hear

The first thing fasting brings is **healing**...and I've seen it both in my body and in my spirit.

When I started fasting, I had physical struggles: low energy, hormone issues, inflammation, thyroid problems. I thought fasting would make me weaker. But the more I fasted, the more my body healed. My blood sugar stabilized. My mind cleared. My sleep improved. My emotions leveled out. There's science behind that, sure...but it's more than science. It's *Spirit*.

Isaiah 58:8 says, "Then your light will break forth like the dawn, and your healing will quickly appear."

Healing comes when we stop trying to fill ourselves and allow God to be our nourishment. But fasting doesn't just heal the body...it heals the soul. Because every time you deny your flesh, you create space for your spirit to listen.

Isaiah 58:9 says, "Then you will call, and the Lord will answer; you will cry for help, and He will say: *Here am I*."

That verse still gives me chills. When you fast, you don't have to beg God to speak. You just become quiet enough to hear Him. Fasting teaches you to listen again. To notice His voice. To stop trying to fill silence with noise. If you've ever said, "I just can't hear God," fasting is the way to tune your heart to His frequency.

Observation Questions

1. According to Isaiah 58:8–9, what connection do you see between fasting, healing, and hearing God's voice?

_____

_____

2. What patterns of physical or spiritual restoration are described as outcomes of fasting in this section?

_____

_____

Application Questions

1. Where do you currently need healing… physically, emotionally, or spiritually… and how might fasting create space for God to work there?

_____

_____

2. What distractions or "noise" might you need to remove so you can better hear God during a fast?

_____

_____

Section 9 - O – Overcome Difficult Times

Fasting doesn't make life easier…but it makes you stronger.

Isaiah 58:10 says, "Your light will rise in the darkness, and your night will become like the noonday."

I love that verse because it's a picture of endurance. When you fast, God gives you inner strength to walk through things that would normally break you. I've gone through business setbacks, personal losses, betrayal, confusion…times when I felt like I had nothing left. And yet, when I fasted, somehow, I found peace that made no sense.

When everything in your world feels uncertain, fasting reminds you that God is still in control. Fasting is spiritual resistance training. Every hunger pang becomes a rep of faith, every craving a moment of surrender. And with each moment, your endurance grows.

There's a verse in Proverbs 16:26 that says, "The appetite of laborers works for them; their hunger drives them on." When you're hungry for God, that hunger drives you forward. It keeps you praying when others would quit. It keeps you hopeful when others lose faith.

Hunger fuels your perseverance.

Observation Questions

1. How does Isaiah 58:10 describe the effect of fasting during seasons of darkness or hardship?

   _____

   _____

2. What imagery in this section illustrates endurance and inner strength produced through fasting?

   _____

   _____

Application Questions

1. What difficult season are you walking through right now where fasting could help you build spiritual endurance?

   _____

   _____

2. How can you intentionally turn moments of hunger into moments of prayer and surrender rather than frustration?

   _____

   _____

Section 10 - P – Provision and Protection

Isaiah 58:11 promises, "The Lord will guide you always; He will satisfy your needs in a sun-scorched land and will strengthen your frame. You will be like a well-watered garden, like a spring whose waters never fail."

There's something about fasting that positions you under the flow of God's provision. When I fast, I don't do it to twist God's arm...I do it to align my heart with His will. Fasting sharpens discernment. It helps you see what to pursue and what to release.

I've fasted before major business decisions, real estate deals, financial choices, and even relationship situations. Every single time, God gave me either peace to proceed or warning to wait. Sometimes His provision looks like a "yes," and sometimes it looks like a closed door that saves you from disaster.

And here's the beautiful part...when you fast, you also experience His **protection.**

Isaiah 58:8 says, "Then your righteousness will go before you, and the glory of the Lord will be your rear guard." That means God goes before you *and* behind you. He leads and He shields. When you fast, you're covered...front, back, and sides.

Observation Questions

1. What specific promises about guidance, provision, and protection are found in Isaiah 58:11 and 58:8?

   _____

   _____

2. How does this section describe the role fasting plays in sharpening discernment and decision-making?

   _____

   _____

Application Questions

1. Where are you currently seeking clarity or direction that fasting could help bring into focus?

   _____

   _____

2. How might trusting God's protection—both in open doors and closed ones... change how you respond to uncertainty?

   _____

   _____

Section 11 - E – Enslaving Sins

This one might be the most powerful of all.

Isaiah 58:6 says, "Is not this the kind of fasting I have chosen: to loose the chains of injustice, to set the oppressed free, and to break every yoke?"

Fasting breaks bondage. Whether your bondage is to food, fear, comparison, addiction, anxiety, or pride...fasting is the tool God uses to break the chains. When I struggled with overeating, I didn't need another diet plan...I needed deliverance. Fasting freed me from a lifetime of using food as comfort, reward, and escape.

I've watched people fast and break free from pornography, from toxic relationships, from anger and resentment. Fasting brings those things to the surface so the Holy Spirit can finally deal with them. Your flesh doesn't like it. The devil doesn't like it. But that's why it's powerful.

Observation Questions

1. According to Isaiah 58:6, what kinds of bondage does God specifically say fasting can break?

   _____

   _____

2. How does this section describe the spiritual conflict that fasting brings to the surface?

   _____

   _____

Application Questions

1. What habit, fear, or pattern might God be inviting you to confront and surrender through fasting?

   _____

   _____

2. How can you rely more fully on the Holy Spirit, rather than willpower alone, to experience freedom during a fast?

   _____

   _____

Section 12 - When You Don't See Results Right Away

One of the hardest lessons I learned about fasting is that the results aren't always immediate. Sometimes the miracle happens in your heart long before it happens in your circumstances.

I remember fasting with two close friends. One was believing for a godly husband. Another was praying for her husband's salvation. And I was praying for healing in my thyroid. We fasted, prayed, and waited. When the fast ended, none of us had seen the answer yet.

A year later, God moved in all three situations. My health began to improve. One friend met the man she'd later marry. And the other saw her husband begin asking questions about faith for the first time.

Fasting doesn't always produce instant gratification. But it always produces spiritual transformation. God moves behind the scenes even when you can't see it.

I won't sugarcoat it...fasting can be painful. You'll feel weak, lightheaded, maybe even emotional. And that's okay.

Psalm 109:24 says, "My knees are weak from fasting, and my body is thin and gaunt."

Fasting humbles your body so your spirit can rise. Don't confuse physical weakness with spiritual failure. God is often doing His greatest work when you feel your weakest. Each hunger pang is an invitation to pray, "God, fill me with what truly satisfies."

That's what fasting does...it empties you of dependence on the physical and fills you with dependence on the spiritual. Don't be surprised when your mind starts giving you excuses.

You'll hear thoughts like:

- "You have a busy week...this isn't the time."

- "You'll get a headache."

- "You can start next month."

- "What if people notice?"

Those aren't just excuses...they're distractions. The enemy knows that a fasting believer is a dangerous believer. That's why you have to decide before you start: *I will finish this fast.*

Once you commit, God gives you strength to endure.

Observation Questions

1. What does this section teach about timing?

   _____

   _____

2. How does fasting work even when results are delayed?

   _____

   _____

Application Questions

1. Are you willing to trust God's timing with what you're fasting for?

   _____

   _____

2. How can patience become part of your faith journey?

_____

_____

HEARING GOD – PERSONAL REFLECTION

Take a moment to slow down before answering these questions. This section is meant to be quiet, personal, and unhurried. Read each question slowly and allow space for God to speak.

1. What is God inviting you to fast for in this season?

2. Where do you need healing, overcoming, provision, or freedom the most?

3. What step of obedience can you take to go beneath the surface with God?

Chapter 18

Fasting for Faith...Breaking Spiritual Monotony and Building Power

ICEBREAKER QUESTIONS

1. Have you ever continued praying, serving, and showing up spiritually, yet still felt like something was missing inside?

2. Have you ever noticed your faith slipping into routine rather than passion, even though you still love God?

3. What spiritual habits in your life feel familiar but no longer feel powerful?

BIBLE PASSAGE

Before discussing, read the following passages slowly and completely in the NIV translation. These Scriptures anchor the chapter and reveal how fasting restores faith, sharpens spiritual sensitivity, and reawakens power.

Romans 12:1 (NIV) A Living Sacrifice

12 Therefore, I urge you, brothers and sisters, in view of God's mercy, to offer your bodies as a living sacrifice, holy and pleasing to God—this is your true and proper worship.

2 Corinthians 12:9 (NIV)

⁹ But he said to me, "My grace is sufficient for you, for my power is made perfect in weakness." Therefore I will boast all the more gladly about my weaknesses, so that Christ's power may rest on me.

James 5:17–18 (NIV)

¹⁷ Elijah was a human being, even as we are. He prayed earnestly that it would not rain, and it did not rain on the land for three and a half years. ¹⁸ Again he prayed, and the heavens gave rain, and the earth produced its crops.

Questions

1. What do these passages show about how God works through surrender, weakness, obedience, and even loss to accomplish something greater than we can see in the moment?

   _____

   _____

2. Where do you notice a contrast between trusting God's process and longing for comfort, control, or familiarity... and how does that challenge the way you respond when life feels hard?

   _____

   _____

Section 1: When Faith Becomes Routine

You can get into a rut even when you love God. You can pray, go to church every week, serve, and still feel like something's missing. You can have all the *forms* of faith without the *fire* of faith.

It's like cooking the same meal every night. One of the easiest dinners for me to make is spaghetti. I've made it so many times, I could do it with my eyes closed. The problem is… when I serve it again and again, my family starts to get tired of it.

That's how our spiritual life can become...predictable, repetitive, bland. We pray the same prayers, sing the same songs, and go through the same motions. We love God, but something feels… stale.

Observation Questions

1. What signs of spiritual monotony are described in this section?

   _____

   _____

2. How does the spaghetti analogy explain routine faith?

   _____

   _____

Application Questions

1. Where has your faith started to feel predictable or stale?

   _____

   _____

2. What routine might God be inviting you to interrupt?

   _____

   _____

Section 2 – Fasting as a Living Sacrifice

Fasting breaks you out of that monotony. It shakes you awake. It reignites your spirit. I call fasting a *faith builder*, because it reintroduces power where routine has dulled passion.

When I fast, even the Sunday service feels different. The songs feel alive again. The Word leaps off the page. The same sermon I might have heard a hundred times suddenly pierces my heart like it's brand new. It's not that God changed...it's that fasting cleared the clutter between my spirit and His.

Paul said in Romans 12:1 (NIV): "Therefore, I urge you, brothers and sisters, in view of God's mercy, to offer your bodies as a living sacrifice, holy and pleasing to God...this is your true and proper worship."

That verse becomes real when you fast. You literally offer your body...your appetite, your energy, your focus...as a living sacrifice. It's your way of saying, "God, I'm hungry for You more than for food."

When you fast, even your senses sharpen. Worship isn't background noise anymore. It's alive. Scripture doesn't feel like ink on paper. It breathes. It resurrects sensitivity to God's presence.

Observation Questions

1. According to this section, what specific changes occur in worship, Scripture, and spiritual sensitivity when fasting removes routine and spiritual clutter?

   _____

   _____

2. How does Romans 12:1 connect fasting with the idea of offering the body as a living sacrifice and true worship?

   _____

   _____

Application Questions

1. Where has spiritual routine or monotony dulled passion in your own walk with God, and how might fasting help reawaken your sensitivity to His presence?

   _____

   _____

2. What would it look like for you to practically offer your body... your appetite, focus, or energy... as a living sacrifice this week in response to God's mercy?

   _____

   _____

Section 3 - Grace in the Weakness

Paul prayed three times in 2 Corinthians for God to take away the thorn in his flesh. Three times! That's not a lot compared to how many times I've prayed for God to remove mine. But the Lord's answer to Paul still stops me in my tracks:

"My grace is sufficient for you, for my power is made perfect in weakness." ...2 Corinthians 12:9 (NIV)

When you fast, weakness becomes your teacher. Fasting doesn't make you strong...it makes you *dependent*. It reveals how much we've relied on comfort, caffeine, or control instead of grace. And it's in that space...where we admit weakness...that God's power rests on us.

That's the paradox of fasting: you give up physical strength, and God gives you spiritual strength. You feel weaker in body but stronger in discernment.

James 5:17-18 (NIV) says: "Elijah was a human being, even as we are. He prayed earnestly that it would not rain, and it did not rain on the land for three and a half years. Again he prayed, and the heavens gave rain, and the earth produced its crops."

I love that it starts with, *"Elijah was a human being, even as we are."*

It's like God wanted to remind us...Elijah wasn't superhuman. He wasn't a spiritual celebrity. He was just a person who prayed and fasted with faith.

So what made Elijah different? He controlled his appetite more than his ambition. His hunger for God outweighed every earthly craving. He was laser-focused on hearing God's direction and obeying it. That's the power of fasting...it aligns your spirit with heaven's rhythm.

When you combine fasting and prayer, it's like clearing static off a radio. Suddenly, you hear the broadcast clearly.

Observation Questions

1. What does God's response to Paul in 2 Corinthians 12:9 reveal about the relationship between weakness and God's power?

   _____

   _____

2. According to this section, how do fasting and prayer change the way weakness, dependence, and spiritual clarity are experienced?

   _____

   _____

Application Questions

1. Where have you been asking God to remove weakness when He may be inviting you to rely more fully on His grace instead?

   _____

   _____

2. How might intentionally surrendering comfort or control through fasting help you hear God more clearly in your current season?

   _____

   _____

Section 4 - When You've Lost Years, Fasting Restores

I can't read Joel 2:25–26 (NIV) without tearing up:

"I will repay you for the years the locusts have eaten... the great locust and the young locust, the other locusts and the locust swarm... my great army that I sent among you.

You will have plenty to eat, until you are full, and you will praise the name of the Lord your God, who has worked wonders for you; never again will my people be shamed."

This verse reminds me that life isn't always fair...but God is always faithful. There are seasons where you feel like you've lost years. You've poured yourself into people who walked away. You've worked hard for doors that never opened. You've prayed for something that seemed delayed forever. But God promises restoration...not just of what you lost, but of *the years* you lost. When you fast, God redeems time. He accelerates healing. He restores clarity, energy, and purpose that you thought were gone for good.

This verse reminds me of my husband's story. He had every reason to walk away from faith. His childhood was rough...his dad was a drug addict who spent time in jail, and his mom, also addicted, eventually died of an overdose.

None of that was fair.

But I've watched God turn all of it into purpose. The compassion, empathy, and strength he carries today are the fruits of what God grew out of pain.

Just like Joseph in the Bible. Sold by his brothers, betrayed, imprisoned...and yet God used it all to position him for purpose.

"You intended to harm me, but God intended it for good to accomplish what is now being done, the saving of many lives." he says, according to Genesis 50:20 (NIV)

Sometimes, what feels like punishment is preparation. Sometimes, the prison is the pathway to purpose. Fasting reminds you of that truth...because it strips away distraction and teaches you to trust that God is doing more than you can see.

Observation Questions

1. According to Joel 2:25–26, what does God promise to restore, and how is that restoration described emotionally and practically?

   _____

   _____

2. How do the examples of your husband's story and Joseph's story illustrate God's ability to redeem painful or lost seasons?

   _____

   _____

Application Questions

1. Where do you feel like "the locusts have eaten" years of your life, and how might fasting help you trust God with restoring what feels lost?

   _____

   _____

2. How could choosing to fast help you release bitterness, regret, or shame and begin seeing past pain as preparation rather than punishment?

   _____

   _____

Section 5 - Breaking Free From What Still Controls You

After God delivered the Israelites from Egypt, you'd think they would have run forward with joy and gratitude. But instead, they looked backward.

In Numbers 11:5 (NIV) they complain, "We remember the fish we ate in Egypt at no cost...also the cucumbers, melons, leeks, onions and garlic."

Did you catch that? They were willing to go back into *slavery* because they missed the *food*. Their stomachs had more authority than their spirit. Fasting exposes those areas in us too...where comfort, routine, or appetite still rules our obedience. God didn't free Israel from Pharaoh just to have them enslaved to cravings. And He doesn't deliver us from sin so we can be ruled by snacks. If you want to live an abundant, Spirit-led life, you can't be a slave to your stomach.

Fasting breaks the cycle of indulgence and teaches you that joy isn't in what you consume, but in Who consumes you.

There's a reason hunger is powerful...it's the posture of pursuit. When you're full, you don't go looking for food. But when you're hungry, you search, you listen, you act. Fasting takes that natural instinct and redirects it toward God.

You stop feasting on comfort and start craving communion. You begin to hear Him more clearly because every distraction has been denied. Your body's hunger becomes your spirit's amplifier. And in that place of longing, you find what routine religion can't give you...a living, breathing relationship with the voice of God.

Every fast builds faith. When you deny yourself, you discover that God really does sustain you. When you press into prayer, you realize He's been speaking all along...you just weren't quiet enough to hear. When you step away from comfort, you find courage. And every single time, your obedience becomes the breeding ground for breakthrough.

Fasting doesn't earn you God's favor...it awakens your awareness of it.

Observation Questions

1. According to Numbers 11:5, what did the Israelites long for after being freed from Egypt, and what does that reveal about what was still controlling them?

   _____

   _____

2. How does this section describe the way fasting exposes hidden areas where comfort, appetite, or routine may still rule a person's obedience?

   _____

   _____

Application Questions

1. What "Egypt" might you be tempted to look back to when following God feels uncomfortable, and how could fasting help break that pull?

_____

_____

2. In what specific area of your life do you sense God inviting you to replace comfort with communion so you can hear His voice more clearly?

_____

_____

HEARING GOD – PERSONAL REFLECTION

1. Where has routine replaced hunger in your relationship with God, and what might fasting awaken in that place?
2. What would it look like to let physical hunger train your spirit to listen more closely to God?
3. What step of obedience could unlock deeper faith for you?

Week 7

Walking It Out with Trust and Obedience

By week seven, hearing God is no longer the hard part. The real challenge becomes living out what He has already shown you.

Clarity has come. Conviction has surfaced. Humility has been practiced. Hunger has been awakened. And now the invitation is simple, but not easy. Obey.

This is the week where faith moves from insight to action. Where listening turns into walking. Where trust is proven not by what you feel, but by what you choose.

Obedience often looks quieter than we expect. It rarely comes with applause or certainty. Sometimes it looks like staying when you want to leave. Waiting when you want to move. Saying yes when the outcome is still unclear. But obedience is where intimacy deepens. It is where hearing God becomes relational, not theoretical.

Many people stop short right here. They love revelation, but hesitate at response. They want reassurance before obedience instead of trusting God enough to move without it. This week gently confronts that hesitation.

God does not speak to overwhelm you. He speaks to guide you. And He walks with you as you respond. You are not expected to have the full picture. You are only asked to take the next step.

As you move through this week, notice where resistance shows up. Not to shame yourself, but to recognize where trust is being stretched. Obedience always reveals what we truly believe about God's character.

Do not rush ahead.

Do not lag behind.

Just walk with Him.

God is faithful in the steps, not just the destination.

And clarity grows as obedience continues.

Chapter 19

Secret Fasting...The Hidden Power That Heaven Rewards

ICEBREAKER QUESTIONS

1. Have you ever done something meaningful for God that no one else knew about? How did it feel compared to something that was publicly recognized?

2. Why do you think it's so easy to pursue spiritual habits that are visible, but harder to commit to ones that stay hidden?

3. When you hear the phrase "secret place with God," what comes to mind?

BIBLE PASSAGE

Matthew 6:16–18 (NIV)

"When you fast, do not look somber as the hypocrites do, for they disfigure their faces to show others they are fasting. Truly I tell you, they have received their reward in full.

But when you fast, put oil on your head and wash your face, so that it will not be obvious to others that you are fasting, but only to your Father, who is unseen; and your Father, who sees what is done in secret, will reward you."

Leviticus 23:27 (NIV)

27 "The tenth day of this seventh month is the Day of Atonement. Hold a sacred assembly and deny yourselves, and present a food offering to the Lord.

Esther 4:16 (NIV)

"Go, gather together all the Jews who are in Susa, and fast for me. Do not eat or drink for three days, night or day. I and my attendants will fast as you do. When this is done, I will go to the king, even though it is against the law. And if I perish, I perish."

Questions

1. What do these passages reveal about the heart posture God is looking for when we fast both privately before Him and corporately with others?

   _____

   _____

2. How do these Scriptures challenge the idea that fasting is just about personal sacrifice, and instead connect it to humility, obedience, compassion, and transformation?

   _____

   _____

Section 1 - A Faith Heaven Sees

There's a kind of faith that whispers, not shouts. A kind of obedience that hides, not flaunts.

And there's a kind of fasting that heaven sees...even when no one else does. This is what Jesus meant when He taught about *secret fasting*. Fasting, at its heart, is not about proving holiness. It's about pursuing closeness. It's not about being noticed by others...it's about being noticed by God.

There are certain spiritual rhythms that people expect Christians to do...give, pray, love. Those are the "obvious" ones. We all nod when someone says, "Christians should be generous," or "Christians should pray." But what many believers don't realize is that Jesus grouped *fasting* right beside those same spiritual disciplines...not as an extra, not as an option, but as an expectation.

Remember, in the Sermon on the Mount, He said "*When* you fast..." (Matthew 6:16) Not *if*. It's the same tone of assumption, the same command structure. In other words: *This is what My people do.*

Yet, in modern Christianity, we've often ignored that third one. We love to talk about prayer and giving, but we skip over fasting like it's a forgotten footnote. If you look closely at Scripture, you'll see that fasting has always been intertwined with hearing from God, receiving breakthrough, and walking in deeper intimacy with Him.

Observation Questions

1. How is secret fasting contrasted with visible faith in this section?

   _____

   _____

2. What word choice from Jesus emphasizes fasting as an expectation?

   _____

   _____

Application Questions

1. What motivates your spiritual disciplines most closeness or recognition?

   _____

   _____

2. How could fasting become more about intimacy than visibility for you?

   _____

   _____

Section 2 - Denying the Flesh, Not Displaying It

So why is it so rare in the church today? Maybe because it's the one discipline that costs us the most. We live in a culture that celebrates indulgence. Everything around us says, *Feed it, buy it, scroll it, satisfy it.*

Fasting is the complete opposite spirit of the world. It says, "Deny yourself so that God can fill you." It's an act of rebellion against self-centeredness. When you fast, you're not punishing yourself...you're positioning yourself. You're saying, "I'm tired of being ruled by cravings. I want to be led by Christ." That's why fasting is so powerful. It's spiritual resistance.

The Bible never gives a formula for how long to fast. That's part of what makes it such a personal act of faith. In Leviticus 23:27 (NIV), God commanded one specific day of fasting for the Israelites:

"The tenth day of this seventh month is the Day of Atonement. Hold a sacred assembly and deny yourselves, and present a food offering to the Lord."

That phrase...*deny yourselves*...is the essence of fasting. It doesn't say "deny social media" or "deny Netflix." Those are fine modern sacrifices, but the Bible is explicit: this is about *denying food*. The physical denial mirrors a spiritual posture...humility. When you fast, you remind your body that it's not in charge. You dethrone your flesh and enthrone your faith. And every time you do, God honors it in ways you can't even measure.

Observation Questions

1. What does "deny yourselves" specifically refer to here?

   _____

   _____

2. How is fasting described as resistance against culture?

   _____

   _____

Application Questions

1. What comforts are hardest for you to deny?

2. How might fasting help re-establish who is leading your flesh or your faith?

_____

_____

Section 3 - What Jesus Actually Meant

Now, let's look again at the words of Jesus: "When you fast, do not look somber as the hypocrites do, for they disfigure their faces to show others they are fasting. Truly I tell you, they have received their reward in full.

But when you fast, put oil on your head and wash your face, so that it will not be obvious to others that you are fasting, but only to your Father, who is unseen; and your Father, who sees what is done in secret, will reward you."...Matthew 6:16–18 (NIV)

When I first read this, I misunderstood it. I thought Jesus meant that if *anyone* found out I was fasting, I ruined it...like I had accidentally "voided the warranty."

But that's not what He meant at all. In the Old Testament, there were many *corporate fasts*...entire communities fasting together. Everyone knew about it! Esther gathered all the Jews to fast (Esther 4:16). The early church fasted together before sending out Paul and Barnabas (Acts 13:2–3).

So, clearly, the problem isn't that people *know* you're fasting.

The problem is *why* you want them to know.

Observation Questions

1. According to Matthew 6:16–18, what behavior does Jesus criticize in those who fast, and what motivates their actions?

_____

_____

2. How do the examples of corporate fasting in Esther 4:16 and Acts 13:2–3 clarify what Jesus did *not* mean about fasting in secret?

179

_____

_____

Application Questions

1. When practicing spiritual disciplines like fasting, what motives might you need to examine to ensure you are seeking God's approval rather than human recognition?

_____

_____

2. How can you approach fasting in a way that keeps your focus on intimacy with God, even if others are aware that you are fasting?

_____

_____

Section 4 - Being Seen vs. Fasting to Be Seen

There's a difference between being _seen fasting_ and _fasting to be seen._

Jesus wasn't rebuking visibility...He was confronting vanity. He was saying, "Don't perform holiness. Pursue humility." When we fast to impress others, we've already received our reward...attention. But when we fast to seek God alone, our reward is intimacy. That's why Jesus said to "put oil on your head and wash your face."

In today's language, that means: Get up. Take a shower. Do your hair. Put on your makeup. Go about your day. Don't walk around miserable and dramatic. If people look at you and think, "Wow, she looks awful," they won't be inspired to fast...they'll be afraid of it! I'll be honest...this one convicted me deeply.

One day, a friend asked another person, "Is Chantel eating today?" And the response was, "She's fasting."

Then my friend said, "Oh… I'll wait to talk to her until she's eating again." That hit me hard. I realized that I was doing fasting wrong.

When you're fasting, you should be _more_ filled with the Spirit, not less. You should be more joyful, more gracious, more peaceful...because you're spending more time in God's presence.

Fasting shouldn't make you unbearable to be around; it should make you *unshakable* in spirit. There will be times in life when sadness is right.

Jesus Himself said, "Blessed are those who mourn, for they will be comforted." (Matthew 5:4)

But purposeful sadness for attention? That's not fasting...that's pride in disguise. If you're going to fast, don't wear misery like a badge. Wear joy like armor. Let people see the light in your eyes, not the hunger in your stomach. Let them see God's strength, not your suffering.

When you fast, you are practicing self-denial for the sake of intimacy with God. So even when your body feels weak, your spirit should radiate life. God's rewards are often invisible at first. He doesn't always hand you the miracle the next day.

Sometimes the reward is peace that can't be shaken. Sometimes it's clarity you didn't have before. Sometimes it's strength to resist a temptation that used to master you.

Observation Questions

1. What distinction does Jesus make between motive and visibility?

    _____

    _____

2. What fruit should fasting produce in a person's attitude?

    _____

    _____

Application Questions

1. Why do you think God cares so deeply about motive?

    _____

    _____

2. How can you guard your heart from turning fasting into performance?

    _____

    _____

Section 5 - The Secret Place Heaven Rewards

Fasting in secret teaches you to value the unseen. It trains your heart to crave what heaven values...purity, humility, endurance, and intimacy. And when God sees that posture, He rewards it. "...and your Father, who sees what is done in secret, will reward you."

That's the only audience that matters. In Isaiah 58, God rebuked Israel for fasting the wrong way. They were fasting while mistreating others...missing the entire point. Fasting should never make you harsh or self-righteous. If your fast leads you to snap at your spouse or coworkers, start over. The purpose of fasting isn't starvation...it's transformation. If it doesn't produce love, it's just a diet. When you fast, make sure your heart stays soft, your tone stays kind, and your spirit stays humble. That's when heaven notices.

Corporate fasting...fasting with others...is powerful. It's not a contradiction to Jesus' command; it's a completion of it. When Esther called the Jews to fast together, it wasn't a publicity stunt. It was a united act of surrender. There's power in agreement. There's strength in shared hunger.

If you have friends or a church community who want to grow spiritually, invite them to fast with you. You don't have to broadcast it online. You don't even need to announce the details. Just link arms in prayer and say, "We're doing this together."

Heaven moves when believers fast in unity. Fasting in today's world is countercultural...especially when everyone is obsessed with pleasure, image, and convenience. We live in a world where skipping breakfast is called "intermittent fasting," but skipping comfort for God's presence is called "extreme." Yet, every time you deny your body and focus on God, you declare war on apathy. The Spirit rejoices when the flesh surrenders.

You don't need to be a monk on a mountain. You can fast while you work, while you parent, while you lead your business. You can fast with joy, grace, and gratitude. Because fasting isn't about punishing yourself...it's about prioritizing God.

Fasting is one of the few spiritual disciplines that truly leads you into the "secret place."

When you pray in private, heaven listens. When you give in private, heaven multiplies. When you fast in private, heaven rewards.

It's in that secret place where revelation comes. Where direction becomes clear. Where God whispers things to your heart that He couldn't say when the noise was loud. That's where fasting leads...not to public applause, but to private intimacy.

I never yet got an "attagirl" from people for fasting. But I do believe one day 'll stand before the Lord and He'll say, "I saw it. Every meal you gave up. Every prayer you prayed. Every moment you denied yourself for Me. I saw it...and I'm proud." That's the reward that never fades away for me.

Observation Questions

1. How is the reward of fasting described differently than worldly rewards?

   _____

   _____

2. What heart posture does heaven respond to?

   _____

   _____

Application Questions

1. Where might God be inviting you into deeper unseen obedience?

   _____

   _____

2. What kind of reward are you truly living for?

   _____

   _____

HEARING GOD – PERSONAL REFLECTION

1. What motivates your obedience when no one is watching?
2. Where might pride subtly try to enter your spiritual disciplines?
3. How could secret fasting deepen your intimacy with God?

Chapter 20

Hearing God in the Stillness

ICEBREAKER QUESTION

1. If you have children, how did you decide what to name them, or how was your own name chosen? If you do not have children, why do you think no one has ever named their daughter Jezebel?

BIBLE PASSAGE

1 Kings 19:1-21 (NIV)

The Lord said, "Go out and stand on the mountain in the presence of the Lord, for the Lord is about to pass by."

Then a great and powerful wind tore the mountains apart and shattered the rocks before the Lord, but the Lord was not in the wind. After the wind there was an earthquake, but the Lord was not in the earthquake.

After the earthquake came a fire, but the Lord was not in the fire. And after the fire came a gentle whisper.

When Elijah heard it, he pulled his cloak over his face and went out and stood at the mouth of the cave.

This chapter follows Elijah after a great victory and shows how God speaks, restores, and redirects him... not through loud signs, but through care, truth, and a still, small voice.

Questions

1. What stands out to you about where God wasn't found in this passage and what does that teach you about how He often chooses to speak?

2. How might learning to recognize God's voice in the whisper, rather than the dramatic moments, change the way you seek His guidance in your own life?

_____

_____

Section 1 - The Power of a Name and the Weight of Influence

When I was pregnant with Kyle, choosing a name felt far heavier than I ever expected. What should have been simple became strangely complicated. Everyone had ideas. Everyone had opinions. Family, friends, well meaning people would ask over and over, "What are you going to name the baby?" And every time the question came, the answer was the same we didn't know.

We even had what I can only describe as a meeting. Names were suggested. Lists were made. Conversations went in circles. Yet nothing felt right. I realized that for me, a name wasn't just a sound or a label it carried meaning, memory, and emotion. I didn't want to give my child a name that already had negative associations attached to it. Because when you hear a name, you don't hear it in isolation. You think of people. You think of experiences. You think of stories.

There were names I simply couldn't choose, not because they were bad names, but because I had known people who carried them poorly. Names like Jennifer or David came with mental images of real people some good, some not. And I knew I didn't want my child's name to come with emotional baggage before he ever had a chance to define it himself.

Then one day, our daughter Shayla spoke up and said, almost offhandedly, "What about Kyle?" Something stopped me. I thought about it for a moment, and then it hit me every person I had ever known named Kyle was kind. Not perfect. Not flashy. Just genuinely nice people. Easy to trust. Easy to like. And in that moment, clarity came. I said, "That's it. That's his name."

We didn't choose the name Kyle because it was trendy or popular. We chose it because of what it represented to us. The name carried a pattern a reputation of goodness, kindness, and character. It mattered to me that my child's name didn't already carry a shadow.

That thought brings us to a very different name one that carries a reputation so dark that it has nearly disappeared from use altogether. Jezebel.

If you pause and think about it, you likely don't know a single person named Jezebel. And that absence is not accidental. The name itself has become synonymous with manipulation, wickedness, and moral corruption. It evokes discomfort. It carries weight. Over time, the name stopped being just a name and became a warning.

Jezebel's story is not simply about a woman in Scripture it is about the power of influence, the legacy of choices, and how a life lived in rebellion against God can leave such a stain that even the name becomes untouchable. Her actions were so destructive, her spirit so opposed to righteousness, that history itself rejected her name.

Names carry meaning. They carry memory. They carry legacy. Some names invite blessing. Others serve as caution. And as we step into the story of Jezebel, we are not just studying a person we are examining what happens when a life becomes so defined by darkness that its very name becomes a symbol of everything God warns us against.

Observation Questions

1. What does the text explain about the name Jezebel and why it is no longer commonly used?

   _____

   _____

2. What themes emerge in this section about how names are formed through association, memory, and lived experience?

   _____

   _____

Application Questions

1. What kind of reputation or influence do my words, actions, or choices leave behind for others to remember?

   _____

   _____

2. If my life were described the way a name is described in this section, what would I want it to represent before God and others?

_____

_____

Section 2 - Hearing God Beyond the Loud Moments

Sometimes we expect God to speak in big, dramatic ways. We wait for something loud, exciting, or overwhelming. But when we do that, we can miss how God often speaks in quiet and simple ways. God does not always shout. Many times, He speaks gently to our hearts in a still, small voice. To hear Him, we need humility and a willingness to listen, not just excitement.

This is the setting of **1 Kings chapter 19**. To understand it, we first need to look at what happened right before it.

At that time, Israel was ruled by a very wicked king named Ahab. He did not follow God. Instead, he led the people into idol worship. His wife, Jezebel, was even worse. She was raised around false gods and brought that influence into Israel. Jezebel hated God's prophets and had many of them killed. She wanted God's voice silenced.

In chapter 18, God used the prophet Elijah to show His power on Mount Carmel. God proved that He alone was real, and the people began to turn back to Him. A spiritual revival started.

But Jezebel was furious. She threatened to kill Elijah. Even after seeing God's power, Elijah became afraid and ran for his life.

This chapter shows us something important: Even strong believers can struggle. Even God's servants can feel afraid. And even after great victories, we may still need to hear God in a quiet way. What happens next will teach us how God speaks... not through noise and fear, but through humility and listening.

Observation Questions

1. According to the section, how does God often speak to people instead of using loud or dramatic moments?

_____

_____

2. What was happening in Israel before 1 Kings 19, and how did Jezebel respond to God's work through Elijah?

_____

_____

Application Questions

1. Do I sometimes expect God to speak in big or exciting ways and miss how He may be speaking quietly to me?

_____

_____

2. When I feel afraid, discouraged, or overwhelmed, what would it look like for me to slow down and listen for God instead of reacting in fear?

_____

_____

Section 3 - When Fear Gets Louder Than Faith

After Jezebel threatened Elijah, fear took over. Even though God had just shown His power in an amazing way, Elijah became scared and ran away. He traveled a long distance to escape danger and left his servant behind.

Elijah felt overwhelmed and alone. He went into the wilderness, sat down under a tree, and prayed something shocking. He asked God to take his life. Elijah felt like he had failed and believed he was no better than anyone else. His fear and discouragement became louder than his faith.

This shows us something important. Even people who love God deeply can feel exhausted and discouraged, especially after intense moments. Big victories can be followed by big emotional crashes.

- God did not scold Elijah.

- God did not shame him.

- [ ] God cared for him.

- [ ] God sent an angel to help Elijah.

The angel told him to get up and eat. Elijah rested, ate, and then slept again. The angel returned and reminded him that the journey ahead was too much to face without strength.

Before God spoke to Elijah's heart, He cared for Elijah's body. This teaches us humility. Sometimes we need to admit that we are tired, afraid, or worn down. Listening to God often begins with slowing down, resting, and letting Him take care of us. God was preparing Elijah for something deeper. But first, Elijah needed rest.

Observation Questions

1. What did Elijah do after Jezebel threatened him, and how did fear affect his actions?

   _____

   _____

2. How did God respond to Elijah when he was exhausted and discouraged?

   _____

   _____

Application Questions

1. When I feel tired, scared, or overwhelmed, do I tend to run in fear or turn to God for help?

   _____

   _____

2. What is one way I can slow down and let God care for me when I feel worn out or discouraged?

   _____

   _____

Section 4 - God Speaks in a Quiet Way

After Elijah rested and ate, he traveled to Mount Horeb, the mountain where God had spoken to Moses long ago. Elijah went into a cave and spent the night there. While he was there, God spoke to him and asked a simple question: "What are you doing here, Elijah?"

Elijah answered honestly. He told God that he felt alone, afraid, and forgotten. He believed he was the only one left who truly followed God. His feelings felt real, but they were not completely true.

Then God told Elijah to stand outside. A powerful wind came, so strong it broke rocks apart. But God was not in the wind.

Then an earthquake shook the ground. But God was not in the earthquake.

Then fire appeared. But God was not in the fire.

After all of that, there was a gentle whisper. That is where God spoke. God did not speak through the loud or dramatic moments. He spoke through a quiet voice. Elijah had to be still and listen.

This teaches us humility. God does not always shout. He often speaks softly. If we are always waiting for something big or exciting, we may miss what God is saying.

To hear God, we must slow down. We must listen carefully. And we must be humble enough to hear Him speak quietly.

Observation Questions

1. What did God use to get Elijah's attention before speaking, and where was God *not* found?

   _____

   _____

2. How did God finally speak to Elijah, and what does that show about how God communicates?

   _____

   _____

Application Questions

1. Do I expect God to speak only through big or dramatic moments, or am I willing to listen quietly?

   _____

   _____

2. What is one way I can slow down and create space to listen for God's gentle voice this week?

   _____

   _____

Section 5 - God Corrects Elijah's Thinking

After God spoke in the quiet voice, Elijah shared his feelings again. He told God that he felt alone and believed everyone else had turned away. Elijah thought he was the only one left who was faithful.

But God gently corrected him.

God told Elijah that he was not alone. There were still **7,000 people** in Israel who had not worshiped false gods. Elijah's feelings felt real, but they were not true. His fear had made him forget what God was still doing.

Then God gave Elijah clear instructions. He told him to go back and keep moving forward. God had more work for him to do. Elijah's story was not over.

This shows us something important. When we feel discouraged or alone, God does not shame us. He speaks truth to us. He reminds us that He is still in control and still working, even when we cannot see it.

Humility means admitting that our feelings do not always tell the full story. Hearing God means trusting His truth over our fear.God was teaching Elijah to listen, trust, and keep going.

Observation Questions

1. What did Elijah believe about himself and the people of Israel, and how did God correct that belief?

    _____

    _____

2. What instructions did God give Elijah after correcting his thinking?

    _____

    _____

Application Questions

1. Are there times when my feelings make me believe things that may not be fully true?

    _____

    _____

2. How can I practice humility by trusting what God says instead of letting fear or discouragement guide my thoughts?

_____

_____

Section 6 - God Gives Elijah a New Assignment

After correcting Elijah, God did not leave him stuck in fear. God gave him **clear direction**.

God told Elijah to go back and anoint new leaders. These leaders would replace the ones who had led Israel into sin. God also told Elijah to choose **Elisha** as the next prophet.

This was important. Elijah thought everything depended on him. But God showed him that His plan was bigger than one person. God was already preparing the next generation.

Elijah learned that he was not carrying the work alone. God was still moving, still calling people, and still guiding the future.

Humility means trusting that God's work does not rise or fall on us. Hearing God means obeying, even when the assignment means passing the responsibility to someone else.

God reminded Elijah that He was always in control... and always preparing what comes next.

Observation Questions

1. What new instructions did God give Elijah after correcting his thinking?

   _____

   _____

2. What did God show Elijah about His plan by choosing new leaders and a new prophet?

   _____

   _____

Application Questions

1. Do I ever feel like everything depends on me instead of trusting that God is in control?

   _____

   _____

2. What might God be asking me to obey or step into...even if it means trusting Him with the outcome or letting someone else take the lead?

_____

_____

Section 7 - God Was Speaking, Even When Elijah Felt Alone

Elijah felt like he was the only one still faithful to God. He told God that everyone else had turned away and that he was all alone. But Elijah was wrong.

God told him that He had kept **7,000 people** who had not worshiped false gods. Elijah was never as alone as he felt.

This teaches an important lesson. Feelings can be strong, but they are not always true. When we are tired, scared, or discouraged, it can be hard to hear God clearly.

God gently corrected Elijah. He reminded him that He was still working, even when Elijah could not see it. Hearing God means trusting Him more than our emotions. Humility means admitting that God sees more than we do. Elijah learned that God was faithful… even in the quiet moments.

Observation Questions

1. What did Elijah believe about himself and others, and what did God reveal to him instead?

_____

_____

2. What does the text say about God's work, even when Elijah could not see it?

_____

_____

Application Questions

1. Are there times when my emotions make me feel alone or forgotten, even though God is still working?

_____

_____

2. How can I practice humility by trusting God's perspective instead of relying only on how I feel?

_____

_____

HEARING GOD - PERSONAL REFLECTION

1. When life feels loud with fear, discouragement, or pressure, do you notice yourself running, shutting down, or slowing down to listen for God's quiet voice? What do you think God might be inviting you to hear right now?

2. Are there any thoughts or feelings you've been believing that God may want to gently correct… like feeling alone, forgotten, or responsible for everything? What truth from this chapter do you need to trust instead?

3. If God is speaking to you through obedience, rest, or serving quietly where you are, are you willing to listen… even if the path feels slow or unseen? What is one small step of obedience you sense God asking of you today?

Chapter 21

Storms That Humble Us

ICEBREAKER QUESTIONS

1. If God asked you to pause and listen right now, what do you think might make it hardest for you to hear Him… being too busy, feeling too confident, or being afraid of what He might say?

2. Can you think of a storm in your life that changed the way you see yourself or others?

BIBLE PASSAGE

Daniel 4:1-37 (NIV)

28 All this happened to King Nebuchadnezzar. 29 Twelve months later, as the king was walking on the roof of the royal palace of Babylon, 30 he said, "Is not this the great Babylon I have built as the royal residence, by my mighty power and for the glory of my majesty?"

31 Even as the words were on his lips, a voice came from heaven, "This is what is decreed for you, King Nebuchadnezzar: Your royal authority has been taken from you. 32 You will be driven away from people and will live with the wild animals; you will eat grass like the ox. Seven times will pass by for you until you acknowledge that the Most High is sovereign over all kingdoms on earth and gives them to anyone he wishes."

33 Immediately what had been said about Nebuchadnezzar was fulfilled. He was driven away from people and ate grass like the ox. His body was drenched with the dew of heaven until his hair grew like the feathers of an eagle and his nails like the claws of a bird.

34 At the end of that time, I, Nebuchadnezzar, raised my eyes toward heaven, and my sanity was restored. Then I praised the Most High; I honored and glorified him who lives forever.

His dominion is an eternal dominion;

   his kingdom endures from generation to generation.

35 All the peoples of the earth

   are regarded as nothing.

He does as he pleases

   with the powers of heaven

   and the peoples of the earth.

No one can hold back his hand

   or say to him: "What have you done?"

36 At the same time that my sanity was restored, my honor and splendor were returned to me for the glory of my kingdom. My advisers and nobles sought me out, and I was restored to my throne and became even greater than before. 37 Now I, Nebuchadnezzar, praise and exalt and glorify the King of heaven, because everything he does is right and all his ways are just. And those who walk in pride he is able to humble.

Questions

1. What do you notice about the moment Nebuchadnezzar's pride peaks... and how quickly God intervenes to remind him who is truly in control?

   _____

   _____

2. How does Nebuchadnezzar's restoration show the difference between being humbled by God and choosing humility before God and what does that teach us about pride in our own lives?

   _____

   _____

Section 1 -When Strength Breaks and Compassion Is Born

I used to think sickness was an excuse.

If someone on my team called in sick, my first thought was, *"Come on, suck it up, buttercup."* I prided myself on being strong...the one who pushed through headaches, exhaustion, anything. I'd show up no matter what, because in my mind, that's what strong people did. Weakness wasn't an option.

And then, God humbled me. A few years ago, I was diagnosed with **psoriatic arthritis**, an autoimmune disease that causes joint pain, fatigue, and inflammation. It hit me like a freight train.

One morning I woke up, and it felt like every joint in my hands was on fire. My fingers were swollen, my knees ached, and I could barely make a fist. Simple things...opening a jar, typing an email, holding a pen...suddenly felt impossible.

I went from being unstoppable to barely functional. And it shattered me. At first, I did what I always do...I tried to *push through it.* I told myself, *"I'm fine. It'll go away."* But it didn't. It got worse.

Stress made it flare up, and no matter how hard I worked, my body kept saying, "Stop." That sickness broke me in ways success never could. It stripped away my illusion of control. It made me realize how fragile this body really is...and how much I'd taken my health for granted.

Before I got sick, when someone said they had chronic fatigue or Lyme disease, I'd smile politely, but inside I was thinking, *"They just need to toughen up."* But pain has a way of softening you.

Now, when someone tells me they're struggling physically, I don't roll my eyes. I don't rush to fix them. I listen. I look them in the eye and say, *"I understand."* Because I do. I know what it's like to feel trapped in your own body. To have energy one day and nothing the next. To pray, *"God, please just help me make it through this day."*

Pain gave me compassion I didn't have before. It made me slower to judge and quicker to love. Sometimes the thing that humbles you the most is the very thing God uses to open your heart.

Observation Questions

1. How did the author's view of strength and weakness change through sickness?

   _____

   _____

2. What role did pain play in developing compassion in this section?

Application Questions

1. Has hardship ever softened your heart toward others in a new way?

   _____

   _____

2. Where might God be using discomfort to grow compassion in you right now?

   _____

   _____

Section 2 - Storms as God's Classroom

I've come to believe we are always in one of three places in life:

- ☐ **BS - Before the Storm:** When life feels peaceful, and you start to think maybe you've got it all figured out.

- ☐ **IMS - In the Middle of a Storm:** When everything hits at once and you're clinging to God just to stay standing.

- ☐ **AMS - After the Storm:** When you're finally catching your breath, trying to rebuild and find your footing again.

The truth? Storms are inevitable. Some are small...an unexpected bill, a hard conversation, a closed door. Others knock the wind right out of you. The kind that leave you gasping, "God, why?" But storms are not punishment. They're classrooms.

They strip away pride and force us to depend on God. They remind us that we're not in control...and that's actually the best news, because He is.

James 4:6 says, "God opposes the proud but gives grace to the humble." And nothing humbles us faster than pain. When you're in the middle of a storm, all the things you thought you could control start to crumble. And that's when you realize...you never had control to begin with. You just had grace.

Here's what I've learned: the storm isn't just something to survive...it's something God speaks through. When my health fell apart, His voice got louder in ways I'd never heard before.

Through pain, He softened my heart. Through fatigue, He taught me rest. Through frustration, He taught me patience. And through suffering, He taught me humility.

The very thing I thought would destroy me became the thing that drew me closer to Him. Looking back, I can see that my illness wasn't just a diagnosis...it was an invitation. An invitation to slow down, to listen, to trust. It was God saying, *"You've spent years running ahead of Me. Now walk with Me."*

Maybe you're reading this in the middle of your own storm. Maybe the pain feels unbearable. Maybe you're tired of praying for answers that haven't come yet. Can I gently tell you this? You're not alone. God is not distant in your storm. He's right there...in the middle of it, holding you steady when you feel like you're falling apart. You may not see it now, but He's using this season to shape you. He's removing what can't go with you into your next chapter. You might not hear His voice the way you used to, but trust me...He's speaking through every wave, every tear, every ache. And when the storm finally passes, you'll come out softer, wiser, and more compassionate than you ever were before. Because storms don't just humble us. They heal us. They make us look a little more like Him.

Observation Questions

1. How are storms reframed in this section...from punishment to purpose?

   _____

   _____

2. What lessons does God teach through different kinds of suffering?

   _____

   _____

Application Questions

1. Which stage before, in, or after a storm do you find yourself in right now?

   _____

   _____

2. How might God be using this season to shape you rather than break you?

   _____

   _____

Section 3 - When Pride Stops Us from Hearing God

Babylon was an amazing city. It was big, strong, and beautiful. Tall walls and colorful gates showed how powerful it was before anyone even walked inside. Everything about the city was meant to impress people.

Inside the city were a huge palace, a large throne room, and a tall temple that reached toward the sky. Babylon also had the Hanging Gardens, filled with trees and plants and flowing water. People talked about these gardens for many years because they were so beautiful.

Babylon was powerful. Babylon was famous. And the man behind it all was King Nebuchadnezzar. Nebuchadnezzar believed the city existed because of him. He wanted people to remember his name, so he even put it on many of the bricks used to build Babylon. Everywhere you looked, the message was the same.

- ☐ Nebuchadnezzar built this

- ☐ Nebuchadnezzar deserved the credit

This is where the problem began. Nebuchadnezzar forgot that God was the one who gave him his power and success. Pride replaced gratitude, and humility disappeared. When that happens, people often stop listening to God.

From the outside, Nebuchadnezzar's life looked perfect. Nothing seemed wrong. But pride was growing quietly in his heart.

Daniel chapter 4 begins here. It shows what happens when someone takes credit for what God has given. Before judging Nebuchadnezzar, we should look at ourselves. It is easy to forget God when things are going well.

This chapter starts with greatness, but it also starts with pride… and pride makes it hard to hear God.

Observation Questions

1. How is the city of Babylon described in the text? What makes it seem powerful and impressive?

   _____

   _____

2. What does the text show about how Nebuchadnezzar felt about the city and who he believed deserved the credit for it?

Application Questions

1. Are there things in my life that I feel proud of where I may forget to thank God or recognize Him as the source?

   _____

   _____

2. Is there an area where I need to stop relying only on myself and start trusting God more?

   _____

   _____

Section 4 - When God Gets Our Attention

Nebuchadnezzar's life did not fall apart during a hard time. It happened when everything was going well. His kingdom was strong, his power felt secure, and his city showed his success. From the outside, his life looked perfect.

This is often when pride grows. Nebuchadnezzar was not looking for God. He was not asking for help or direction. He felt comfortable and in control. Then God gave him a dream that scared him and took away his peace. The dream showed him something important... he was not as powerful as he thought.

Nebuchadnezzar called his wise men and advisors to explain the dream, but they could not help him. They had no answers and no understanding. This showed that even his greatest resources had limits.

That is when he remembered Daniel. Daniel had helped him before, not because Daniel was special, but because God revealed the truth through him. Daniel made it clear that the answer came from God, not from human wisdom.

Nebuchadnezzar was impressed and even spoke well of Daniel's God. But being impressed is not the same as being humble. Knowing about God is not the same as listening to Him.

Nebuchadnezzar had already seen God work. He had seen dreams explained and lives saved from the fire. But his heart had not changed. He still believed he was in control, and he still had not learned humility.

That is why this chapter matters. God is patient, but He does not ignore pride. When people stop listening, God knows how to get their attention. Sometimes He interrupts comfort so His voice can be heard.

Daniel chapter 4 reminds us that ignoring God does not stop Him from speaking. It only delays the lesson He wants to teach.

And sometimes, the most loving thing God can do is interrupt a comfortable life so we can learn humility and truly hear Him.

Observation Questions

1. What was Nebuchadnezzar's life like when God gave him the dream, and why is it important that everything seemed to be going well?

    _____

    _____

2. What happened when Nebuchadnezzar asked his wise men to explain the dream, and what does that show about their ability to help him?

    _____

    _____

Application Questions

1. Are there times when I stop seeking God because life feels comfortable or easy?

    _____

    _____

2. When something interrupts my plans or comfort, do I ignore it or ask God what He might be teaching me?

    _____

    _____

Section 5 - The Dream That Revealed the Truth

Nebuchadnezzar had a dream that scared him. It was clear and hard to ignore.

In the dream, he saw a huge tree. It was tall, strong, and full of fruit. People were fed by it. Animals rested under it. Birds lived in its branches. The tree showed power and success.

Then a messenger from heaven said the tree must be cut down. The branches were removed, and everything left. What once looked strong was brought low.

The tree was not destroyed completely. The stump stayed in the ground, showing that limits were being placed.

The tree represented a man. That man would lose his right thinking until he learned an important lesson. The message was simple: God is in charge, and He gives power to whomever He chooses.

Daniel understood the dream and knew it was about Nebuchadnezzar. The dream was not meant to hurt him. It was a warning.

God was giving Nebuchadnezzar a chance to humble himself and listen.

God still works this way today. Before He corrects us, He warns us.

The question is not whether God is speaking. The question is whether we are listening.

Observation Questions

1. How is the tree described in the dream, and how does it help people, animals, and the land?

   _____

   _____

2. What happens to the tree, and what reason is given in the dream for why this happens?

   _____

   _____

Application Questions

1. Are there things in my life that I depend on more than God, like success, popularity, or being in control?

   _____

   _____

2. When God shows me something about my heart that is hard to hear, do I listen or try to ignore it?

_____

_____

Section 6 - The Warning That Was Ignored

Daniel did not speak right away after hearing the dream. He understood how serious it was and who it was about. When he finally spoke, he was clear and honest. Daniel told Nebuchadnezzar the truth. The great tree in the dream was the king himself. His power, influence, and kingdom had grown because God allowed it. Many people benefited from his rule. But the same God who raised him up could also bring him down. Daniel explained what would happen next. Nebuchadnezzar would be taken away from people. He would live like an animal and lose his right thinking for a time. This would continue until he admitted one important truth.

Daniel made it clear:

- God rules over all kingdoms

- God gives power to whomever He chooses

Even in the warning, there was mercy. The stump would remain. The kingdom would not be destroyed forever. If Nebuchadnezzar humbled himself, he could be restored. Daniel did more than explain the dream. He gave the king advice. He urged Nebuchadnezzar to turn away from pride. He told him to do what was right and to show kindness to others. Daniel begged the king to humble himself so the punishment could be delayed or avoided.

It was wise advice.

It was loving advice.

And it was ignored.

Nebuchadnezzar listened, but he did not change. Months passed. God gave him time to respond. But the king went back to his life as usual. The city was still beautiful. The palace still shined. And Nebuchadnezzar still believed it all belonged to him. One night, the king walked on the roof of his palace and looked out over Babylon. He spoke proudly about the city and said it was built by his power for his glory. Before he even finished speaking, God answered. The warning became real. Nebuchadnezzar lost his authority. He lost his sanity. He was driven away from people and lived like an animal, eating grass and living outside. The most powerful man in the world became completely helpless.

This teaches an important lesson. Hearing God's warning is not the same as obeying it. Knowing the truth is not the same as changing. God is patient, but patience does not mean we can ignore Him forever.

When warnings are ignored, consequences follow. And sometimes, God must remove what we refuse to surrender in order to teach us humility. Nebuchadnezzar learned humility the hardest way. Not because God was cruel, but because pride left him no other way to learn.

Observation Questions

1. What warning did Daniel give Nebuchadnezzar, and what did he say would happen if the king did not humble himself?

   _____

   _____

2. How did Nebuchadnezzar respond to the warning, and what happened after God gave him time to change?

   _____

   _____

Application Questions

1. Has God ever warned me about something that I chose to ignore or put off?

   _____

   _____

2. Is there an area in my life where I need to let go of pride or control before it causes bigger problems?

   _____

   _____

Section 7 - Learning Humility the Hard Way

Nebuchadnezzar's fall was real. For a time, the most powerful king on earth lived like an animal. He ate grass, slept outside, and lost control of his mind. The king who once sat on a throne lost everything.

This really happened. Even historians wrote that Nebuchadnezzar became very sick near the end of his reign. God did exactly what He said He would do.

But the story did not end there. At the right time, Nebuchadnezzar looked up toward heaven. In that moment, his right thinking returned. The change did not come from strength or effort. It came from humility.

For the first time, Nebuchadnezzar admitted the truth. He praised God and said that God rules forever and that all power belongs to Him. This was no longer the voice of a proud king. It was the voice of a humbled man. God responded. Nebuchadnezzar's sanity returned, his kingdom was restored, and he became even greater than before.

This is the heart of Daniel chapter 4. God was not trying to destroy Nebuchadnezzar. He was trying to save him. All power comes from God. All success is allowed by God. All glory belongs to God.

When we choose humility, God lifts us up. When we refuse, He may still teach us ... but the lesson becomes much harder.

Observation Questions

1. What happened to Nebuchadnezzar during his time of humiliation, and how does the text describe how he lived?

   _____

   _____

2. What change happened that led to Nebuchadnezzar getting his right mind and kingdom back?

   _____

   _____

Application Questions

1. What could humility look like in my life right now, before I have to learn it the hard way?

   _____

   _____

2. How can I better remember to give God credit for the good things in my life instead of taking the credit myself?

_____

_____

Section 8 - A Lesson We Still Need Today

Nebuchadnezzar did not share his story to make himself look good. He shared it so people would know the truth. He wanted everyone to understand what he learned the hard way.

Human success does not last forever. God's authority does.

Nebuchadnezzar learned that humility is not about losing everything. It is about seeing clearly. He finally understood that everything he had came from God...his power, his success, and even his ability to think and rule.

Humility does not mean pretending you are worthless. It means knowing where your gifts and success come from. All credit belongs to God.

- ☐ Every breath

- ☐ Every opportunity

- ☐ Every achievement

When Nebuchadnezzar accepted this truth, God restored him and lifted him up again. This lesson still matters today. It is easy to believe we earned everything ourselves. But Daniel chapter 4 reminds us that nothing lasts unless God sustains it. God will teach humility one way or another. We can learn it gently through gratitude and obedience, or we can learn it the hard way through loss. The choice is ours.

Daniel chapter 4 is not just a story from the past. It is an invitation... to listen to God, walk humbly, and give Him the glory now, before pride has to be corrected later.

Observation Questions

1. Why did Nebuchadnezzar share his story with everyone in his kingdom, and what lesson did he want them to learn?

_____

_____

2. How does the text explain what true humility is and who deserves the credit for everything?

_____

_____

Application Questions

1. When am I tempted to take credit for good things in my life instead of thanking God?

_____

_____

2. What is one simple way I can practice humility this week by trusting or obeying God?

_____

_____

HEARING GOD - PERSONAL REFLECTION

1. Let me be honest. Are you in a season where life feels comfortable and under control, or a season where God has disrupted your plans? How might God be using this season to get your attention?

2. If hearing God begins with humility, what is one area of pride or self...reliance you may need to surrender so you can listen more closely and obey more fully?

Week 8

Freedom Begins Beneath the Reaction

By week eight, many of us start to notice something important. We are hearing God more clearly. We are learning to obey. We are practicing humility. But there are moments when our reactions still feel louder than His voice.

This week is about triggers.

Triggers are not failures. They are signals. They reveal places where healing is still needed, not places where God has abandoned us. Often, the moments that feel most overwhelming are not about what is happening right now. They are connected to something older. Something unresolved. Something that still hurts.

God is not intimidated by those places. He is not frustrated by your reactions. He is gentle and intentional, and He meets you right there. Every trigger is an invitation to pause instead of react. To listen instead of defend. To let Him touch what has been buried beneath the surface.

When triggers go unexamined, they can quietly distort how we hear God. Old vows, past wounds, and unresolved pain can filter His voice and shape our decisions without us realizing it. But when those places are brought into the light, freedom begins.

This week invites you to stop shaming yourself for your reactions and start paying attention to them. Not to relive the pain, but to allow God to heal it. Healing does not erase your story. It redeems it.

As you move through this chapter, give yourself permission to slow down. To notice what rises up in you. To ask God to search your heart with kindness. He does not expose wounds to embarrass you. He reveals them so He can restore you.

Freedom does not come from controlling your reactions.

It comes from healing what fuels them.

And when healing takes place, God's voice becomes clearer, calmer, and easier to trust.

Chapter 22

Freedom from Triggers

ICEBREAKER QUESTIONS

1. Can you think of a moment when your reaction surprised you because it felt bigger than the situation itself?

2. Growing up, how were emotions like anger, sadness, or frustration handled in your home?

3. When you feel emotionally overwhelmed, do you tend to shut down, speak up, or push through?

BIBLE PASSAGE

Psalm 139:23-24 (NIV)

"Search me, God, and know my heart;

test me and know my anxious thoughts.

See if there is any offensive way in me,

and lead me in the way everlasting."

Questions

1. What stands out to you about David's willingness to invite God to search his heart?

   _____

   _____

2. How does this passage change the way you think about bringing uncomfortable emotions to God?

   _____

   _____

Section 1 - What Triggers Really Are

Have you ever been in a situation where something small sets you off...a tone, a look, a phrase...and suddenly you're overwhelmed with emotion? That's a trigger.

Triggers are not just reactions to what's happening in the moment. They're echoes of old wounds, unresolved pain, unmet needs, or unhealed trauma. Our bodies remember pain even when our minds want to move on.

The beautiful thing is this: The Holy Spirit doesn't ignore our triggers. He meets us in them. Every trigger is an invitation from God to stop, reflect, and allow Him to heal what lies beneath the surface.

God doesn't want you to live at the mercy of your reactions. He wants you to be free...to walk in peace and wisdom, to respond with the fruit of the Spirit. But in order to live in that freedom, you have to invite Him into the places that still feel stuck, scared, or angry.

Psalm 139:23-24 says: *"Search me, God, and know my heart; test me and know my anxious thoughts. See if there is any offensive way in me, and lead me in the way everlasting."*

That's the prayer we need to pray when we feel triggered. One of the things about hearing from God is this...you've got to make sure your triggers aren't getting in the way.

Observation Questions

1. How does this section describe the difference between a trigger and a normal emotional reaction?

_____

_____

2. What does this section say about how God views our triggers?

_____

_____

Application Questions

1. What is one emotion you tend to react to quickly without stopping to reflect?

_____

_____

2. How could praying Psalm 139:23-24 help you respond differently the next time you feel triggered?

_____

_____

Section 2 - Listening to the Holy Spirit Instead

Now, let me share another story...this time where I actually did listen to the Holy Spirit. We were at a hotel, and the baggage guy was walking us up to our room. On the way, he started telling us about the restaurants on the property. He got especially excited about the steakhouse. He said, "Everyone says it's amazing. I can't wait to try it...but I haven't been able to yet."

In that moment, I felt the Holy Spirit nudge me: *Get him a gift certificate for the steakhouse.*

And my first thought was, *How in the world am I going to do that?* I never carry cash in my purse, and honestly, I didn't know if I'd even see him again. But the nudge didn't go away. I felt the Spirit say, *Just give him a hundred dollars so he can go.*

So I reached into my wallet, pulled out $100, and handed it to him. "This is for you," I told him. "Go enjoy that steakhouse."

You would've thought he had just won the lottery. His face lit up like it was the best day of his life.

Observation Questions

1. What emotions did the author experience when she followed the Holy Spirit's prompting?

   _____

   _____

2. How does this story contrast with the previous example?

   _____

   _____

Application Questions

1. When was the last time you felt a nudge from the Holy Spirit and hesitated?

   _____

   _____

2. What might change if you responded more quickly to those promptings?

   _____

   _____

Section 3 - Where Triggers Are Formed and Why They Linger

When I was younger, my mom would never complain about anything. I remember sitting in a restaurant one night when I was about ten years old. We had been waiting for our food for over an hour. The room smelled like fried chicken and mashed potatoes, and other people who came after us were already eating. I looked over at my mom, who was just sitting quietly, smiling politely as if everything was fine.

Finally, I whispered, "Mom, are you not going to say anything?" She looked at me softly and said, "I don't want to complain. You say something."

So I did. I flagged down the server, my little heart pounding, and said, "Excuse me, we haven't gotten our food in over an hour. Can you please check on it?" that moment on, something shifted in me. I became the one who spoke up. I was the one who asked questions, made phone calls, followed up, and took charge. Even with small things like deciding where to eat, it was always me. I'd ask my mom and stepdad, "Where do you want to go?" They'd both say, "I don't know." Finally, I'd sigh and say, "We're going to Red Lobster. Let's go."

I didn't realize it then, but that simple dynamic shaped me. It made me responsible, decisive, and bold...but it also planted something deeper. Over time, I developed a trigger toward passivity. When people won't step up, when they stay silent and let things slide, something inside me stirs. I don't like it. It takes me back to that little girl at the restaurant, watching someone I loved choose silence when she deserved to be heard.

Another deep wound in my story came from my real dad.

I remember one day, I found him doing drugs. I didn't fully understand what I was seeing...I just knew it wasn't right. Another time, I went to visit him in jail, but they told me he was "sick." I had to talk to him through a plastic divider, and they said it was to keep me from catching his sickness. But I knew deep down it wasn't sickness...it was sin. It was prison.

The hardest part wasn't the lies...it was the promises. My dad would say, "I'll see you this weekend," or "Next time, I'll take you to the park." I'd wait by the window for hours, watching cars drive by, hoping one would stop. Most weekends, he never came.

Those disappointments shaped me more than I realized. Even today, when someone says they'll do something and then doesn't follow through, it stings more than it should. It's not just about the missed promise...it reopens an old wound that whispers, *You're not worth showing up for.*

But healing has taught me something powerful: God's promises are the opposite. He's the Father who *always* shows up. He doesn't forget. He doesn't cancel. When He says He'll do something, He does it...and that reliability has been the anchor for my heart ever since.

Observation Questions

1. What childhood experiences helped shape the author's triggers?

   _____

   _____

2. How do broken promises connect to deeper emotional wounds?

   _____

   _____

Application Questions

1. What past experiences might still be influencing how you react today?

   _____

   _____

2. How can trusting God's consistency help heal lingering wounds?

   _____

   _____

Section 4 - The Night the Salt Was Missing

One of the moments that marked me forever happened over something as small as salt. My stepdad was an alcoholic, and my mom was the sweetest, most gentle person you could ever meet. One night, she forgot to put the salt on the dinner table. That's it...just the salt. But he exploded. He slammed his fist on the table and yelled, "I've told you before...don't forget the salt!" The room went silent. My mom's hands trembled as she reached for the shaker. I stood there frozen, my stomach in knots, thinking, *This is ridiculous. She doesn't deserve this.*

That night I made a silent vow: *No one will ever treat me like that. Ever.* From that point on, disrespect became one of my biggest triggers. If someone talks down to me, especially in front of others, I can feel that ten...year...old girl rise up inside me again. My voice gets sharper. My guard goes up. I'm ready to protect the people I love...and the little girl in me who once felt powerless.

But through healing and God's grace, I've learned to pause before reacting. I remind myself that not every situation is my stepdad yelling about salt. God has taught me that standing for respect doesn't have to mean carrying resentment. I can honor truth and still walk in peace.

Observation Questions

1. What specific childhood moment shaped the vow about respect, and how did that experience influence emotional reactions later in life?

   _____

   _____

2. How does this section show the difference between reacting from past wounds versus responding from healing and grace?

Application Questions

1. What situations or behaviors trigger strong emotional reactions in you, and how might they be connected to unresolved experiences from your past?

_____

_____

2. How can you pause and invite God into a triggering moment so you can respond with truth and peace instead of fear or resentment?

_____

_____

Section 5 - When Words and Promises Become Sacred

For me, one of my biggest triggers has always been broken commitments. When someone doesn't do what they say they're going to do, it hits me on a deep level. It's not about the task...it's about trust.

I think that's one of the reasons I fell in love with my husband. When he says he's going to do something, he does it...every single time. And he knows I'm the same way. My word means something.

We both came from painful pasts filled with inconsistency and disappointment. So, for us, keeping our word became sacred. We respond quickly. We follow through. We don't ghost each other or leave things unresolved. That reliability isn't just about discipline...it's about love.

When someone keeps their promises, it builds a safe space for your soul. And that's what I found in my husband: safety. We both had to unlearn old pain and rebuild new patterns together. But now, that sense of consistency...of showing up no matter what...has become one of the strongest foundations in our marriage. It's the quiet, everyday way we remind each other: _You're safe here. You can count on me._

Observation Questions

1. Why do broken commitments carry such emotional weight in this section, and how are they connected to trust and safety?

_____

_____

2. How does consistency and follow...through become a form of love and healing within this relationship?

_____

_____

Application Questions

1. How do you personally respond when someone breaks a promise, and what past experiences might be shaping that response?

_____

_____

2. In what ways can keeping your word...both to others and to God...be an act of love, safety, and spiritual maturity?

_____

_____

Section 6 - The Office Move That Exposed the Trigger

About ten years ago, we were moving offices. We had hired a moving company and I was trying to arrange all the furniture in a new, smaller space.

By the third time I asked the mover to reposition something, he snapped in front of my whole staff: "This is the last time I'm moving this for you. I'm not moving it again." I went from calm to level...10 mad in seconds. I looked at him and said, "I'm paying you hourly, and if I need you to move that fourteen times, we'll move it fourteen times. I'm the customer. If you disrespect me one more time, you'll be out of here so fast your head will spin."

Afterward, I talked with a friend about it. She asked, "What do you think made you so mad?"

And I realized...it wasn't just about the furniture. It was about my past. My stepdad had been very disrespectful to my mom. He was an alcoholic, and he constantly belittled her. And she just took it.

So I made a vow as a child: *I will not let anyone disrespect me.*

That vow came roaring back in that office. It wasn't about the mover...it was about my trigger. It's funny because in other areas, I don't get triggered at all. For example, I'm literally the nicest driver you'll ever meet. You could cut me off in traffic, honk at me, or even give me a dirty look, and I'll just assume you didn't see me. I'm like, "Oh, they must be in a rush," or, "Maybe they're having a bad day." I don't take it personally at all. Driving isn't a trigger for me...it just rolls right off my back.

But broken promises? Or disrespect? Oh, that's a whole different story. Those things can take me from zero to a hundred real quick. It's like all the emotions from my past come rushing right back in that moment.

And here's what I've learned about triggers: they're not really about what's happening in the moment. They're about the old stuff...old vows we made, old wounds that never got fully healed, old stories we keep carrying around. When someone disrespects me, it's not just about that person in front of me...it's about the little girl inside of me who watched her mom get disrespected. When someone breaks a promise, it's not just about them...it's about my real dad who made promises to me and never kept them.

That's why triggers feel so big. They're not just emotions; they're echoes. They're memories our hearts and bodies are still holding onto. And until we invite God into those places, those old wounds will keep bleeding into our present.

Observation Questions

1. What event triggered the intense emotional response during the office move, and what deeper issue did it reveal?

   _____

   _____

2. How does the contrast between reactions to disrespect versus reactions while driving highlight how triggers work?

   _____

   _____

Application Questions

1. When you react strongly in certain situations, how can you ask God to reveal whether the response is about the present moment or a past wound?

   _____

   _____

2. What old vows or beliefs might God be inviting you to revisit, surrender, or replace with His truth and healing?

_____

_____

Section 7 - Anger Demands Our Attention

I don't know if you keep up with the boxing world very much, but there's a fellow named James Toney who not long ago became the IBF middleweight boxing champion of the world. He was a 25...year...old man with a punch like a howitzer, and he won the middleweight title by knocking out Michael Nunn, who was the defending champion and a 20...to...1 favorite against him.

James Toney was powerful and successful, but he was also an angry man… deeply angry at his father. In an interview with *Sports Illustrated*, Toney explained why. He said his father did his mother wrong. He left them. He beat his mother repeatedly. He shot her and left a permanent mark on her leg. He made her work two jobs and then walked away from his responsibilities.

Toney went on to say that he fights with his anger. Everything is about that anger. When he looks at his opponent, he sees his dad. He said he has to take him out. He has to kill him. He said he will do whatever it takes to get him out of the ring. He even said he knows where his father is, and if his father ever comes out of hiding, he will be ready for him.

That is what anger looks like when it is never dealt with.

Anger is a powerful emotion, and it demands our attention. As we see from the life of James Toney, anger that is not handled properly… anger that is not handled biblically… becomes a smoldering cancer that slowly eats away at a person's life.

That is why we need to talk about anger, and that brings us to the question this passage forces us to ask.

How do we handle anger so it does not destroy us?

To answer that question, we turn to Scripture. At this point in the story, Jesus has just completed the triumphal entry. He has entered the city of Jerusalem during the final week of His earthly life. The Bible tells us that when He entered the city, He went through the eastern gate and went straight to the temple.

Luke 19:45...46 (NIV)

When Jesus entered the temple courts, he began to drive out those who were selling. "It is written," he said to them, " 'My house will be a house of prayer'; but you have made it 'a den of robbers.' "

John's Gospel gives us an even fuller picture of what was happening inside the temple.

John 2:13...17 (NIV)

When it was almost time for the Jewish Passover, Jesus went up to Jerusalem. In the temple courts he found people selling cattle, sheep and doves, and others sitting at tables exchanging money. So he made a whip out of cords, and drove all from the temple courts, both sheep and cattle; he scattered the coins of the money changers and overturned their tables.

To those who sold doves he said, "Get these out of here! Stop turning my Father's house into a market!" His disciples remembered that it is written: "Zeal for your house will consume me."

Here is what Jesus saw when He walked into the temple:

- ☐ People selling cattle, sheep, and doves

- ☐ Money changers seated at tables

- ☐ Worship replaced with commerce

- ☐ God's house turned into a marketplace

This moment matters, because it shows us something many people struggle with.

Jesus gets angry. His anger was not random. His anger was not selfish. His anger was not sinful.

Observation Questions

1. What do we learn about James Toney's anger, and where did it come from?

_____

_____

2. What did Jesus see when He entered the temple, and how did He respond?

_____

_____

Application Questions

1. Are there areas in my life where anger has been left unresolved and allowed to grow?

_____

_____

2. When I feel angry, do I stop to examine it and bring it to God, or do I ignore it and move on?

_____

_____

Section 8 ... What Was Really Happening in the Temple

Jesus entered the city of Jerusalem during the last week of his earthly life. And the Bible says when he enters the city, he goes through the eastern gate of the wall and right to the temple. And let's pick up the story there.

In Luke 19:45 it said, and then he entered the temple area and began driving out those who were selling. Now, John chapter 2 gives us a little fuller picture of what these guys were doing that he drives out.

It says in John's chapter 2 that in the temple courts, Jesus found men selling cattle and sheep and doves and others sitting at tables exchanging money. Now, what's really going on here? Well, the answer is there's two things going on here. First of all, if you remember from other passages in the Bible, according to Jewish law, every male Jew had to pay a temple tax once a year to support the work of the temple.

You remember when Jesus sent Peter to catch this fish and inside of its mouth was a coin and he said, now go take that coin and pay for your tax and mine. That was this temple tax that had to be paid once a year. Now, the problem was that Palestine had five or six different currencies floating around at this time.

There was Roman currency, Greek currency, Egyptian currency, but the rabbis insisted that the temple tax could only be paid in shekels. And so people, in order to come and pay their tax, had to convert whatever money they had into shekels. It was the only acceptable form of money in which you could pay your temple tax.

And thus, money changers sat at the gate of the temple and they would exchange your money for you, whatever kind of money you brought, into shekels so you could pay your temple tax. That was the first thing going on here. The second thing going on is that, remember, Jewish people would come from all over the world to sacrifice to God at the temple.

And of course, that meant they had to have a bull or a lamb or a goat or pigeons or whatever to sacrifice. Now, one option was to schlep the animal from wherever you were coming from, drag that animal across hundreds of miles to bring him to the temple so you could sacrifice him. And don't forget, even after you got there, the animal had to be without blemish.

The animal had to meet the exacting requirements of the priest in order to be sacrificed. So you took the risk of schlepping some animal hundreds of miles across the wilderness, getting there, finding out that the animal wasn't acceptable and you couldn't use it. The other option is to wait till you got to the temple, buy an animal right there on the spot that the priest had already said was okay, and then, you know, that was kind of easier.

And so that's what the people were sitting out there doing. They were selling bulls and goats and sheep and pigeons for people to sacrifice. And you say, well, Lon, why was Jesus so torqued off? I mean, here were these nice people sitting at the temple just trying to help worshipers when they came.

I mean, just trying to provide a nice service. What was he so upset about? Friend, listen, do you really think that Jesus was against the legitimate helping of foreign worshipers? If that's all that was going on here, you think he would have really overturned the tables and run these people out? No, of course not. But there's some clue into why Jesus did what he did that's found in the next thing that he said.

Look at verse 46. And when he drove them out, he said, it is written, my house will be a house of prayer, but you have made it into a den of robbers. Look what he called the guy.

He called them robbers. And it's clear that what we have here is a bunch of carpetbaggers victimizing people, exploiting people, charging rates that were akin to raw thievery because they had people at their disposal. They had people right in the palm of their hand.

Now, the Jewish Talmud actually records, and if you really care, I can give you the reference, come up afterwards and go look it up, records an instance, for example, where the sellers of pigeons were actually selling those pigeons at 90 times, that's right, 9...0, 90 times the real worth of the pigeons. And it was so bad, it even scandalized the rabbis. That's how bad it was.

And they got upset and said, you can't sell pigeons for that much. So there was extortion going on here. Do you understand what's going on? Here come these poor people from foreign countries.

They don't know squat about how the temple works. And these people are just gouging them beyond belief. Kind of sounds like going to RFK Stadium, doesn't it? You ever go down there, they sell peanuts for a dollar on the street, five dollars inside the stadium.

You say, golly, what happened to these peanuts when they went through the gate? I mean, did these become divine peanuts? What happened to these things? You ever had that experience? All right, well, they know once you're in, you can't go back out on the street to buy peanuts for a dollar, so they got you. And there's a sense in which you say, this is not right. This is not fair.

The priests were the ones who ran this thing. They controlled who was allowed to set up shop in the temple. They got huge kickbacks, the Talmud tells us, from these people who were selling there.

It kind of sounds like the mafia in Atlantic City, doesn't it? Yeah, well, it wasn't a whole lot different. And in fact, Josephus, the great historian, tells us that Annas, the high priest who's mentioned in the New Testament, became filthy rich by running this scheme out there and getting all these kickbacks from all of these people who were selling and extorting the people. And the bottom line is, this was a monopoly that was being run by the family of the high priest, and it generated a fortune.

And I like what one commentator said. He said, instead of praying for the people, the priests were praying on the people. You got the point? Yeah.

Now, that's why Jesus went crazy and did what he did. And when Jesus saw this, he was incensed. He was outraged.

And the Bible says he drove them out. He threw them out. And Matthew gives a little fuller picture. Matthew's gospel says, he overturned the tables of the money changers and the benches of those selling doves. And you get the picture, don't you? Mr. Scrooge sitting there with his little neat piles of coins all over his table. And here comes Jesus just flipping these tables over and coins go rolling all over everywhere.

And the merchants and the pilgrims and the rabbis and the priests were all down on the floor scrambling for the money, fighting for one another. It's like a mud wrestling contest without the mud, if you can picture that. Like total bedlam. To make this easier to understand, think about going to FedEx Field, which used to be RFK Stadium. I am a Washington Commanders fan, back when they were the Washington Redskins. When you go into the stadium, they might charge you ten dollars for a bottle of water. That same bottle of water costs about fifty cents or less at Costco. Nothing changed about the water. The price changed because once you are inside, you are trapped.

That is exactly what was happening in the temple.

Once worshipers entered, they had no choice. They could not leave to exchange money elsewhere. They could not buy animals cheaper somewhere else. The leaders knew this and used it to make money. It was price gouging in God's house.

What made it even worse was who was behind it. Historical records, including the writings of Josephus, tell us that the high priest and his family controlled this system and became extremely wealthy through it. The priests allowed it, managed it, and profited from it.

That is why Jesus became angry. His anger was not impulsive. His anger was not sinful. His anger was righteous.

Matthew records in **Matthew 21:12 (NIV)** that Jesus overturned the tables of the money changers and the benches of those selling doves. Coins scattered. Tables fell. The system was exposed.

Jesus was defending God's honor and protecting people who were being hurt in the name of religion. This moment shows us that anger, when guided by truth and love for God, can confront injustice instead of creating it.

And this sets the foundation for the rest of the chapter.

Observation Questions

1. What practices were taking place inside the temple that caused Jesus to react so strongly?

   _____

   _____

2. According to the passage, who benefited from the system that was set up in the temple, and who was being harmed?

   _____

   _____

Application Questions

1. Are there ways people today can misuse religion or authority for personal gain instead of helping others?

   _____

   _____

2. When I see injustice or unfairness, do I respond with God...guided concern or do I ignore it because it is uncomfortable?

Section 9 - What Anger Really Is

Seeing Jesus angry in the temple forces us to ask an important question. If Jesus was angry, does that mean anger itself is wrong?

The answer is no.

The Bible is very clear that Jesus never sinned. **Hebrews 4:15 (NIV)** tells us that Jesus was tempted in every way just as we are, yet He did not sin. That means His anger in the temple was not sinful. It was righteous.

So what is anger?

Anger is an emotion. It is a strong feeling that shows up when something hurts us, feels unfair, threatens something we value, or violates what we believe is right. Anger is not something you decide to feel. It happens before you have time to think it through.

When anger shows up, our bodies respond immediately. Doctors tell us that anger is not only emotional, it is physical. When someone gets angry:

• Adrenaline is released

• Heart rate increases

• Blood pressure rises

• Muscles tighten

• Energy surges

• Vision sharpens

That is why anger feels so powerful and so fast.

The Bible never says that feeling angry is a sin. In fact, **Ephesians 4:26 (NIV)** says, "In your anger do not sin." That verse alone tells us something important. Anger is not automatically sin, but it brings us very close to it.

Anger is like standing at the edge of a cliff. You are not over the edge yet, but it does not take much to fall.

Scripture gives us many examples of this.

Cain became angry and killed his brother in **Genesis 4**.

Moses became angry and struck the rock in **Numbers 20**, which cost him entry into the Promised Land.

Absalom became angry and murdered his brother in **2 Samuel 13**, setting in motion his own destruction.

Anger itself was not the sin. What they did with it was.

Even in our own lives, we see this pattern. It is usually when we are angry that we:

• Say words we cannot take back

• Lash out at people we love

• Damage our witness

• Make decisions we regret

Anger is not the problem. Anger is a signal.

It tells us that something is wrong. It alerts us to injustice, pain, betrayal, or brokenness. But anger does not tell us what to do next. That is where we need God.

This is why hearing God matters so much when anger shows up. Without God's voice, anger leads us. With God's voice, anger is guided.

Observation Questions

1. What does the Bible say about Jesus and sin that helps us understand His anger in the temple?

   _____

   _____

2. How does the section describe what happens in our bodies and actions when anger shows up?

   _____

   _____

Application Questions

1. When I feel angry, do I usually pause and think, or do I react quickly?

_____

_____

2. How could listening to God change the way I respond the next time I feel angry?

_____

_____

Section 10 - When Anger Crosses the Line

Anger does not stay neutral for long. If it is not handled carefully, it will move somewhere. The question is not whether anger will act, but how.

The Bible teaches that anger becomes sinful when it stops being guided by God and starts guiding us.

James Dobson explains that anger crosses the line in three specific ways. Scripture supports each one.

1. **First, anger becomes sinful when it leads us to hurt other people.**

When anger moves from feeling to action, damage follows. This can happen through words, physical actions, or even silent treatment meant to punish someone.

The Bible warns us about this clearly. **Proverbs 29:22 (NIV)** says, "An angry person stirs up conflict, and a hot...tempered person commits many sins." Anger does not just express itself once. It creates a chain reaction.

We see this throughout Scripture. Cain's anger led to murder. Moses' anger led to disobedience. Absalom's anger led to revenge. In each case, anger was allowed to move unchecked.

2. **Second, anger becomes sinful when it turns inward and stays there.**

Some anger explodes outward. Other anger settles inward. This kind of anger does not shout. It simmers.

When anger is held onto, it turns into bitterness, resentment, and rage. **Hebrews 12:15 (NIV)** warns that a bitter root can grow and cause trouble, defiling many.

This is the kind of anger we saw in James Toney's story. His anger did not disappear. It shaped how he saw people. It fueled his identity. It followed him into every fight.

Anger that is not released in a healthy way will eventually control the person holding it.

3. **Third, anger becomes sinful when it damages our relationship with God.**

Anger crosses the line when it pushes God out of the conversation. When we justify our reactions instead of surrendering them. When we stop praying because we feel entitled to our feelings.

Psalm 66:18 (NIV) says, "If I had cherished sin in my heart, the Lord would not have listened." Unchecked anger dulls our spiritual hearing.

Anger does not just affect how we treat people. It affects how clearly we hear God.

That is why anger is never the solution. Anger is information. It tells us something is wrong, but it cannot tell us how to fix it.

When anger is left alone, it becomes destructive. When anger is brought to God, it becomes instructive.

Observation Questions

1. What are the three ways anger crosses the line and becomes sinful according to this section?

   _____

   _____

2. What happens to anger when it is not brought to God or handled carefully?

   _____

   _____

Application Questions

1. Which of the three areas do I struggle with most when I get angry...hurting others, holding it inside, or pulling away from God?

   _____

   _____

2. What is one step I can take to bring my anger to God instead of letting it control me?

   _____

   _____

Section 11 - How God Teaches Us to Handle Anger

God never tells us to pretend anger does not exist. He tells us how to deal with it before it deals with us.

The Bible does not say, "Do not feel angry." It says, **"In your anger do not sin" (Ephesians 4:26, NIV)**. That verse alone tells us something important. Anger will happen. Sin does not have to.

Jesus shows us this clearly. When Jesus cleared the temple, His anger had direction. It had purpose. It had restraint. He did not lose control, and He did not act selfishly. His anger was rooted in obedience to God.

God teaches us to handle anger by slowing us down. Anger pushes us to react quickly. God calls us to pause. **James 1:19...20 (NIV)** says we should be quick to listen, slow to speak, and slow to become angry, because human anger does not produce the righteousness God desires. Before anger turns into action, God invites us to bring it to Him. God teaches us to handle anger by bringing it into the light instead of hiding it. Many people pretend they are fine when they are not. They push anger down and hope it goes away. But anger does not disappear when it is ignored. It grows.

The Psalms show us a different pattern. David often brought his anger, confusion, and frustration straight to God. He spoke honestly, then waited for God to respond. God teaches us to handle anger by choosing obedience over impulse. Anger wants immediate release. God wants faithful response. **Proverbs 16:32 (NIV)** says, "Better a patient person than a warrior, one with self...control than one who takes a city."

Self...control does not mean silence. It means surrender. God also teaches us to handle anger by letting Him deal with justice. **Romans 12:19 (NIV)** reminds us not to take revenge, because God says, "It is mine to avenge; I will repay." When we hold onto anger, we often believe we must fix the situation ourselves. God asks us to trust Him instead. Anger handled God's way does not destroy us. It refines us. When anger is surrendered to God, He uses it to reveal wounds that need healing, boundaries that need wisdom, and truth that needs to be spoken with humility. The goal is not to never feel angry. The goal is to hear God clearly when anger shows up. When we listen, anger becomes a tool for growth instead of a weapon of destruction.

Observation Questions

1. What does the Bible say we should do when we feel angry instead of pretending it is not there?

   _____

   _____

2. According to this section, what are some ways God teaches us to respond to anger differently than our natural impulse?

   _____

   _____

Application Questions

1. When I feel angry, do I usually react quickly or pause and bring it to God first?

   _____

   _____

2. What is one practical way I can practice self...control and obedience the next time anger shows up?

   _____

   _____

HEARING GOD - PERSONAL REFLECTION

1. What trigger has been showing up most often in your life lately?
2. What memory, vow, or wound might be connected to that trigger?
3. What would it look like to pause and invite God into that moment instead of reacting?
4. How do you want to respond differently when that trigger shows up again?

Chapter 23

Buried or Planted? Trusting God in Hidden Seasons

ICEBREAKER QUESTIONS

1. Have you ever reached a goal you worked hard for, only to feel strangely empty once you got there? What surprised you about that feeling?

2. When you face uncertainty, do you tend to focus more on the obstacles in front of you or on the promises of God?

BIBLE PASSAGES

Hebrews 10:38 (NIV)

"And, 'But my righteous one will live by faith. And I take no pleasure in the one who shrinks back.'"

Hebrews 11:6 (NIV)

"And without faith it is impossible to please God, because anyone who comes to him must believe that he exists and that he rewards those who earnestly seek him."

Romans 1:17 (NIV)

"For in the gospel the righteousness of God is revealed...a righteousness that is by faith from first to last, just as it is written: 'The righteous will live by faith.'"

Read Numbers chapters 13...14 in full before continuing.

Questions

1. Why do you think Scripture highlights certain people as especially pleasing to God?

   _____

   _____

2. What do these passages collectively reveal about how God defines righteousness and the central role faith plays in pleasing Him?

Section 1 - When God Says No...and Means Love

There comes a moment in life when you realize that unanswered prayer isn't always rejection. You can pray sincerely, passionately, and faithfully...and still not receive what you asked for. That realization often doesn't come in the moment of disappointment, but years later, when clarity replaces confusion and gratitude replaces frustration.

Many of us assume that if a prayer is heartfelt, God's answer should be yes. But Scripture shows us repeatedly that sincerity does not equal wisdom, and desire does not always equal destiny. God is not obligated to grant every request simply because it was emotional or intense. His responsibility is not to fulfill our preferences, but to accomplish His purposes.

We often pray from a limited perspective. We see what we want in the moment, while God sees what that answer would cost us in the long run. What feels like delay or denial is often divine protection. God answers prayer through wisdom, not impulse. And sometimes the most loving thing He can do is refuse what would ultimately harm us or distract us from what He has prepared.

Unanswered prayer forces us to confront an uncomfortable but necessary question:
"Do I trust God's character even when I don't understand His decisions?"

God's silence is not absence. His refusal is not indifference. Just because God doesn't answer the way we expect does not mean He doesn't care. In fact, unanswered prayers often reveal the depth of His care. They are evidence that He sees beyond the moment and loves us enough to guide us toward something better.

True faith is not proven when God says yes...it is revealed when He says no and we continue to trust Him anyway.

Observation Questions

1. What does this section reveal about the difference between sincere prayer and God's greater wisdom?

   _____

   _____

2. How does this teaching reframe the idea that unanswered prayer means God is distant or uncaring?

   _____

   _____

Application Questions

1. Is there a prayer in your life that may require renewed trust in God's wisdom rather than immediate understanding?

   _____

   _____

2. How might your prayer life change if you truly believed that God's "no" can be an expression of love?

   _____

   _____

Section 2 - Failure Isn't Always Failure and Success Isn't Always Success

There's a powerful truth hidden in this statement: failure is simply succeeding at the wrong goal. You can do something well, pour your energy into it, and even be applauded for it yet still miss what God was actually asking you to do. It's possible to climb quickly and successfully, only to discover your ladder was leaning against the wrong wall.

The world celebrates achievement without questioning alignment. God does the opposite. Heaven may call what the world applauds a loss, and what the world ignores a victory. You can excel at something God never assigned, and you can walk away from something impressive because obedience requires it. From God's perspective, obedience always outweighs outcome.

Scripture makes this clear in Hebrews 11, where men and women are remembered not for visible success, but for faith. Many of them never saw the fulfillment of what they were promised in their lifetime. Yet they are honored because they trusted God completely. Their obedience mattered more than their results.

Legacy is another place where our measurements often conflict with God's. The world asks, "What did you build?" God asks, "Who did you become?" Legacy is not fame passed down or success remembered it is faithfulness reproduced in others. It is the quiet transfer of trust, obedience, and integrity from one life to the next.

Scripture reminds us that everything visible is temporary. Records will be broken. Titles will be forgotten. Trophies will fade. But obedience produces eternal fruit. God is not impressed by speed, applause, or scale. He is moved by consistency, humility, and trust.

Observation Questions

1. How does this section challenge the way the world defines success and failure?

   _____

   _____

2. What examples from Hebrews 11 support the idea that obedience matters more than outcomes?

   _____

   _____

Application Questions

1. Are there areas in your life where you may be succeeding at something God never asked you to pursue?

   _____

   _____

2. What would it look like for you to redefine success based on obedience rather than visible results? _____

_____

Section 3 - Heaven's Final Audit

One day, every life will be evaluated not by resumes, but by stewardship. Scripture is clear that each of us will give an account before God (Romans 14:12). This evaluation will not be based on what we accumulated or how impressive our lives appeared to others, but on how faithfully we handled what God placed in our care.

That final assessment will not center on titles, income, platforms, or influence. Instead, it comes down to two eternal questions that cut through every distraction: What did you do with Jesus? And what did you do with what God entrusted to you? These questions move the focus from performance to responsibility, from success to faithfulness.

Everything we are given time, gifts, relationships, influence, resources, opportunities comes with purpose. None of it is random. All of it is entrusted. Success, in God's eyes, is not using everything for ourselves, but using everything for His purposes. Stewardship is the measure, not visibility.

When this truth settles in, competition loses its grip. Comparison fades. Anxiety lifts. We stop racing others and start walking faithfully with God. Life becomes less about proving ourselves and more about pleasing Him.

The world measures by visibility.
God measures by surrender.

Observation Questions

1. What does this section reveal about how God evaluates a life differently than the world does?

_____

_____

2. Why is stewardship emphasized more than achievement in God's final evaluation?

_____

_____

Application Questions

1. If your life were evaluated today, how faithfully are you stewarding what God has entrusted to you?

_____

_____

2. What areas of comparison or competition might God be inviting you to release so you can walk more faithfully with Him?

_____

_____

Section 4 - When God Uses Pain to Redirect Purpose

Some of the most formative seasons in life feel like rejection, loss, or unexpected detours. In the moment, they can seem pointless or unfair. Yet Scripture shows us repeatedly that God often uses painful interruptions as divine redirection. What feels like life falling apart may actually be God realigning our path.

Romans 8:28 does not promise that all things are good...it promises that God works all things together for good for those who love Him. Pain itself is not the goal, but God never wastes it. Pain refines empathy. Hardship deepens compassion. Loss reshapes priorities. These difficult seasons often form in us what comfort never could.

What feels like failure in the moment frequently becomes clarity in hindsight. God uses uncomfortable seasons to detach us from false goals and re...anchor us in our true calling. When plans collapse or doors close, it is often because God is preventing us from building a life that looks successful but lacks alignment.

Sometimes God does not remove the pain because the pain is doing a holy work within us. It is shaping our character, sharpening our discernment, and preparing us for a purpose that requires depth, humility, and dependence on Him. In those seasons, pain is not punishment...it is preparation.

Observation Questions

1. How does this section explain the difference between pain being meaningless and pain being purposeful?

    _____

    _____

2. What roles do hardship and loss play in shaping character and calling according to this teaching?

    _____

    _____

Application Questions

1. Is there a painful season in your life that God may be using to redirect your purpose rather than derail it?

    _____

    _____

2. How might your perspective change if you viewed discomfort as preparation instead of punishment?

    _____

    _____

Section 5 - Vision Requires Faith Before Validation

When God gives vision, it rarely comes with immediate confirmation. Often, others will not see what you see, and affirmation may be absent altogether. Scripture is filled with men and women who obeyed God long before any visible results appeared. Vision always precedes validation.

Vision is not logical it is spiritual. It requires obedience without applause and faith without proof. God often asks us to move before the outcome is clear, trusting that clarity will follow obedience, not precede it. Faith steps forward while questions remain unanswered.

Scripture reminds us that without vision, people drift (Proverbs 29:18). Vision provides direction, but faith provides movement. Direction alone is not enough; obedience is what turns vision into action. God rarely reveals the entire plan at once He reveals the next step and asks us to trust Him with the rest.

However, vision must come from God, not desire alone. Before imagining outcomes or building plans, Scripture calls us to commit our ways to the Lord (Proverbs 16:3). God...breathed vision carries peace, even in uncertainty. When the vision is from Him, there is alignment without striving and confidence without control.

Observation Questions

1. What does this section teach about the relationship between vision, faith, and obedience?

   _____

   _____

2. How does Scripture distinguish between God...given vision and personal desire?

   _____

   _____

Application Questions

1. Is there a vision God has given you that requires obedience before validation?

_____

_____

2. What step of faith might God be asking you to take before you receive clarity or confirmation?

_____

_____

Section 6 - The Hidden Work of God

Before anything blooms, it goes underground. Growth begins in places that are unseen, unnoticed, and often uncomfortable. Jesus explained this spiritual law clearly when He said, "Unless a grain of wheat falls into the ground and dies, it remains alone. But if it dies, it produces many seeds" (John 12:24). What looks like loss is often the beginning of multiplication.

Hidden seasons are not wasted seasons...they are formative seasons. God does some of His deepest work where no one is watching. In those quiet places, He reshapes motives, strengthens character, and deepens dependence. What is built in secret will eventually sustain what is revealed in public.

Isolation often feels like abandonment, but Scripture shows that it is frequently protection. God hides what He values. He covers what He is preparing. He plants what He intends to multiply. When God removes visibility, He is often increasing capacity.

You are not buried you are planted. What feels like delay is actually development. Roots must grow before fruit appears, and depth must be established before influence is released. Public impact is sustained by private obedience, and lasting fruit is always the result of hidden faithfulness.

Observation Questions

1. What spiritual truths does Jesus reveal about growth and multiplication in John 12:24?

_____

_____

2. How does this section redefine isolation and hidden seasons in light of God's purposes?

_____

_____

Application Questions

1. Are you currently in a hidden season where God may be developing roots before fruit?

   _____

   _____

2. How can you remain faithful and obedient in private, trusting God with the timing of what He will reveal publicly?

   _____

   _____

Section 7 - Biblical Examples of Hidden Seasons

Scripture makes it clear that hidden seasons are not accidents they are patterns. Before God releases public purpose, He often leads His people into private preparation. The Bible is filled with men and women who were called by God long before they were seen by people.

Joseph's calling was undeniable, but so was his waiting. Scripture tells us that while he was confined, "the word of the Lord tested him" (Psalm 105:18...19). God used isolation, betrayal, and confinement to shape Joseph's character before entrusting him with influence. The delay was not punishment it was preparation.

David was anointed king while still a shepherd, yet years passed before the promise was fulfilled. Psalm 78:70...71 reminds us that God took David from tending sheep to shepherding a nation. Leadership was learned in obscurity. Private victories over fear, faithfulness, and responsibility prepared him for public battles he would later face.

Moses experienced a similar process. After being raised in power, God removed him from influence and placed him in the desert (Exodus 3:1). It was there...far from status and recognition...that Moses learned humility. Only after that hidden season did God call him to lead a nation. Authority followed surrender.

Even Jesus modeled this pattern. Before stepping into public ministry, He withdrew into the wilderness (Matthew 4:1). Identity was affirmed before impact was released. Power flowed from obedience, not visibility.

If God hid Joseph, David, Moses, and even Jesus, He may be hiding you too...not to delay you, but to prepare you. What feels like obscurity may actually be God's mercy, ensuring that when purpose is revealed, character is ready to sustain it.

Observation Questions

1. What similarities do you notice in the hidden seasons of Joseph, David, Moses, and Jesus?

   _____

   _____

2. How does Scripture portray waiting as preparation rather than punishment?

   _____

   _____

Application Questions

1. Which biblical example most reflects your current season, and why?

   _____

   _____

2. How might God be using your present hidden season to prepare you for future responsibility?

   _____

   _____

Hearing God - Personal Reflection

1. What season of waiting or obscurity are you currently in, and how might God be working beneath the surface?

2. Are there areas where impatience is competing with trust in God's timing?

3. What has God been teaching you privately that may one day support public obedience?

4. How can you intentionally listen for God's voice in this season instead of rushing toward the next one?

Chapter 24

Why We Don't Receive When We Ask

ICEBREAKER QUESTION

1. Have you ever prayed consistently for something and felt like God was not answering? How did that affect your faith, emotions, or trust in Him?

BIBLE PASSAGE

James 4:1-3 (NIV)

What causes fights and quarrels among you? Don't they come from your desires that battle within you? 2 You desire but do not have, so you kill. You covet but you cannot get what you want, so you quarrel and fight. You do not have because you do not ask God. 3 When you ask, you do not receive, because you ask with wrong motives, that you may spend what you get on your pleasures.

These verses address conflict, desire, and prayer. James focuses on two common reasons believers fail to receive what they ask from God. While unanswered prayer can have many causes, James highlights issues that often go unnoticed in our hearts.

Questions

1. According to James 4:1-3, how can unchecked desires lead not only to conflict with others but also to broken communication with God?

   _____

   _____

2. What desires or motives in your own life might God be inviting you to examine or realign before you pray for certain outcomes?

SECTION 1- The Question Behind Unanswered Prayer

James is a practical writer. While his letter can be difficult to outline, the message itself is straightforward and direct. In James chapter 4, he shifts his focus to prayer...not every aspect of prayer, but one specific and deeply personal question: Why don't we receive what we ask for from God?

This is a struggle many believers face. We pray repeatedly, sometimes over long periods of time, and yet nothing seems to change. James does not deny that unanswered prayer can have many explanations. God's timing, His greater purposes, spiritual growth, or unseen circumstances may all play a role. However, James deliberately narrows his focus to two common reasons that frequently explain why prayers go unanswered.

James's purpose is not to discourage prayer, but to correct misunderstandings about it. His intent is not to shame believers, but to help them pray more effectively by addressing what may be happening beneath the surface of their requests.

Unanswered Prayers Lyrics by Garth Brooks

Just the other night, at a hometown football game

My wife and I, ran into my old high school flame

And as I introduced them, the past came back to me

And I couldn't help but think, of the way things used to be

She was the one, that I'd wanted for all times

Each night I'd spend prayin', that God would make her mine

And if he'd only grant me this wish, I wished back then

I'd never ask for anything, again

Sometimes, I thank God, for unanswered prayers

Remember, when you're talkin' to the man upstairs

And just because, he doesn't answer, doesn't mean he don't care

Some of God's greatest gifts, are unanswered prayers

She wasn't quite the angel, that I remembered in my dreams

And I could tell, that time had changed me

In her eyes too, it seemed

We tried to talk about the old days

There wasn't much, we could recall

I guess the Lord knows what he's doin', after all

And as she walked away, and I looked at my wife

And then and there, I thanked the good Lord

For the gifts, in my life

Sometimes, I thank God, for unanswered prayers

Remember, when you're talkin' to the man upstairs

That just because he may not answer, doesn't mean he don't care

Some of God's greatest gifts, are unanswered

Some of God's greatest gifts, are all too often unanswered

Some of God's greatest gifts, are unanswered prayers

The song opens with a moment that feels almost ordinary: "Just the other night, at a hometown football game / My wife and I ran into my old high school flame." There's nothing dramatic or emotional about it at first...it's casual, familiar, and unexpected. But when he introduces his wife to the woman from his past, something deeper stirs. "As I introduced them, the past came back to me." That's such a real human moment. All at once, memories rush in, and he finds himself reflecting on "the way things used to be." Not with longing, but with awareness.

He admits that at one point in his life, this woman was everything to him. "She was the one that I'd wanted for all times." His prayers weren't shallow or half...hearted. He prayed earnestly, night after night, asking God to make her his. He even tells God that if He would just answer this one request, "I'd never ask for anything again." That line reveals something so honest about the way we often pray...we don't just want God's will; we want God's approval of our will. We genuinely believe that what we're asking for is best, and we bargain with God from that place.

Then the chorus hits, and it reframes everything: "Sometimes, I thank God for unanswered prayers." This is the spiritual turning point of the song. He acknowledges something most of us don't realize until much later...that unanswered prayer doesn't mean God is distant. "Just because He doesn't answer doesn't mean He don't care." In fact, the opposite is true. The song boldly states what Scripture teaches again and again: some of God's greatest gifts are unanswered prayers.

As the conversation with his old flame continues, reality sets in. "She wasn't quite the angel that I remembered in my dreams." Time has a way of stripping away fantasy and revealing truth. And he can see that it wasn't just her who changed..."time had changed me." When they try to talk about the past, there isn't much to hold onto. What once felt so significant now feels distant and unclear. And that's when the quiet confession comes: "I guess the Lord knows what He's doing after all."

The most powerful moment in the song happens when she walks away. He doesn't follow her with his eyes or his heart. Instead, he looks at his wife. "And then and there, I thanked the good Lord for the gifts in my life." This is where the song stops being about a past relationship and becomes a testimony. Standing in the present, he realizes that what he once prayed for would have cost him the very blessings he now cherishes.

The song closes by repeating its central truth: "Some of God's greatest gifts are all too often unanswered." Not because God withholds good things, but because He knows which things are truly good. The unanswered prayer wasn't a loss...it was protection. It wasn't rejection...it was redirection. And only with time, maturity, and hindsight could he see that God answered him in the best way possible.

Observation Questions

1. What question is James addressing in this passage?

   _____

   _____

2. What does James assume about the prayer struggles of believers?

   _____

   _____

Application Questions

1. How do you typically respond when prayer feels unanswered?

   _____

   _____

2. Do you tend to examine your heart when prayer feels stalled, or do you assume God is simply saying no?

   _____

   _____

SECTION 2 - When Desire Turns Into Conflict

James begins by addressing conflict among believers. He asks where fights and quarrels come from and immediately directs attention inward. Conflict does not originate with other people or external circumstances; it begins with desires that wage war within the heart.

James explains that envy, coveting, and frustration grow when desires go unmet. These desires are often connected to material things, personal advancement, or a desire for control. While these desires are not always sinful in themselves, they become harmful when they take priority over trust in God. When desires dominate the heart, peace is replaced by tension, and relationships begin to suffer.

James then makes an important clarification. The reason believers do not have what they want is not because someone else has taken it from them or because life has been unfair. The reason is that God has not given it. This truth removes comparison and blame and shifts the focus squarely onto our relationship with God.

Observation Questions

1. According to James, where do conflicts originate?

   _____

   _____

2. What desires does James say are fueling these conflicts?

   _____

   _____

Application Questions

1. Are there desires in my life that are creating tension or dissatisfaction?

_____

_____

2. How do I typically respond when I do not receive what I want?

_____

_____

SECTION 3 - Reason One: We Do Not Ask

James states the first reason prayer goes unanswered with blunt clarity: "You do not have because you do not ask." One of the most common reasons believers lack what they desire is simply because they never bring the request to God. Instead of praying, they often carry frustration, worry, or disappointment on their own, assuming that prayer will not make a difference or forgetting to invite God into the situation at all.

This does not mean prayer exists to inform God of our needs. Scripture is clear that God already knows what we need before we ask. Jesus Himself taught that the Father is fully aware of every need, concern, and desire long before it ever reaches our lips. Prayer does not educate God, nor does it alert Him to something He has overlooked. In the same way, prayer does not make us worthy of receiving anything from God. We are never worthy of God's gifts, and we never earn His blessings through spiritual effort. Everything we receive from God comes by grace, not by merit.

Prayer exists because God desires relationship with His people. He requires asking not because He lacks knowledge, but because He is shaping the hearts of those who ask. Asking teaches dependence. It forces believers to slow down, humble themselves, and acknowledge that provision, strength, and direction do not come from self...sufficiency. Through prayer, we confess that we cannot provide for ourselves apart from Him, and we learn to rely on God rather than on our own ability, resources, or control.

Observation Questions

1. What does James identify as the first reason believers do not receive?

_____

_____

2. What does Jesus teach about asking in Matthew 6 and Matthew 7?

_____

_____

Application Questions

1. Are there needs or frustrations I complain about but never pray over?

_____

_____

2. What does my prayer life reveal about my dependence on God?

_____

_____

SECTION 4 - Why God Requires Asking

God does not want to be treated as a spiritual convenience someone we acknowledge only when we need something and ignore the rest of the time. He is not interested in a transactional relationship where prayer becomes a last resort or an emergency option. God desires a relationship marked by trust, humility, and ongoing dependence. He wants His people to know Him, rely on Him, and walk with Him daily, not only when circumstances feel overwhelming.

Asking teaches believers that true strength does not come from human effort alone. While God does call His people to act responsibly, make wise decisions, and live faithfully, He consistently reminds us that real effectiveness does not originate in our ability, discipline, or determination. It comes from Him. Prayer keeps this truth in front of us. It anchors us in the reality that even our best efforts are powerless apart from God's involvement and blessing.

At times, God requires persistent asking so that when the answer finally comes, we do not forget where it came from. Repeated prayer guards against pride and self...sufficiency. It deepens humility by reminding us that we are not in control and reinforces reliance on God rather than on ourselves.

Through persistence in prayer, God shapes the heart of the one who asks, teaching dependence long before the answer is ever given.

Observation Questions

1. Why does God insist on asking, even though He already knows our needs?

   _____

   _____

2. How does prayer guard against self...reliance?

   _____

   _____

   Application Questions

1. In what areas of my life do I rely more on myself than on God?

   _____

   _____

2. How could intentional prayer reshape my sense of dependence?

   _____

   _____

SECTION 5 - Reason Two: Asking with Wrong Motives

James introduces the second reason prayer goes unanswered: "You ask and do not receive, because you ask wrongly." The problem is not the request itself, nor is it the act of asking. The issue lies deeper, in the motive behind the request. James directs attention away from the surface of the prayer and toward the condition of the heart from which it comes.

God examines the heart. He is far more concerned with why we ask than with what we ask. Scripture consistently teaches that God looks beyond words and actions to the intentions that drive them. When requests are motivated by personal pleasure, a desire for control, or self...exaltation, they drift away from the true purpose of prayer. Even when the request itself appears reasonable, the motive can quietly redirect prayer away from dependence on God and toward self...centered outcomes.

James does not say that these requests are always sinful. Instead, he reveals that they are misaligned. Prayer that centers on self rather than on God's glory loses its power, not because God is unwilling to give, but because the request no longer reflects the purpose for which prayer exists. When motive shifts away from honoring God, prayer becomes disconnected from the very relationship it was meant to strengthen.

Observation Questions

1. What does James mean by "asking wrongly"?

    _____

    _____

2. What motive does Jesus connect to answered prayer?

    _____

    _____

Application Questions

1. When I pray, what outcome am I hoping for personally?

    _____

    _____

2. How often do I consider whether my request honors God?

    _____

    _____

SECTION 6 - Praying with Proper Motives

Scripture encourages believers to ask specifically. Clear, honest requests are not wrong, and they are not discouraged by God. Throughout Scripture, God invites His people to bring real needs, real concerns, and real desires before Him. However, while specificity in prayer is biblical, every request must ultimately be surrendered to God's greater purpose and wisdom.

A properly motivated prayer acknowledges desire while yielding control. It communicates trust rather than demand. It says, "This is what I desire. This is what I believe may honor You. But I trust You to decide what ultimately brings You the most glory." This posture of surrender does not weaken prayer; it strengthens it. God delights in answering prayers that are offered with humility and a sincere desire to honor Him rather than to promote self.

God answers prayer not simply to meet needs, though He is faithful to care for His people. He answers prayer to glorify Himself. When prayer aligns with that purpose, believers can pray boldly and confidently, knowing their requests are rooted in trust rather than control. Prayer becomes less about getting what we want and more about participating in what God is doing, confident that His glory and our good are never in conflict.

Observation Questions

1. What does a surrendered prayer sound like?

   _____

   _____

2. Why does surrender strengthen prayer rather than weaken it?

   _____

   _____

Application Questions

1. What prayer request in my life needs a motive check?

   _____

   _____

2. How can I begin praying with God's glory as my primary goal?

   _____

   _____

HEARING GOD - PERSONAL REFLECTION

1. What prayers in your life might need deeper honesty or surrender?
2. Are there requests God may be using to teach you dependence, patience, or humility?
3. How might God be inviting you to adjust not just *what* you ask for, but *why* you ask?
4. In what area of your prayer life is God inviting you to trust Him more deeply, even if the answer looks different than you expected?

Week 9

Obedience That Moves Before It Understands

By this point in the journey, you may be noticing something about how God works. He rarely explains everything upfront. He speaks, and then He waits. Not to test your intelligence, but to test your trust.

Week 9 is about immediate obedience.

There is a kind of obedience that says, "I will follow once I understand." And there is another kind that says, "I will follow because I trust You." Scripture shows us again and again that God responds to the second posture.

Delayed obedience often feels reasonable. We tell ourselves we need more clarity, more confirmation, or better timing. But many times, what we call wisdom is actually fear wearing a softer name. The longer we wait, the louder doubt becomes. And the quieter God's voice feels.

Immediate obedience does not mean reckless action. It means responding while the invitation is still clear. It means moving before excuses take root. It means trusting that God already sees what we cannot.

This week invites you to notice where God has already spoken. Not vaguely. Not someday. But clearly. It may be a nudge to forgive, to speak up, to let go, to give, to move, or to stop something that no longer aligns. The question is not whether God has spoken. The question is whether we are willing to respond.

God's voice is not meant to be debated endlessly. It is meant to be followed. And when we obey quickly, we position ourselves to experience Him more deeply. Not just as a guide, but as a provider, protector, and faithful Father.

As you step into this week, resist the urge to overthink. Ask God to show you the next right step. Then choose obedience while your heart is still soft. Because often, the breakthrough is waiting on the other side of your yes.

Chapter 25

When God Rewrites Your Story

ICEBREAKER QUESTIONS

1. Have you ever looked back and realized God was working in your life long before you recognized His voice?

2. Do you believe God can redeem parts of your story that began in pain, confusion, or chaos?

3. What does it mean to trust God as the Author of your story rather than the one trying to control it?

BIBLE PASSAGE

2 Corinthians 12:9 (NIV)

9 But he said to me, "My grace is sufficient for you, for my power is made perfect in weakness." Therefore, I will boast all the more gladly about my weaknesses, so that Christ's power may rest on me.

Proverbs 3:5–6 (NIV)

5 Trust in the Lord with all your heart and lean not on your own understanding; 6 in all your ways submit to him, and he will make your paths straight.

Questions

1. How does 2 Corinthians 12:9 encourage you to view your weaknesses, past mistakes, or painful experiences as opportunities for God's power to be displayed in your life? How might God be "rewriting" areas of struggle into something that brings glory to Him?

   _____

   _____

2. Proverbs 3:5–6 reminds us to trust God even when we don't understand our circumstances. In what ways can you submit past disappointments, regrets, or negative experiences to Him, trusting that He can use them to guide your path toward purpose and good works?

_____

_____

Section 1 - God Speaks Before We Understand the Story

Before I ever learned to recognize God's voice, I learned to recognize chaos.

The sound of slammed doors. The shaking in my mother's voice. The silence that followed arguments too big for a little girl to understand. Those were my first lessons in listening...not to peace, but to pain. Not to truth, but to survival.

I was born in Tehran, Iran, a place I don't often tell people about. My father was Iranian, and my mother was American. When Khomeini came into power, everything changed. My parents fled the country with me when I was four years old. We moved to New York City, carrying fear in one hand and hope in the other.

My father was a drug addict. My mother was the definition of resilience...strong, determined, and trying to hold everything together. We lived in a beautiful home, not because of honest work, but because of money that came from the wrong places. On the outside, it looked perfect...the kind of neighborhood where Washington Redskins players lived. I still remember going to Magruders grocery store and running into John Riggins, or passing Joe Theismann's house like it was normal.

But inside our home, there was a fracture. And when my parents divorced, that fracture split wide open. I was losing everything I thought made me safe.

Observation Questions

1. What specific sounds, images, and moments are described as the author's "first lessons in listening," and what do they reveal about the environment she grew up in?

_____

_____

2. How does the contrast between the outward appearance of the home and the inner reality of the family shape the tension in this section?

_____

_____

Application Questions

1. What kinds of "voices" did you learn to listen to early in life… peace or chaos, truth or survival… and how do they still influence the way you respond to stress or conflict today?

   _____

   _____

2. Where might you be mistaking outward stability or success for true safety, and how could God be inviting you to redefine what security really means?

   _____

   _____

Section 2 - When Vows Become Chains

When we moved from that beautiful neighborhood into a simple, middle-class one, I made a vow to myself. I remember standing there, looking at our new home, and thinking, *This will never happen to me again.* No one will ever have the power to move me from my home. I will make enough money so no man ever decides where I live.

I didn't realize it at the time, but that vow…born out of pain…was also the beginning of a quiet chain around my heart. It felt like determination, but underneath it was fear. I was trying to protect myself from ever feeling that powerless again.

So I grew up strong, driven, and fiercely independent. I learned how to work hard, how to make things happen, how to never need anyone. And in many ways, that strength became a gift. It pushed me to succeed, to build, to lead. But it also came with a cost.

When you live in survival mode long enough, control starts to feel like safety. I wanted to plan everything, fix everything, manage every outcome. It made me an achiever, but it also made it hard for me to trust God fully. Because surrender felt like weakness.

It took years...decades, really...for God to show me that control and calling can't coexist. He began whispering to my heart, *You don't have to carry this alone anymore.* I had spent so long proving I could do it all that I forgot the beauty of letting Him lead.

Eventually, I learned that real security doesn't come from control. It comes from peace. It comes from knowing that even if everything changes again, I'm held by Someone who never will.

Observation Questions

1. What vow does the author make in response to loss, and how does the language of "determination" slowly shift into the language of fear and control throughout the section?

   _____

   _____

2. What contrasts does the author draw between strength and surrender, and how are success and security defined differently as the story unfolds?

   _____

   _____

Application Questions

1. What vows... spoken or unspoken... have you made in response to pain or instability, and how might those vows be shaping your need for control today?

   _____

   _____

2. In what areas of your life does control feel safer than trust, and what would it look like to exchange that control for the peace God offers?

   _____

   _____

Section 3 - Searching For Identity in the Wrong Places

Around the same time, my mom was trying to find her own form of peace. She was lost and searching...dabbling in astrology and tarot cards. I remember her taking me to an astrologer who told her, "You need to change your name and your daughter's name immediately."

My birth name was *Angela Panahinia*. After that visit, she changed mine to *Chantel Coveyci Vochan*. I'll never forget the humiliation of going to school and having to explain that my name...my identity...had changed overnight because of something a stranger said. Kids didn't understand. Honestly, neither did I.

But now, when I look back, I see something sacred buried in that confusion. Even then, God was showing me what it means to *search for identity outside of Him*...and how empty it feels. We were both chasing meaning, but in the wrong places. My mom in tarot cards, me in self-reliance. Both of us desperate to control a story we didn't yet understand was being written by Someone far greater.

By sixteen, I had moved out. My mom had read *Tough Love* by James Dobson and decided to put it into practice. I was rebellious, angry, and impossible to reason with. I was smoking. I was mouthy. I was determined to prove I didn't need anyone. So I packed up and moved in with my best friend. For two years, my mom and I barely spoke. I graduated high school living on my own, thinking I was winning the battle of independence...when in reality, I was just running further from healing.

Observation Questions

1. What actions in this section reveal the different ways both the author and her mother were searching for peace, meaning, and control?

   _____

   _____

2. How does the name change function as a symbol in the story, and what emotions and consequences does it create for the author?

   _____

   _____

Application Questions

1. Where have you been tempted to search for identity, direction, or peace outside of God, and what has that pursuit ultimately produced in you?

   _____

   _____

2. In what ways might independence, rebellion, or self-reliance be masking unresolved pain or delaying healing in your own story?

Section 4 - When God Redeems What We Resist

But God was still there. Even in the silence between us, He was working in the background...mending what anger had ripped apart. In my early twenties, my mom and I reconciled. And that moment taught me something profound: when you stop fighting to be *right*, God can finally make things *right*.

I went to Virginia Wesleyan College and majored in mathematics...not because I loved numbers, but because they were easy. Numbers made sense. They were clean, clear, predictable. One plus one was always two. There was comfort in that. Numbers didn't lie, they didn't confuse you, and they didn't change their minds.

Reading, on the other hand, made me squirm. Words could twist. Stories could shift. Feelings could change from one page to the next. With math, I could control the outcome. With reading, I couldn't.

So naturally, in true God fashion, He later called me to write...not just an article or a devotional...but five full books. *Five*. I still laugh every time I think about it. I, the girl who hated reading, somehow became a published author whose words have impacted lives around the world.

But I'll be honest...I didn't sit down with a laptop and write them word-for-word. Most of my books started as spoken words. I dictated them on Zoom calls, pouring my heart out to whoever was helping me that day. I'd tell stories, share lessons, and talk about what God was showing me, and then hand the messy transcript off to a ghostwriter or editor who would help organize my thoughts into something readable.

It's funny, because people often assume writing a book means sitting in silence with a pen in hand, but for me, it looked like conversation, coffee, and a lot of laughter over my unfiltered sentences.

And that's exactly how God works. He takes our limitations and turns them into testimonies. He uses the very things we think disqualify us to show that His strength is made perfect in our weakness.

I never would've chosen writing as my calling. But God did. And in doing so, He reminded me that His power doesn't depend on my preferences. Sometimes, the very thing we resist becomes the very thing God uses to reach others.

When I look back now, I realize God had been preparing me all along. Math taught me structure, logic, and problem-solving...and I've used those same skills to break down complex spiritual truths in my books. The clarity I loved in numbers became the clarity I now strive for in words.

God didn't change my wiring. He redeemed it. *"But He said to me, 'My grace is sufficient for you, for My power is made perfect in weakness.'", 2 Corinthians 12:9*

When you surrender your weakness to God, He doesn't remove it...He rewrites it.

Observation Questions

1. What evidence does this passage give that God was at work even during seasons of silence, discomfort, and resistance—both in relationships and in calling?

   _____

   _____

2. How does the contrast between mathematics and writing highlight the author's desire for control versus God's method of using weakness and surrender?

   _____

   _____

Application Questions

1. What abilities, preferences, or comfort zones have you relied on for a sense of control, and how might God be inviting you to trust Him beyond them?

   _____

   _____

2. What weakness, limitation, or resistance in your life might God be asking you to surrender— not to remove, but to redeem for His purposes?

   _____

   _____

Section 5 - The Holy YES

So, if you ever feel like the thing you're least good at could never be used for His glory, remember this: God used a math major who hated reading to write books that would change lives. If He can do that, there's no limit to what He can do with your story, too.

After college, I became a math teacher. On paper, it made perfect sense. I was good at numbers, I liked structure, and it seemed like a stable, respectable career. But two years in, I dreaded walking into that classroom. Every day, I'd grab my coffee, drive to school, and feel this quiet ache in my chest...like I was living someone else's life.

One day, while I was sitting at my desk grading papers, I felt a gentle whisper deep in my spirit: *Ministry*. At first, I honestly laughed. I didn't even know what that meant. I wasn't a Bible scholar. I hadn't gone to seminary. I didn't see myself as "pastor material." But I knew that voice...that quiet nudge from God that didn't make sense but carried peace anyway.

So, in faith, I said yes. That single word...*yes*...changed everything. Before I knew it, I became a youth pastor. Then later, a children's pastor. My new life was nothing like what I'd imagined for myself. I worked twenty hours a week making nine dollars an hour. That's not a typo...*nine dollars an hour*. I also waitressed at a restaurant called Pargo's to help pay the bills, and let me tell you, I was not good at it. I mixed up orders, spilled drinks, and forgot tables more times than I can count. My tips weren't really tips...they were sympathy donations.

I remember one night standing in the grocery store with a half-empty cart, counting items and swiping a credit card I wasn't sure would go through. I'd whisper under my breath, "God, please help me make it another week."

It was humbling. It was exhausting. But it was also holy. That season stripped away everything that made me feel self-sufficient. I couldn't rely on my paycheck, my plans, or even my skills. I had to rely on Him.

Looking back, I see what God was doing. He wasn't punishing me; He was preparing me. That season of lack was teaching me something I never could have learned in abundance...*dependence*.

God was showing me how to hear His voice in the middle of the stretch. When I had nothing else to lean on, His whispers became louder. His guidance became clearer.

That's the thing about detours...they don't always make sense while you're in them. They look like setbacks, but they're actually setups. God was using that detour into ministry to train my ears to listen, my heart to trust, and my faith to grow.

If I had stayed comfortable, I might never have discovered my calling.

Observation Questions

1. What contrasts does the author draw between what looked "right on paper" and what felt true in her spirit, and how does that tension guide her next steps?

_____

_____

2. How does the season of financial lack and discomfort function in the story—not as punishment, but as preparation—and what does it reveal about how God teaches dependence?

_____

_____

Application Questions

1. Where might God be inviting you to say a quiet but costly "yes," even if the outcome feels uncertain or uncomfortable?

_____

_____

2. How do you typically interpret detours or seasons of lack—as setbacks to escape or as opportunities God might be using to deepen your trust and sensitivity to His voice?

_____

_____

Section 6 - Learning the Sound of Trust

"Trust in the Lord with all your heart and lean not on your own understanding; in all your ways submit to Him, and He will make your paths straight."...Proverbs 3:5–6

What I thought was a step backward was actually God redirecting me toward purpose. He was rewriting my story...one humble, dependent prayer at a time.

It was in that season of ministry, I was learning what it really meant to depend on God. When you don't have much, you learn to listen closely...every bill, every need becomes a chance to trust Him again.

One Sunday, my pastor preached about tithing, and honestly, I just sat there thinking, *This can't be for me.* I was already barely making it. But deep down, I felt God whisper, *Trust Me here too.*

The verse came to mind..."*Test Me in this,*" from Malachi 3:10. So I did. I wrote a check for $30, even though my account was almost empty.

The next day, I opened the mail and found a refund check from Dominion Power...for exactly $300. It wasn't luck. It was God.

That moment changed me. It wasn't just about money...it was about learning to hear His voice. The kind of voice that asks you to trust when logic says, "Don't."

It was the day I realized God doesn't just speak in big miracles...sometimes, He speaks through a $30 step of faith.

Even though I had already learned that God provides, I still found myself caught in the hustle to provide it all myself. I left ministry and entered real estate and in that first year I sold fifty-four homes...more than anyone else in Hampton Roads. I hired a team before I even finished training. I built an empire before I built rest.

I became the head of the Chantel Ray Team which changed to Canzell Team, leading one of the biggest real estate groups in Virginia. From the outside, it looked like a dream. Inside, I was exhausted. When success came, so did the noise. Meetings. Sales goals. Expansions. Growth. I grew the company into twenty states...and somewhere in the chaos, I stopped listening to the One who gave me the calling.

And that's when I started hearing another whisper: *Merge it. Let it go.*

I didn't want to let go. But I couldn't ignore the peace that came with obedience. So I merged my company with eXp Realty...a $2 billion organization. It was a business decision, yes, but it was really a spiritual one. God was teaching me that sometimes, the "biggest" thing you build is actually the one you're willing to release.

Right before that, God said, "*It's time to move.*"

We'd been visiting Florida almost every month to escape the cold. Every trip felt like a deep exhale. Finally, we realized: *Why keep visiting your promise land when you can live in it?* So we packed up, left Virginia, and started over. That move didn't just change my zip code...it changed my perspective. Florida became the physical picture of what obedience feels like: warmth replacing striving.

Looking back, I see God's fingerprints all over my story...from Iran to New York, from broken homes to restored hearts, from debt to overflow. Every chapter that looked like an ending was really a redirection. Every loss was a lesson in listening. Every no became a sacred "not yet." And now, when people ask me, "How do you hear God's voice so clearly?"... I tell them this: Because I know what it sounds like when I don't. If I could go back and talk to that little girl who lost everything she thought made her safe, I'd tell her this:

"You don't have to control the story, because the Author is still writing." Every vow I made out of fear, He has rewritten with grace. Every label the world tried to stick on me, He's replaced with purpose. My story began in chaos. But the voice of God...steady, patient, and kind...has been guiding it toward peace all along.

Observation Questions

1. What patterns emerge in how God speaks throughout this section—from seasons of lack, to success, to moments of release—and how does the author respond each time?

   _____

   _____

2. How do the contrasts between abundance and exhaustion, provision and striving, shape the author's understanding of obedience and dependence on God?

   _____

   _____

Application Questions

1. Where might God be asking you to take a small but uncomfortable step of trust—one that doesn't make sense logically but requires obedience?

   _____

   _____

2. What "success," role, or season might God be inviting you to release so you can return to listening more closely to His voice?

   _____

   _____

HEARING GOD - PERSONAL REFLECTION

1. Looking back over your own story, where do you see patterns of God speaking, guiding, or protecting you—even in seasons that felt chaotic, silent, or painful at the time? (What might He have been forming in you before you understood the purpose of it?)

2. What part of your life still feels driven by survival, control, or striving—and what would it look like to trust God as the Author of that chapter instead of trying to manage the outcome yourself?

Chapter 26

The Pattern of God's Direction

ICEBREAKER QUESTIONS

1. Have you ever noticed that God tends to lead you one step at a time rather than all at once?

2. How do you usually respond when something familiar begins to feel uncomfortable or unstable?

3. Do you find it easier to trust God after you see the outcome, or while you are still waiting?

BIBLE PASSAGE

Proverbs 3:5-6 (NIV)

5 Trust in the Lord with all your heart

and lean not on your own understanding;

6 in all your ways submit to him,

and he will make your paths straight.

Psalm 37:23 (NIV)

The Lord makes firm the steps

of the one who delights in him;

Questions

1. What area of your life are you most tempted to rely on your own understanding rather than fully trusting the Lord, and what would it look like—practically—to surrender that area to Him this week?

_____

_____

2. What decision are you facing right now where you need God's direction, and how can you intentionally quiet other voices so you can recognize and follow His leading?

_____

_____

Section 1 - Steps of Faith in Every Season

One of the most important things I've learned about walking with God is that His direction almost never comes all at once.

He doesn't hand you the full blueprint.

He gives you a single step...and waits to see if you'll take it.

He leads us through a rhythm I've come to recognize...a divine pattern that repeats in every season of life:

1. **Discomfort**...when God stirs your heart and makes what once felt comfortable feel too small.
2. **Disruption**...when He removes what can't go with you into the next season.
3. **Direction**...when His whisper gives you the next small step of faith.
4. **Decision**...when obedience requires courage to act before you fully understand.
5. **Deliverance**...when hindsight reveals how every detour was part of His perfect plan.

Once you see this pattern, you stop fearing change...because you realize every shift is just God leading you closer to purpose.

If you've walked with Him long enough, you start to recognize His rhythm. There's a divine pattern to how He leads...not just in your faith, but in your finances, your relationships, your calling, your purpose. Let me show you what I mean.

Observation Questions

1. What are the five steps in the divine pattern the author identifies (Discomfort, Disruption, Direction, Decision, Deliverance), and how does each step function in the process of God leading someone closer to purpose?

_____

_____

2. How does the author illustrate the difference between immediate understanding and step-by-step guidance from God, and what does that reveal about His timing and methods?

_____

_____

Application Questions

1. Reflect on a time when God led you through a step-by-step process rather than giving the full picture. How did discomfort, disruption, or decision play a role in bringing you closer to His purpose?

_____

_____

2. In which area of your life—faith, relationships, career, or finances—might God be inviting you to take a next small step of obedience, even if you don't yet see the whole path?

_____

_____

Section 2 - Disruption...The Divine Interruption

Once God has your attention through discomfort, He often allows _disruption_.

This is when something shifts...sometimes suddenly, sometimes painfully. It could be a door closing you thought would always stay open. A friendship ending. A plan unraveling.

We think disruption means we've failed. But often, it's God removing the things that can't go with us into our next season. Sometimes He has to break our rhythm to reset our direction. When disruption comes, don't cling to what's leaving...ask Him what's coming.

Observation Questions

1. How does the author define "disruption," and what examples are given to illustrate the kinds of shifts God might allow in our lives?

_____

_____

2. What distinction does the author make between seeing disruption as failure versus seeing it as God's redirection, and how does that perspective change the way we respond?

_____

_____

Application Questions

1. In what areas of your life have you experienced disruption that felt like loss, and how might God be using it to remove what can't move with you into your next season?

_____

_____

2. How can you practice asking God what's coming next instead of clinging to what is leaving, and what might that teach you about trust and obedience?

_____

_____

Section 3: Direction...The Gentle Whisper

After the noise of disruption, comes direction. It doesn't usually arrive as a neon sign or a thunderclap. It comes as a whisper...a thought, a scripture, a conversation, a peace that doesn't make sense.

This is the stage where God speaks most clearly...but only to the hearts quiet enough to listen. Direction rarely looks like clarity at first. It looks like a single step. He says, *"Start the business." "Make the call." "Move to the new city."*

And you don't get the next instruction until you act on the first one. God doesn't reveal the map until you start walking.

Observation Questions

1. How does the author describe the way God gives direction, and what role does quietness of heart play in receiving it?

_____

_____

2. What examples of "single steps" are mentioned, and how does the author show that God's guidance often comes progressively rather than all at once?

_____

_____

Application Questions

1. In what areas of your life might God be inviting you to take a first step of faith, even if the full path isn't clear yet?

_____

_____

2. How can you cultivate a heart quiet enough to hear God's whispers amidst life's noise and distractions?

_____

_____

Section 4 - Decision...The Step of Faith

Once He gives direction, the next stage is *decision*. This is where obedience becomes real. This is where faith stops being theoretical and starts becoming visible. And honestly, this is where most people get stuck. Because obedience almost never feels convenient.

It rarely makes sense. It usually costs something. But if you've ever obeyed when it didn't make sense...and then watched everything align...you know what I mean when I say: *obedience is the key that unlocks peace.*

You don't need to see the whole staircase to take the first step. You just need to trust the voice of the One who built it.

Observation Questions

1. How does the author define the stage of decision, and what challenges or costs are associated with obedience in this context?

_____

_____

2. What contrast does the author make between seeing the whole path and taking the first step, and how does that illustrate trust in God?

_____

_____

Application Questions

1. In what areas of your life is God calling you to take a step of obedience, even when it doesn't make sense or feels inconvenient?

_____

_____

2. How can you cultivate the faith to trust God with the "staircase" you cannot yet see?

_____

_____

Section 5 - Deliverance...The Reward of Obedience

Then comes *deliverance*. This is the moment when everything finally makes sense. It's when you look back and realize, "That disruption wasn't rejection...it was redirection." It's when you see the way God used every delay, every detour, every disappointment to position you exactly where you were meant to be.

Deliverance doesn't always look like rescue. Sometimes it looks like peace. Sometimes it looks like purpose. And sometimes it looks like you...standing in the very place you once cried about, now realizing it was all part of His plan.

Observation Questions

1. How does the author describe deliverance, and what distinctions does she make between rescue, peace, and purpose?

_____

_____

2. In what ways does the text show that what once felt like disappointment or delay was actually part of God's redirection?

_____

_____

Application Questions

1. Looking back on your own life, where can you recognize God's deliverance in situations that once felt like setbacks or detours?

   _____

   _____

2. How might viewing challenges as part of God's redirection change the way you respond to current difficulties or delays?

   _____

   _____

Section 6 - The Flow of Faith

This five-step pattern repeats itself throughout our lives. It's the rhythm of relationship with God...not a one-time lesson, but a lifelong process.

Discomfort → Disruption → Direction → Decision → Deliverance.

Once you recognize it, you stop panicking when things fall apart. You stop questioning God every time He shifts something in your life. You start saying, "Okay, I know what this is. I'm in the middle of the pattern. I may not see the finish line yet, but I know Who's leading me."

The next chapters will show you how to walk in that rhythm...how to live in alignment with God's voice, how to hear Him not just in moments, but in movements. Because your purpose isn't something you chase...it's something you *become* as you follow His lead, one obedient step at a time.

When you learn the pattern of His direction, you'll stop striving for answers and start walking with confidence. You'll stop asking, *"God, where are You?"* and start declaring, *"God, I trust You, even here."* Because purpose isn't a destination. It's the peace that comes when your heart beats in rhythm with His.

Observation Questions

1. How does the author summarize the five-step pattern, and what significance does she place on recognizing it as a repeating rhythm rather than a one-time lesson?

   _____

   _____

2. What contrasts does the text make between striving for answers and walking in alignment with God's rhythm, and how does that illustrate spiritual growth?

_____

_____

Application Questions

1. How can you identify the current stage of God's rhythm in your own life, and what step might He be inviting you to take next?

_____

_____

2. In what areas of your life do you tend to panic or question God, and how could embracing this rhythm help you respond with trust and peace instead?

_____

_____

HEARING GOD - PERSONAL REFLECTION

1. When you look back at your own life, can you identify a season of discomfort, disruption, or decision where God was leading you step by step, even if you didn't realize it at the time? How does seeing that pattern change your perspective on current challenges?

2. Are there areas in your life right now where you feel stuck, uncertain, or resistant to God's direction? How might you intentionally take one small step of obedience, trusting that He is guiding you toward deliverance and purpose?

Chapter 27
Discovering God's Purpose for You

ICEBREAKER QUESTIONS

1. Have you ever wondered whether God's purpose for your life is something you might miss or get wrong?

2. Do you tend to think of purpose as a future destination or a present journey?

3. How comfortable are you with the idea that your purpose may change across seasons?

BIBLE PASSAGE

Psalm 139:16 (NIV)

Your eyes saw my unformed body;

   all the days ordained for me were written in your book

   before one of them came to be.

Ephesians 2:10 (NIV)

For we are God's handiwork, created in Christ Jesus to do good works, which God prepared in advance for us to do.

Questions

1. When you don't know your next step or feel lost, this verse reassures you that God already has your path outlined. Discovering your purpose is often a process of listening and stepping into what He's already prepared. How can you apply this in your everyday life?

   _____

   _____

2. We can make goals, set ambitions, and plan our careers or relationships—but ultimately, God directs the steps we take. Think of a time you had to sit back while God took control of a situation for the better?

   _____

   _____

Section 1 - Your Story, Written Before You Were Born

I can't tell you how many times I've sat across from someone...sometimes over coffee, sometimes at church...and heard them say, *"I just wish I knew what God's purpose for my life was."* And every time, I smile, because I've asked that same question more times than I can count.

But here's the good news: **God is not hiding His purpose from you.** He's not playing some divine game of hide-and-seek. He wants you to know it. He designed you with it in mind before you were even born.

Psalm 139:16 says, "All the days ordained for me were written in Your book before one of them came to be." That means before you ever took your first breath, God already wrote your story.

Observation Questions

1. What does Psalm 139:16 reveal about God's knowledge and involvement in your life even before birth?

   _____

   _____

2. How does the author describe the common human desire to know purpose, and what contrast does she make with God's perspective?

   _____

   _____

Application Questions

1. In what ways could you trust God's plan more fully, knowing He has already written your story and knows your days?

   _____

   _____

2. How might viewing your experiences—both challenges and blessings—as part of God's pre-written story change how you approach your purpose and daily decisions?

   _____

   _____

Section 2 - God Shapes Purpose Through Your Story

Your purpose is usually hiding inside your story. Look back at your life...the highs, the heartbreaks, the twists that didn't make sense. Every season, even the messy ones, were shaping something in you. When I look at my own journey, I see how God used every piece.

My early financial struggles taught me faith. The discouraging years grew endurance. My success in business gave me a platform to reach people I never would've met otherwise.

And my health battles...like living with psoriatic arthritis...broke my pride and filled me with compassion for those in pain. At the time, none of it felt purposeful. But now I see it: God wastes nothing. Every victory, every scar, every closed door was raw material for His purpose in my life.

If you're still wondering *what exactly God wants you to do,* start by looking at the clues He's already placed inside you.

- ☐ **Your Gifts:** What do you do well without even trying? What do people thank you for?

- ☐ **Your Passions:** What lights a fire in you? What could you talk about for hours and never get tired?

- ☐ **Your Pain:** What breaks your heart or makes you angry enough to take action?

- ☐ **Your Opportunities:** Where has God already opened doors or given you influence?

Your purpose is usually where those four things overlap. When your gifts, passions, pain, and opportunities collide, that's where your calling lives. Discovering purpose isn't a one-time lightning bolt moment. It's a daily walk. Sometimes God gives you a big vision, but most of the time He just gives you *the next step.*

I used to pray, *"God, show me my whole purpose."* Now I pray, *"God, what's one thing You want me to do today that lines up with Your purpose for me?"*

One shift changed everything. It keeps me from striving and keeps me surrendered. Because purpose isn't something you chase...it's something you *walk out* with Him, one obedient step at a time.

Observation Questions

1. How does the author describe the way God uses both victories and struggles to shape purpose, and what examples does she provide from her own life?

   _____

   _____

2. What are the four areas the author identifies as clues to discovering purpose, and how do they interact to reveal one's calling?

_____

_____

Application Questions

1. Looking at your own life, what patterns of gifts, passions, pain, or opportunities has God already placed that might point to your purpose?

_____

_____

2. How can you shift your prayers from seeking a full vision of your life's purpose to asking God for the next obedient step today?

_____

_____

Section 3 - Finding Your Purpose is God's Assignment in Every Season

If there's one thing I've learned, it's this: Your purpose doesn't stay the same forever. The assignment that once gave you life can become the very thing God asks you to lay down in the next season. That doesn't mean you missed it...it means you've *completed it*.

Purpose evolves. It matures as you do. What God called you to build in your twenties might not be what He asks you to carry in your forties. And that's okay. The key is to stay *tuned in*...to keep asking, "Lord, what are You doing in this season, and how can I partner with You in it?"

When you start asking God to reveal your purpose, He'll usually start by revealing your *motives*. He might ask you, "Why are you chasing what you're chasing?" Are you trying to prove something? Impress someone? Live out someone else's expectations?

I grew up in a family where success was almost part of your DNA. My mom's side was Jewish, and we used to joke that you were expected to be one of three things: a doctor, a lawyer, or a failure.

It was funny...but also true. Many of us spend years trying to live up to someone else's dream. But calling can't be copied. God won't anoint a version of you that you're pretending to be. Ask yourself, "Is this dream really mine, or was it handed to me? If no one expected anything of me, what would I still want to do?

Observation Questions

1. How does the author describe the evolution of purpose across different seasons of life, and what examples illustrate that purpose can change without being lost?

_____

_____

2. What role do motives play in discovering God's purpose, and how does the author connect personal and familial expectations to the way we chase dreams?

_____

_____

Application Questions

1. Are there areas in your life where you might be pursuing someone else's expectations instead of God's calling for you, and how can you discern the difference?

_____

_____

2. How can you actively ask God to reveal your motives and align your current season with His evolving purpose for your life?

_____

_____

HEARING GOD - PERSONAL REFLECTION

1. Looking back at your own life, how has God used your past struggles, victories, or unexpected twists to shape the person you are today and prepare you for your purpose?

2. Are there areas of your life where you may be chasing someone else's expectations or dreams instead of what God is calling you to do, and how can you begin to discern what is truly your own purpose in this season?

Week 10

When God Rewrites What You Thought Was Final

By Week 10, something becomes clear. Hearing God is not just about direction. It is about redemption.

This week is about story. Not the version you tell people. The one you lived. The one that shaped how you see yourself, how you trust, how you survive, and how you listen.

Many of us learned how to read a room before we learned how to read Scripture. We learned how to anticipate chaos before we learned how to recognize peace. We learned to listen for danger long before we learned to listen for God. And those early lessons quietly shape the way we live long into adulthood.

But God is not limited by the chapters that came before Him.

Week 10 invites you to look back, not to relive pain, but to recognize redemption. To see where survival turned into strength. Where fear turned into drive. Where vows made in pain shaped your choices without you realizing it. And most importantly, to see how God has been present even when you did not know His name yet.

This week is about letting God rewrite meaning, not erase memory. He does not waste your past. He redeems it. He does not shame your coping. He transforms it. What once protected you may no longer need to lead you. And what once felt like weakness may be the very place His power shows up most clearly.

As you move through this chapter, notice the themes that repeat in your own life. The patterns. The vows. The moments that redirected you. Ask God not just where He is taking you, but what He is reinterpreting along the way.

Because when God rewrites your story, He does not change who you are.

He reveals who you have always been becoming.

Chapter 28

Hearing God in Every Season...From Obedience to Purpose

ICEBREAKER QUESTIONS

1. Can you recall a time when you felt God nudging you to do something that didn't make logical sense?

2. What season of life are you currently in—waiting, stretching, leading, or stepping into something new?

3. When have you experienced clarity only **after** taking a step of faith?

BIBLE PASSAGE

Luke 5:1–11 (NIV)

One day as Jesus was standing by the Lake of Gennesaret, the people were crowding around him and listening to the word of God. He saw at the water's edge two boats, left there by the fishermen, who were washing their nets. He got into one of the boats, the one belonging to Simon, and asked him to put out a little from shore. Then he sat down and taught the people from the boat.

When he had finished speaking, he said to Simon, "Put out into deep water, and let down the nets for a catch." Simon answered, "Master, we've worked hard all night and haven't caught anything. But because you say so, I will let down the nets."

When they had done so, they caught such a large number of fish that their nets began to break. So they signaled their partners in the other boat to come and help them, and they came and filled both boats so full that they began to sink.

When Simon Peter saw this, he fell at Jesus' knees and said, "Go away from me, Lord; I am a sinful man!"

For he and all his companions were astonished at the catch of fish they had taken, and so were James and John, the sons of Zebedee, Simon's partners.

Then Jesus said to Simon, "Don't be afraid; from now on you will fish for people."

So they pulled their boats up on shore, left everything and followed him.

Question

1. Peter didn't understand how lowering the nets again after a fruitless night would produce a miraculous catch. But he obeyed Jesus' voice anyway. Similarly, God often gives one step at a time, and obedience—even when it doesn't make sense—is what positions you to experience His provision and guidance. Can you think of a time this scenario happened in your life?

   _____

   _____

Section 1 - His Voice can be Heard in Every Season

There are moments in life when God's voice doesn't sound like comfort...it sounds like a command. And those commands don't always make sense.

Sometimes, God's direction will contradict your logic, your experience, and even your emotions. But when you obey...when you take Him at His word...you unlock miracles that logic could never explain. This chapter is about those moments. It's about learning to hear God in every season: when He's silent, when He's stretching you, when He's calling you to lead, and when He's pulling you into the deeper waters of your purpose.

Observation Questions

1. How does the author describe the tension between God's commands and human logic, experience, or emotions?

   _____

   _____

2. What examples or language suggest that God's direction can be both challenging and transformative in different seasons of life?

   _____

   _____

Application Questions

1. When have you felt God calling you to do something that didn't make sense at the time, and how did you respond?

   _____

   _____

2. In what area of your life might God be inviting you to step into deeper waters of purpose, even if it feels uncomfortable or uncertain?

   _____

   _____

Section 2 - Sometimes God's Instructions Don't Make Sense

Luke 5:5 says: "Simon answered, 'Master, we've worked hard all night and haven't caught anything. But because You say so, I will let down the nets.'"

I love this story. It's one of the most vivid pictures of what obedience looks like when faith is tested. Let's set the scene.

Jesus is standing by the Lake of Gennesaret, better known as the Sea of Galilee...a familiar place to every fisherman in Israel. Peter, James, and John are there, washing their nets after a long, disappointing night. Their boats are empty, their hands are raw, and their spirits are tired.

Then Jesus does something unusual...He steps into Peter's boat. He doesn't ask if Peter feels ready. He doesn't wait until Peter has recovered from failure. He simply says, *"Put out a little from shore."* And Peter...weary, confused, and probably embarrassed...obeys.

Jesus teaches the crowd from that boat, and when He's finished, He turns to Peter with an even stranger instruction: "Put out into the deep water, and let down the nets for a catch."...Luke 5:4

Now, this made absolutely no sense to Peter. He was a professional fisherman. He knew the rules...you caught fish at night, not during the day. You fished in the shallows, not in the deep.

And yet, Jesus was asking him to do the *wrong thing at the wrong time in the wrong place*. Still, Peter replied, *"Because You say so."* Those five words...*because You say so*...have changed my life more times than I can count. There have been seasons when God told me to forgive someone who didn't deserve it, to give when I had little, or to stay silent when I wanted to fight back. Every time, my logic said no. But obedience said yes. That's the moment where faith grows...the space between what makes sense and what God says.

Isaiah 55:8 reminds us, "For My thoughts are not your thoughts, neither are your ways My ways," declares the Lord.

God's instructions don't always align with human understanding because His perspective stretches beyond our sight. When you can't see the outcome, obedience becomes the bridge between your problem and His promise.

So Peter pushes the boat into the deep, throws his nets back into the water, and waits.

And suddenly...movement. The water ripples. The nets tighten. The boat starts to lurch forward from the weight of hundreds...maybe thousands...of fish.

They pull with all their might until their nets begin to tear. They wave for their partners...James and John...to bring their boat. And before long, both boats are so full they begin to sink.

Historians say Peter's fishing boat was roughly 27 feet long, 7.5 feet wide, and 4.5 feet deep. That's nearly 900 cubic feet. Multiply that by two boats, and you're looking at over 1,700 cubic feet of fish...all caught at the wrong time, in the wrong place, using the wrong method.

But when Jesus speaks, even the fish obey. That's how Peter knew this wasn't a coincidence...it was a calling.

The same sea that mocked his efforts all night had just bowed to the voice of God. When Peter saw the miracle, he didn't celebrate...he broke.

"When Simon Peter saw this, he fell at Jesus' knees and said, 'Go away from me, Lord; I am a sinful man.'"...Luke 5:8

That's what happens when obedience meets revelation. Peter suddenly saw who Jesus was...and who he was not. He was undone. He said, "Get away from me." Jesus said, "Come closer." Peter said, "I'm a sinner." Jesus said, "You're chosen."

And in that moment, Peter's entire life changed. He went from catching fish to catching people...from provision to purpose.

"Then Jesus said to Simon, 'Don't be afraid; from now on you will fish for people.'"...Luke 5:10

When you obey God in the little things, He opens the door to the bigger things. There's something beautiful about surrendering your logic to God. Faith doesn't mean ignoring reality...it means trusting a higher one. Faith says, "This may not make sense, but His voice is more reliable than my experience."

Every miracle begins with an act of obedience that seems small or strange. The widow pours oil into empty jars. Naaman dips seven times in a dirty river. Peter casts his net into deep water. And in each story, obedience becomes the doorway to breakthrough.

Maybe your "deep water" moment looks like starting that business, apologizing first, giving even when you're behind, or stepping into a ministry when you feel unqualified. You may feel like saying, "Lord, I've already tried that."

But if He's saying, *"Cast again,"* then cast again. Because obedience in the deep always leads to abundance in the Spirit. Hearing God isn't just personal...it's *positional*. When you lead others, you have to hear not just for yourself but for those who follow you.

Observation Questions

1. How does Peter's response, "Because You say so," illustrate the tension between human logic and divine instruction?

   _____

   _____

2. What is the significance of Peter's reaction after the miraculous catch, and how does it reveal his understanding of Jesus' authority and his own identity?

   _____

   _____

Application Questions

1. In what area of your life is God asking you to step into "deep water," even when it doesn't make sense logically, and how can you respond in obedience?

   _____

   _____

2. How might practicing obedience in small, uncomfortable steps prepare you for greater opportunities to influence and lead others in alignment with God's purpose?

   _____

   _____

Section 3 - Leadership in the Kingdom

It's never about control...it's about clarity. It's not about titles...it's about trust.

It's not about status...it's about surrender. God speaks to leaders who listen...not to be admired, but to guide.

Proverbs 29:18 says, "Where there is no vision, the people perish."

Vision begins with hearing. And hearing begins with humility. *"Speak, Lord. Your servant is listening."* Jesus didn't overanalyze. He saw Peter's boat and got in. He didn't wait for a perfect moment...He created one.

Leadership requires movement. Sometimes God's direction will come in the form of a nudge, not a neon sign. When He says, "Push out a little from shore," don't ask for a map...just row.

Many people miss their miracle because they hesitate. But hesitation is often the enemy of hearing. When God speaks, move. Even if it's one small step of faith...that's where clarity comes.

Observation Questions

1. How does the passage contrast human ideas of control, status, and titles with God's principles of clarity, trust, and surrender in leadership?

   _____

   _____

2. What examples from Peter's encounter with Jesus illustrate the importance of moving in obedience even when the full plan is not visible?

   _____

   _____

Application Questions

1. In what area of your life or leadership is God prompting you to take a small step of faith, even if you don't yet see the full picture?

   _____

   _____

2. How can cultivating humility and a listening heart improve the way you discern God's direction in your work, relationships, or ministry?

   _____

   _____

Section 4 - The Obedience Test

Peter didn't understand the instruction...but he obeyed it. Every leader God uses must pass this test: Can you follow God when it doesn't make sense to others? That's what separates those who hear from those who only talk about hearing.

Obedience unlocks wisdom that analysis never will. Sometimes God won't explain until after you obey. He'll ask for movement first, understanding later. Because He's more interested in your *trust* than your comfort. When the nets filled, Peter could have taken the credit.

He could have said, "Look what my persistence produced." But instead, he fell to his knees. He knew the catch wasn't the result of effort...it was the result of obedience. That's the mark of a true leader: they don't touch the glory. They redirect it back to God.

If success ever makes you self-sufficient, you've stopped hearing. Jesus didn't just give Peter fish...He gave him purpose. He said, "From now on, you'll catch people."
never blesses you to make you comfortable...He blesses you to make you *useful*. He expands your vision beyond survival to significance.

Maybe the miracle you're living right now isn't just for you...maybe it's to draw others into His story. That's leadership. Seeing beyond what you get, and focusing on who you're becoming.

"So they pulled their boats up on shore, left everything and followed Him."...Luke 5:11 This verse always gets me. They didn't just leave the boats...they left *the best day of their careers.* They walked away from success to follow significance.

If we want to truly hear God, we have to hold everything loosely...the money, the recognition, the comfort, even the good things. Sometimes the loudest noise in your life is the clinking of your own nets...your plans, your productivity, your pride. But when you let them go, your ears open to heaven again. Hearing God is the beginning. Obedience is the bridge. Purpose is the destination.

Psalm 92:13 says, "Those who are planted in the house of the Lord shall flourish in the courts of our God."

That's what happens when you obey. You get *planted*. You grow roots that sustain you through every season. God doesn't want you drifting from miracle to miracle...He wants you rooted in relationship.

Death Valley is known as the hottest, driest place in America. It looks lifeless...cracked ground, nothing growing, nothing blooming. Just heat, dust, and silence.

But one winter in 2004, something remarkable happened. Over the course of a few days, seven inches of rain fell across Death Valley. For a while, it didn't look like much changed. The ground still looked dry, still looked dead.

Then spring came. Almost overnight, the desert exploded with color...millions of wildflowers covered the valley floor. It was breathtaking. Scientists realized Death Valley wasn't dead after all. It was *dormant*.

The seeds were there the whole time. They were just waiting for the right conditions to awaken. I think a lot of us are like that. We go through seasons that feel barren...nothing's happening, nothing's growing, and we start to wonder if maybe our purpose dried up somewhere along the way.

But the truth is, you're not dead. You're dormant. The calling, the potential, the voice of God...it's still in you. It's just waiting for the right rain. Sometimes that "rain" looks like obedience. Sometimes it's surrender, fasting, forgiveness, or finally trusting God enough to take that next step. When His Spirit pours out, the things in you that looked lifeless start to come alive again. The desert doesn't stay barren when the rain comes...and neither will you.

Observation Questions

1. How does Peter's obedience, despite not understanding, illustrate the connection between trust and receiving God's purpose?

    _____

    _____

2. What parallels does the author draw between the dormant seeds in Death Valley and the potential in our own lives waiting for God's "rain"?

    _____

    _____

Application Questions

1. In what area of your life might God be calling you to surrender comfort, control, or recognition in order to activate your purpose?

    _____

    _____

2. How can you cultivate obedience and trust now so that the "dormant seeds" in your life begin to grow and bear fruit in alignment with God's calling?

_____

_____

Section 5 - The Four Steps of Purpose

That's how purpose works. It starts with a seed that's already in you...God planted it before you were even born. But it takes the right environment to make it grow.

God's pattern for every believer is simple but powerful:

1. **Know God**...personally, not religiously. It starts with relationship, not rules.
2. **Find Freedom**...let Him heal what's been holding you back.
3. **Discover Your Purpose**...begin to see what He created you for.
4. **Make a Difference**...use it to change lives and bring glory to Him.

That's the journey from hearing to doing, from listening to leading. Just like Death Valley, you already have everything you need inside you. You're just waiting for the right rain...the moment of surrender...to bring it all to life.

I discovered that freedom is not about perfection...it's about progress. Nor is it the absence of struggle...it's the presence of healing. You can't hear God clearly if your heart is clogged with pain, bitterness, or guilt. That's why James 5:16 says, "Confess your sins to one another and pray for one another so that you may be healed."

You go to God for forgiveness. You go to people for healing. Isolation will muffle God's voice. Community will amplify it. Once you know God and find freedom, your purpose begins to unfold naturally.

Ephesians 1:18 says, "...that you may know the hope to which He has called you."

Hope and calling are connected. If you feel hopeless, it's because you've lost sight of your calling. Your purpose is not hidden...it's planted. It's in your gifts, your passions, your burdens, your story.

Ask yourself: What do I love doing that makes others come alive? That's often where purpose begins. To me, this is the ultimate goal...not just to _hear_ God's voice but to _echo_ it, to live in such a way that your obedience helps others find their own. You were made to make a difference. The world doesn't need more noise...it needs more people who hear God and act on what they hear. Hearing

God's voice from the surrendered position of one willing to obey gives you the freedom to *actually take action* for a greater good.

There comes a time when you've prayed enough, analyzed enough, waited enough...and it's time to move. Like sitting behind someone at a green light...you're waiting, waiting, waiting...and finally, God gives a gentle "beep beep."

It's His way of saying, *"Let's go."* Don't wait for the perfect moment. Don't let fear of failure hold you back. Don't stay in the shallow water when He's calling you to the deep. You've been equipped. You've been prepared. Now it's time to obey. *Because you say so, Lord.*

That one phrase can move you from confusion to clarity, from hesitation to harvest, from hearing God to fulfilling your purpose.

Observation Questions

1. How does the author describe the connection between knowing God, finding freedom, and discovering purpose?

   _____

   _____

2. What role does community and confession play in amplifying God's voice according to this passage?

   _____

   _____

Application Questions

1. What areas of your life might be cluttered with pain, bitterness, or guilt that could be muffling God's voice, and what practical step can you take toward healing and freedom?

   _____

   _____

2. How can you identify and begin acting on the "seed" of purpose God has planted in your life, even if the timing or circumstances aren't perfect?

   _____

   _____

HEARING GOD - PERSONAL REFLECTION

1. In what areas of your life might you be holding onto comfort, control, or recognition instead of fully surrendering to God's voice, and how might releasing them open you to His purpose?

2. Thinking about seasons where you felt "dormant" or barren, what steps of obedience or surrender could serve as the "rain" to awaken the seeds of purpose God has already planted in you?

Chapter 29

The Reason Behind Kindness

ICEBREAKER QUESTIONS

1. When was the last time someone showed you unexpected kindness, and how did it make you feel?

2. Who is someone in your everyday life who serves quietly and might feel unseen?

3. Have you ever done something kind and later realized it meant more than you expected?

BIBLE PASSAGE

Matthew 5:16 (NIV)

"In the same way, let your light shine before others, that they may see your good deeds and glorify your Father in heaven."

Question

1. This passage reminds us that our actions… especially acts of kindness, generosity, and integrity… are a reflection of God's love. By intentionally doing good for others, we not only meet practical needs but also point people to God. How do you like to do good for others?

   _____

   _____

Section 1 - Letting God Shine Through Your Actions

"Kindness isn't random…it's a reflection of God's love." If you've known me for more than five minutes, you've probably heard me say that line. It's not just a tagline or something cute to post on Instagram…it's a life truth I've seen play out over and over again. Because kindness is never random. It's not an accident or a coincidence. It's intentional. It's how God shows up in people's lives…through people who are willing to listen to His nudges.

I'll never forget the day a woman said to me, "You're so kind…are you vegan or something?"

At first, I laughed. I mean, what does kale have to do with kindness? But later that night, while I was brushing my teeth, her comment hit me differently. People will come up with every explanation in the world for goodness…except the one that's true. They'll think you're spiritual, moral, peaceful, or "into energy." But almost never will they say, "She must be a Christian."

That realization changed something in me. Because as believers, we don't just want to do good things…we want people to know the reason we do them. We want our actions to point back to the Source.

And so I made a quiet promise to God: "Lord, whenever I show kindness, help me also show why. Help me connect the good back to You."

One night during our family devotional, we gathered in the living room, Bibles scattered across the coffee table, our kids cozy and half-snuggled in blankets.

We weren't talking about theology. We were talking about love…real, practical, do something-about-it love.

I said, "Okay, who in our life helps us every week...someone we might overlook...and how can we show them God's love?" Kyle paused, thoughtful, and said, "Our mail lady. Mrs. Helena." And instantly, everyone nodded. Because she wasn't your average mail carrier.

This woman radiated joy. Every single day, rain or shine, she showed up with the biggest smile. If she had a package too heavy to carry, she'd ring the doorbell to make sure we got it. When she drove by in her mail truck, she'd wave like she was greeting an old friend. And even when it poured, she'd walk up our driveway, drenched, making sure our mail didn't get ruined.

God used that moment to remind me how easy it is to take faithful people for granted...the ones who show up, serve quietly, and rarely get recognized.

So we decided to do something special. We declared it "Mrs. Helena Mail Lady Day."

We piled into the car...me, Kyle, and the rest of the family...and headed out to the Dollar Store. I handed Kyle a little envelope with cash and said, "Go for it. Pick whatever you think would make her smile."

He carefully walked down each aisle, picking out things that just screamed joy: bright-colored pens, scented candles, a cute notebook, a cross keychain, and even a mini card that said, "You make a difference."

Then we stopped at the health food store and added a few special things...some organic snacks, a beach bag, and a gift certificate to one of her favorite spots.

When we got home, we spread everything out on the table and packed it with tissue paper, ribbon, and love. I told her to stop by on Saturday when Kyle would be home.

That day, when she arrived, she was her usual cheerful self...smiling, waving, completely unaware of what was about to happen. Kyle stood there holding the bag, grinning from ear to ear. "This is for you," he said. "Because you always make us smile."

She looked confused for a second...then opened the bag. One by one, she pulled out the gifts, her hands starting to tremble. By the time she reached the bottom, her eyes were filled with tears. "Oh my goodness," she said softly, "this is one of the nicest things anyone's ever done for me." She hugged Kyle tight. "People usually say thank you around Christmas," she said, "but no one ever goes out of their way like this. This means so much."

Observation Questions

1. How did the author connect acts of kindness to pointing others toward God?

2. What specific behaviors or attitudes did Mrs. Helena demonstrate that made her an example of faithful service?

_____

_____

Application Questions

1. Who in your life serves faithfully and may be overlooked, and how can you intentionally show them God's love this week?

_____

_____

2. How can you ensure that your acts of kindness reflect not just generosity, but also the heart of God to those who receive them?

_____

_____

Section 2 - Love First, Speak Later

And right there, in that moment, God's presence filled our little front porch. No sermon. No scripture verse. Just pure, tangible love.

That one act of kindness started something in our family. It became a rhythm. Each week, we'd ask: Who's someone in our life who helps us, but we haven't shown love to yet?

The woman who gives us massages. The nail salon team. The barista who always gets our order right. We started making baskets, writing notes, and finding small ways to bless people who might never expect it. It wasn't about making a statement. It was about living one. Because kindness, when done consistently, becomes worship. Then there's the beach story...another one that changed me. We rent our beach chairs from a man who works tirelessly every week. He's there before sunrise, setting up rows of chairs and umbrellas so families can relax without a worry.

Every time we'd go down to the beach, I'd see him...quiet, sweaty, hardworking. And one day, as I watched him dragging another heavy umbrella through the sand, I felt that same whisper from God: "Show him My love."

So the next weekend, instead of just smiling and waving, I packed a small cooler. Inside were bottles of cold water, organic snacks, grilled chicken, fruit...everything I knew he liked.

When I handed it to him, he looked stunned. "You brought this for me?" "Yes," I said. "You make our weekends easier. It's the least I can do." He smiled...that kind of surprised, speechless smile...and said, "You really didn't have to." And I told him, "I know. But that's what makes it love."

From then on, it became our routine. Every Saturday, I'd bring him something new...sometimes sandwiches, sometimes smoothies, always something thoughtful. After about five weeks, he finally said, "You know, I've never had anyone do this for me before. Not once." And in that moment, I knew he wasn't just talking about food. He was talking about being seen. He felt noticed, cared for, valued. And all of that came before a single invitation to Bible study, because I wanted him to know love before he heard about God. Eventually, after months of kindness, I invited him. "Hey," I said, "we have a Bible study at our house on Tuesdays at six. You'd be so welcome." And because love had already softened the soil, the invitation didn't feel forced...it felt like a natural next step.

That's the pattern I've learned: Love first. Speak later. Because when people have tasted love, they're already halfway to meeting the One who is love.

The Bible says in Matthew 5:16, "Let your light shine before others, that they may see your good deeds and glorify your Father in heaven." Notice that last part...and glorify your Father.

It's not about the good deeds. It's about the direction they point people in. If we're kind but never say why, we leave people impressed with us instead of changed by Him. Kindness by itself is good. Kindness with clarity...that points back to Jesus...is transformational. So now, when someone says, "You're so kind," I'll gently respond, "Thank you...it's because of how kind God has been to me." It's not preachy. It's honest. And honesty, when seasoned with love, opens hearts like nothing else.

Observation Questions

1. How did the author and her family create a rhythm of kindness in their daily lives, and who were some of the people they chose to bless?

   _____

   _____

2. What role did love play in preparing others to hear about God, according to the beach story?

   _____

   _____

Application Questions

1. How can you intentionally create opportunities to show consistent, thoughtful kindness to people in your daily environment before sharing your faith?

   _____

   _____

2. In what ways can you ensure that your acts of kindness point others to God rather than just impressing them with your actions?

   _____

   _____

Section 3 - A Simple Prayer that Changes Everything

If you've ever wondered if God is real, you don't need to have all the answers. Start with this: "God, if You're real, show Yourself to me." He'll meet you where you are...through people, peace, or moments that feel too perfect to be coincidence. If you're ready to take the next step, pray this:

"Dear God,

I know I've made mistakes.

I can't fix everything on my own.

But today, I open my heart to You.

I believe that Jesus died for me and rose again.

Please forgive me, wash me clean, and fill me with Your love.

I give You my life, and I choose to follow You from this day forward.

In Jesus' name, Amen."

If you just prayed that, Heaven is celebrating...and so am I.

Kindness is contagious. One person's obedience can set off a chain reaction of grace that travels farther than you'll ever see. That's what happened with Mrs. Helena. Her joy changed the tone of our neighborhood. Her gratitude reminded us how good it feels to give. And her tears reminded us that the smallest act can have eternal impact. That's what happened with the man on the beach too. One cooler of snacks turned into a friendship...and a doorway for God's Word. This is how revival starts.

Not always in church pews or crusades...but in grocery aisles, mail routes, and beach chairs. One act of kindness at a time.

Observation Questions

1. How did small acts of kindness, like the gifts for Mrs. Helena and the beach cooler, lead to deeper connections and opportunities to share God's love?

    _____

    _____

2. What does the passage suggest about how God meets people who are seeking Him?

    _____

    _____

Application Questions

1. How can you intentionally practice small acts of kindness in your own community to create opportunities for God's love to be seen?

    _____

    _____

2. In what ways can your obedience in simple acts of service spark a "chain reaction" of grace around you?

    _____

    _____

HEARING GOD - PERSONAL REFLECTION

1. How intentional am I in showing kindness to the people around me, especially those whose efforts often go unnoticed?

2. When I perform acts of kindness, do I point others to God as the source of my love, or do I let the focus remain on myself?

Chapter 30

Finding and Pursuing Your Purpose in Life

ICEBREAKER QUESTIONS

1. When you think about your future, what is one thing you hope you never regret not doing?

2. What makes you feel most alive when you are doing it, even if it feels risky or uncomfortable?

3. Have you ever sensed God nudging you toward something but hesitated? What held you back?

BIBLE PASSAGE

Jeremiah 29:11 (NIV)

"For I know the plans I have for you," declares the Lord, "plans to prosper you and not to harm you, plans to give you a hope and a future."

Ephesians 2:10 (NIV)

"For we are God's handiwork, created in Christ Jesus to do good works, which God prepared in advance for us to do."

Questions

1. Even when life feels uncertain or difficult, this verse reminds you that God has a plan for your life—one designed for your good, not your harm. You can trust that your current struggles are not the end of your story. How can you share this truth with others?

   _____

   _____

2. Knowing that God has already prepared these good works for you can give you confidence to step into opportunities, serve others, or try new things, because He has equipped you for the task. Have you seen this play out in your life? Give an example.

   _____

   _____

Section 1 - Stepping Into God's Purpose

Have you ever had a moment where you looked back and thought, *"I wish I had done that,"* or *"What would've happened if I had taken that chance?"* I think we all have. The truth is, most of our deepest regrets don't come from the mistakes we made...but from the things we *didn't* do. The risks we didn't take. The dreams we never pursued. The conversations we were too afraid to have.

And if I'm being really honest, I've had those moments too. Times when I knew God was nudging me in a direction, but fear or doubt held me back. And later, I'd look back and think, *"Why didn't I just trust Him? Why didn't I step out?"*

But here's the good news: it's *not too late.* God doesn't hold our past against us. He doesn't shame us for the times we hesitated. He's always inviting us forward.

Jeremiah 29:11 reminds us: "For I know the plans I have for you," declares the Lord, "plans to prosper you and not to harm you, plans to give you a hope and a future."

God has a purpose for your life. You're not here to just survive...you're here to *thrive*. You're here to walk out the calling He's uniquely designed for you. And part of that is learning how He's wired you...your gifts, your passions, your strengths...and then using those to make a difference in the world.

Here's the thing: so many people spend their lives chasing things that will never satisfy. More clients. More money. More recognition. More "likes" online. And listen, I get it...I've been there.

When I first started in real estate, I thought the goal was more, more, more. More houses sold, more awards, more growth. And while those things aren't bad, they weren't what really fueled me. I'd hit one milestone, celebrate for about five minutes, and then feel empty again. I'd immediately be on to the next thing.

That's the hamster wheel of life. Running hard but never feeling fulfilled. And the truth is, if you're chasing success without purpose, you'll always feel like something's missing.

So let me ask you this: *what really fuels you?* What's the thing that makes you feel alive? The thing that you could talk about for hours without getting tired? That's where you need to lean in. Because your purpose is always tied to what makes you come alive.

Observation Questions

1. According to the passage, why do many people feel unfulfilled even after achieving success?

   _____

   _____

2. How does Jeremiah 29:11 encourage us about God's plans and our future?

   _____

   _____

Application Questions

1. Are there areas in your life where fear or doubt have held you back from following God's calling? How can you take a step of faith this week to move forward?

   _____

   _____

2. What gifts, passions, or strengths has God given you that you can start using intentionally to make a difference in the world?

_____

_____

Section 2 - The Four Questions of Ikigai

One of my favorite tools for understanding purpose is something called **Ikigai.** It's a Japanese word that means *"reason for being."* And when I first learned about it, I thought...wow, this is such a beautiful picture of how God created us.

1. **What do I love?** What excites you, energizes you, and makes you feel alive?

2. **What am I really good at?** What skills or talents come naturally to you...things people always compliment you on?

3. **What has God called me to do?** What do you sense He's asking of you? What assignments has He placed on your life?

4. **What can I get paid for?** How can you use your gifts in a way that also provides for your life?

When you bring those four things together...that's Ikigai. That's the purpose.

But here's what I've seen: most people only focus on one or two of those. They chase money but hate their work. Or they do something they love but feel burned out because it doesn't sustain them. True purpose comes when all four line up...when your passion, your skills, your calling, and your provision come together.

For me, that's been a journey. It's taken years of trial and error, listening to God, and sometimes failing miserably. But when I started aligning my gifts and passions with what He was asking me to do, everything shifted. Work didn't feel like just work anymore...it became ministry. It became legacy.

Observation Questions

1. What are the four questions that make up Ikigai, and how do they work together to form a picture of purpose rather than a single calling or job?

_____

_____

2. According to this section, what tends to happen when people focus on only one or two of the Ikigai questions instead of all four?

Application Questions

1. Which of the four Ikigai questions feels most clear in your life right now, and which one feels the most unresolved or confusing?

   _____

   _____

2. What is one practical step you could take this season to better align what you love, what you're good at, what God is calling you to do, and how you provide for your life?

   _____

   _____

Section 3 - Learning From Your Design: The DISC Test

Another thing that's been huge for me is understanding how I'm wired. One of the best tools I've used is the **DISC Personality Test.** Now, let me tell you...I am a high D. If you know DISC, you know what that means. I move fast. I make decisions quickly. I like to cross things off my list and keep it moving. That's just me.

And for a long time, I felt like maybe that was "too much." Maybe I was too strong, too direct, too driven. But then I realized...that's exactly how God made me. And He didn't make a mistake. My "high D" isn't a flaw. It's part of my calling.

Maybe you're not a D. Maybe you're more of an "I"...inspiring, relational, people-oriented. Or maybe you're an "S"...steady, dependable, a peacemaker. Or maybe you're a "C"...detail-oriented, precise, organized. The point is, God wired all of us differently.

And when you know how you're wired, it helps you understand where you'll thrive best. For example:

- If you're naturally outgoing, maybe God will use you in leadership or in building relationships.
- If you're more reserved, maybe your strength is in strategy, creativity, or support.
- If you're more people-focused, you'll thrive in environments of connection.
- If you're more task-focused, you'll thrive in areas that require precision and execution.

None of these are "better" or "worse." They're just different. And knowing who you are helps you see where God wants to use you.

Let me tell you something I've learned: at the end of your life, you're not going to regret the mistakes you made nearly as much as the opportunities you didn't take because you didn't think you had what it took. I've talked to people in their later years who said, "I wish I had traveled more. I wish I had written that book. I wish I had started that business. I wish I had told that person I loved them." It's almost never about the things they did...it's about the things they didn't do. And I don't want that for you. I don't want you to get to the end of your life and look back with a list of "what-ifs."

So here's what I've learned about living without regrets:

- **Take action:** Stop waiting for the perfect moment. It doesn't exist. Start now.
- **Build confidence:** Don't be afraid of failure. Failure is just a lesson on the way to success.
- **Take risks:** If it feels scary, but God is leading you...step out. Fear is not a stop sign.
- **Create moments:** Don't put off spending time with people you love. Don't wait to say the words that matter.

Life is too short to live on autopilot. Purpose requires intentionality.

Observation Questions

1. According to the passage, why do people often regret the things they didn't do more than the mistakes they made?

   _____

   _____

2. How does knowing your personality type help you identify where you'll thrive and how God might use you?

   _____

   _____

Application Questions

1. How can understanding your natural personality traits or "wiring" help you pursue the opportunities God has prepared for you?

   _____

   _____

2. What is one area of your life where fear or hesitation has held you back, and what step can you take this week to act boldly in that area?

_____

_____

Section 4 - Success that Matters

At the end of the day, I've learned that success isn't about how much money I made or how many trophies I collected. It's about whether I lived the life God called me to live. Success is alignment. It's when your gifts, your passions, and His calling all come together. That's when you can look back with peace instead of regret. And here's the beautiful thing: you don't have to wait until you "have it all figured out." You can start today. Start by asking God: *What did You put me on this earth to do?* Then take one step in that direction. And then another. And another.

Your purpose isn't just about you. It's about the impact you leave on others. That's your legacy.

Observation Questions

1. According to the passage, how is success defined differently than by money or achievements?

_____

_____

2. Why does the author emphasize taking small, consistent steps toward your purpose rather than waiting until everything is figured out?

_____

_____

Application Questions

1. What is one step you can take today to align your gifts and passions with God's calling for your life?

_____

_____

2. How can you use your talents and purpose to make a positive impact on others in your daily life?

_____

_____

HEARING GOD - PERSONAL REFLECTION

1. What is one area of your life where fear or doubt has held you back from stepping into what God is calling you to do, and what's one small step you can take this week to move forward?

2. Considering your gifts, passions, and personality, how can you begin aligning them with God's purpose for your life so that your daily actions reflect His calling and create a meaningful impact on others?

Week 11

From Hearing to Living With Purpose

By Week 11, something important has shifted. Hearing God is no longer unfamiliar. Obedience is no longer theoretical. Now the question becomes how to live this way in every season of life.

This week is about integration.

It is about learning how God speaks not just in moments of crisis or clarity, but in daily rhythms. In seasons of waiting and seasons of abundance. In leadership and in quiet faithfulness. In moments when obedience feels costly and moments when it feels joyful.

God's voice does not change with circumstances. But how we respond to it often does.

Sometimes His voice comforts. Other times it challenges. Sometimes it reassures. Other times it calls you deeper, farther, or into places that stretch your faith. And often, His instructions do not make sense right away. They may even contradict your logic, experience, or emotions.

This week invites you to trust His voice beyond understanding. To obey even when clarity feels incomplete. To recognize that obedience is not the end goal, but the pathway into purpose.

As you move through this chapter, you will see how God uses obedience to reposition your life. How listening leads to leadership. How surrender opens doors you could never force open yourself. And how purpose is often revealed not through planning, but through faithful response.

Purpose is not something you chase. It unfolds as you walk with God, step by step, season by season.

This week asks a simple but powerful question.

What might God be building through your obedience right now?

Because when hearing and obedience come together, they do more than guide your life.

They shape it.

Chapter 31

The Buoy of Wisdom

ICEBREAKER QUESTIONS

1. When you are faced with a big decision, what do you usually rely on first, emotion, urgency, or wisdom?
2. Have you ever made a choice that seemed right in the moment but caused stress later?
3. Who do you typically turn to when you need advice or clarity?

BIBLE PASSAGE

Proverbs 1:1–7 (NIV)

The proverbs of Solomon son of David, king of Israel:

for gaining wisdom and instruction,

for understanding words of insight,

for receiving instruction in prudent behavior,

doing what is right and just and fair;

for giving prudence to those who are simple,

knowledge and discretion to the young—

let the wise listen and add to their learning,

and let the discerning get guidance—

for understanding proverbs and parables,

the sayings and riddles of the wise.

The fear of the Lord is the beginning of knowledge,

but fools despise wisdom and instruction.

Question

1. In light of this passage, where in your life might God be inviting you to move from simply knowing what is right to actively receiving and applying His wisdom—and what practical step can you take this week to listen more closely and respond with humility and obedience?

_____

_____

Section 1 - Walking in Wisdom

One of the things that Jesus said constantly over and over in Scripture is something so wise that it continues to shape the way I think about every decision in my life... both personally and professionally. There's a verse in Matthew 10:16 that says, *"Behold, I send you forth as sheep in the midst of wolves: be ye therefore wise as serpents, and harmless as doves."*

That one verse captures a massive part of the Christian life...that tension between wisdom and innocence, between discernment and purity. Jesus was reminding us that in this world, we have to be both spiritually aware and strategically smart. We need to listen to the Holy Spirit but also walk in practical wisdom.

The entire book of Proverbs is constantly reminding us to pursue wisdom. Over and over, it compares the wise person and the fool:

 The wise one loves knowledge, while the fool hates it.

 The wise one practices gentle speech, while the fool uses harsh words.

☐ The wise live blamelessly, while the fool is utterly corrupt.

Proverbs 9:9 says, "Instruct the wise and they will be wiser still; teach the righteous and they will add to their learning." Wisdom is not something we achieve once...it's something we continually seek. It's a lifelong pursuit, with constant check-ins: *Where in my life do I need wisdom right now? Have I paused today to ask God for wisdom before making a decision? What's the difference between worldly wisdom and godly wisdom in this experience?*

Now, obviously I've been in real estate for a long time, and I now do business coaching with people. But during my years in real estate, I had so many couples come to me in different stages of life, all making big decisions that required wisdom. One example that stands out is a good friend of mine who wanted to buy a house about $100,000 more than what they felt comfortable doing. I remember sitting down with them and saying, "It's really not worth it for you to be spending this much money, because then you're just going to be constantly stressed and house poor." I told them, "You won't be able to enjoy life...you won't want to go out to eat, you won't be able to give, travel, or relax...because your mortgage payment will own you."

I reminded them that once you're locked into a house that's $100,000 more than you can afford, you're signing up for years of financial tension. I see so many people fall into this trap because they listen to pressure instead of peace. If you have an agent that's telling you, "You're going to lose this house if you don't get it right away," pause and ask yourself...what would the Word of God tell you? What would wisdom tell you?

Wisdom says: stick to a budget that you set prayerfully and wisely. Don't let emotion or fear drive your choices. Proverbs 21:5 says, "The plans of the diligent lead surely to abundance, but everyone who is hasty comes only to poverty." Wisdom always involves patience, planning, and peace. Have you ever made a financial or life decision out of fear or urgency? What was the result? What would it have looked like if you had applied Proverbs 21:5 in your financial decisions? I bet you agree with me that God's peace guides us better than pressure.

Another example...I've seen people meet someone new and, within two weeks, decide to get married. Do you remember Tommy Lee and Pamela Anderson? They got married after just three days of knowing each other, and of course, it ended in divorce. Was that a wise decision? Probably not. And while that's an extreme example, it happens more often than you'd think...emotionally driven decisions that lack wise counsel and patience.

I've also known people who cashed in all their savings to buy properties or start businesses because they got caught up in the excitement of opportunity without counting the cost. One good friend of mine told me that before he met me, back in 2008, he had over-leveraged himself. He bought several properties with borrowed money, putting all his savings on the line...and when the market crashed, he lost everything. Why? Because he didn't use the principle of wisdom. He didn't stop to ask, "What if these tenants don't pay? Do I have enough to cover the mortgage?" Proverbs 27:12 says, *"The prudent see danger and take refuge, but the simple keep going and pay the penalty."*

Observation Questions

1. What examples does the author give of people making unwise decisions due to pressure, emotion, or lack of counsel?

   _____

   _____

2. Which Bible verses does the passage reference to illustrate the importance of prudence, planning, and seeking wisdom?

   _____

   _____

Application Questions

1. How can I apply the principle of seeking God's wisdom before making big decisions in my personal, financial, or professional life?

   _____

   _____

2. Are there areas in my life where I've acted out of fear, urgency, or emotion instead of patience and planning? How can I change that moving forward?

   _____

   _____

Section 2 - Making Wise Decisions by Aligning with Your God-Given Design

Wisdom means thinking ahead...preparing for the unseen. It's not fear; it's stewardship.

And then there's another layer of wisdom we often overlook...alignment with your personality and design. God created each of us with unique wiring, gifts, and strengths. Sometimes people make unwise choices simply because they're stepping into something that doesn't align with how God made them.

I see this all the time in real estate. People look at real estate agents and think, "Oh, that looks fun! I get to look at luxury homes, tour beautiful properties, and talk to people all day." But what they don't realize is that real estate is a business. You have to generate clients, negotiate contracts, handle conflict, and manage pressure. If you're not wired for sales or relationships, it's going to feel like pushing a boulder uphill. The Bible says in Romans 12:6, *"We have different gifts, according to the grace given to each of us."*

There are some people who are complete introverts...they love quiet, alone time, and predictability. And they'll say, "I want to be in real estate." But they don't enjoy being with people, networking, or following up constantly...and that's a red flag. So one of the buoys you need to look at when you're trying to discern if something is from God is this: *does it match your personality and your God-given design?*

Remember the DISC personality test I shared about earlier in this book? At CanZell, every new agent takes a DISC assessment before joining. You can take it at joiningcanzell.com/disc. The DISC test helps us understand our natural tendencies:

☐ D stands for Dominant or Doer...you're determined, decisive, and driven by results.

☐ I stands for Influencer...you love people, relationships, and being the life of the party.

☐ S stands for Steady...you value consistency, loyalty, family, and you don't love change.

☐ C stands for Compliant...you're analytical, detail-oriented, and love structure and order.

How has God uniquely wired you? Which DISC type do you most relate to? When you understand how you're wired, you can make wiser decisions. For example, if you're a strong S or C, starting a business that requires constant change and chaos might not be your best fit. But if you're a D or I, you'll thrive in environments with risk, people, and momentum. Are there areas where you've been striving outside your God-given strengths?

I interview people all the time for coaching or career changes, and so many of them are simply burnt out. Maybe they've been chiropractors, teachers, or nurses...and now they're ready for a change.

But before jumping into a new calling, I ask them a few key questions: Does this align with your strengths? Does this fit your lifestyle? Is this truly your purpose...or just an escape from frustration? Do you tend to isolate your decisions or involve wise voices? Another buoy of wisdom is godly counsel. Proverbs 11:14 says, *"Where there is no counsel, the people fall: but in the multitude of counselors there is safety."* One of the wisest things you can do when you're trying to make a big decision is gather a group of people who truly know you...people who are godly, trustworthy, and spiritually mature. I like to call it a "Purpose Council."

Observation Questions

1. How does the author describe the connection between personality type (using DISC) and making wise life or career choices?

   _____

   _____

2. Which Bible verses are referenced to support the importance of alignment with God's design and seeking counsel?

   _____

   _____

Application Questions

1. How can I better understand my unique gifts, strengths, and personality to make decisions that align with God's design for my life?

   _____

   _____

2. Who are the godly, trustworthy people I can involve in a "Purpose Council" to provide wise counsel for important decisions?

   _____

   _____

Section 3 - Seeking Counsel and Aligning with God's Word

Who are your "wise counselors" you can seek when you need clarity? You can gather them on Zoom or in person and say, "Here's what I'm sensing. Here's what I feel like God is telling me. What do you see?" And here's something important...always choose an odd number of counselors so there can't be a tie. Ask people who are further along spiritually than you, not just your peers. Describe what you're planning, and then let them speak into it. Invite them to speak truthfully, even if it's not what you want to hear. God often confirms His will through the wisdom and peace of others.

And the most critical buoy of all...does it align with the Word of God? Remember the W in WIIIDOH? There's a reason it's first. If what you're hearing contradicts Scripture, it's not from Him. If you think God told you to cheat on your spouse, drop out of school three weeks before graduation, or quit your job even though you have three kids to support...that's not His voice. God's Word is never going to contradict His will.

Proverbs 23:2 says, *"Put a knife to your throat if you are given to gluttony."* So if you think God told you to eat the whole cake, that's not Him! Or if you think He's telling you to sin or act in selfishness...He's not. God's guidance will always line up with His Word.

And one last step...go back to God and ask Him again: "Lord, is this truly for me?" Sometimes we hear a message, a prophecy, or advice that sounds right but isn't meant for us. Take it back to Him. Confirm it in prayer. Sit quietly and ask, "God, does this align with Your plan for me?" Because true wisdom never rushes...it is a way of walking in peace. Wisdom listens before speaking, prays before acting, and tests everything by Scripture and peace. It is the fruit of intimacy with God, not the reward for perfection. To live wisely is to walk closely with Him. As Psalm 90:12 says, *"Teach us to number our days, that we may gain a heart of wisdom."* When you make decisions from that posture, your life becomes a steady testimony of faith and discernment.

Let wisdom be your buoy. Let it hold you steady when the world demands reaction. And above all, let it draw you deeper into the voice of the One who never leads astray.

Observation Questions

1. What role does confirming guidance through prayer and Scripture play in discerning God's will according to this passage?

_____

_____

2. How does the author suggest handling advice or prophecy that may sound right but doesn't align with God's plan?

_____

_____

Application Questions

1. Who are the spiritually mature counselors in my life that I can seek for guidance when making important decisions, and how can I involve them effectively?

_____

_____

2. How can I ensure that the decisions I'm making align with Scripture and reflect God's will for my life?

_____

_____

HEARING GOD - PERSONAL REFLECTION

1. Who are the godly, spiritually mature counselors I can turn to for guidance when I face important decisions, and how can I intentionally involve them in my decision-making process
2. How can I ensure that the choices I make align with Scripture and reflect God's wisdom, rather than being driven by emotion, fear, or outside pressure?

Chapter 32

Living for Eternity...Keeping Heaven in View

ICEBREAKER QUESTIONS

1. When was the last time you were reminded that life is shorter than we like to admit?

2. What is something you have worked very hard for that no longer feels as important as it once did?

3. If you were honest, what tends to shape your decisions more right now…earthly success or eternal impact?

BIBLE PASSAGE

Matthew 6:19–21 (NIV)

Do not store up for yourselves treasures on earth, where moths and vermin destroy, and where thieves break in and steal.

But store up for yourselves treasures in heaven, where moths and vermin do not destroy, and where thieves do not break in and steal.

For where your treasure is, there your heart will be also.

Question

1. What does the way you currently spend your time, money, and energy reveal about where your true treasure is—and what is one intentional change you could make to invest more in eternal things rather than temporary ones?

Section 1 - Living for God's Approval, Not the World's

We live in a world obsessed with the temporary...success, recognition, comfort, and control. But when you start walking closely with God, He begins to shift your focus from what's fleeting to what's forever. This chapter is about that shift. It's about trading earthly trophies for eternal treasures, learning to see every decision in light of forever, and living for the smile of God rather than the applause of people.

I'll never forget the day I stood up to speak at my friend's funeral. It was one of the hardest things I've ever done...not just because I loved her deeply, but because I could feel God asking me to speak a truth that most people don't want to think about: life is short.

Before the service, I brought a long, white rope...about 300 feet of it. When it came time to speak, I began to roll it out across the floor. It went down the aisle, past the front row, and kept going, all the way toward the back of the room. I remember people whispering, wondering what in the world I was doing. Then I took a tiny piece of red tape...barely an inch wide...and wrapped it around the very tip of that rope.

"Now," I said, holding it up, "pretend this rope doesn't stop here. Pretend it stretches all the way to the moon and back a trillion times... and keeps going. That's eternity. This little red part right here...that's your life on earth."

The room went silent. You could feel the weight of it. Because that's the truth we forget...earth is not our home. We're just passing through.

David prayed it beautifully in Psalm 39:4–5: "Lord, help me to realize how brief my time on earth will be. Help me to know that my days are numbered...that my life is but a breath."

And Peter echoed it in 1 Peter 1:17, saying, "If you call God your Father, live your time here as foreigners in reverent fear."

That verse wrecked me in the best way. Because we really are just temporary residents here. We're travelers, visitors, ambassadors. And yet... most of us live like this little red tape is the whole story.

We chase after success. We fight for recognition. We obsess over being the best...the best mom, the best businessperson, the best anything. But the truth is, one day we'll stand before God and realize that almost everything we worked so hard for... didn't last.

When my husband and I moved from Virginia to Florida, we made a radical decision. We threw away every single trophy, ribbon, plaque, and award we'd ever won.

I'm not exaggerating...boxes and boxes of them. "Top Agent," "Rookie of the Year," "Salesperson of the Month," "Million-Dollar Club." You name it. They all went in the trash.

At first, it felt strange. I mean, we had worked hard for those achievements. They represented years of effort, long nights, and sacrifice. But then, as the boxes emptied, a strange freedom filled the room.

Because we realized...those trophies weren't eternal. They didn't mean a thing in heaven. There's not one award we'll ever receive on earth that compares to hearing, *"Well done, good and faithful servant."*

Now, in our home, there isn't a single trophy on a shelf. Not one ribbon hanging in a shadow box. Because we decided the only award we want is the smile of God. We're not trying to please the world anymore...we're living for an audience of One. If we make the mistake of assuming that God's main goal for our life is material prosperity or worldly success, we'll spend our days chasing things that never satisfy. We'll think we're running after "abundance," but really, we're running on a treadmill...moving hard, going nowhere.

The world says, "Get more." God says, "Give more." The world says, "Build your platform." God says, "Build My Kingdom." I think about all the years I spent trying to be "number one." Number one in real estate. Number one in business. Number one in productivity. But when I picture standing before Jesus, I can't imagine Him saying, "Wow, Chantel, great job on your sales numbers!" No. He's going to ask, *"Did you love people well? Did you obey Me when it didn't make sense? Did you bring anyone closer to Me?"* That's what counts.

Observation Questions

1. What illustration did the author use at her friend's funeral to show the brevity of life compared to eternity?

_____

_____

2. How did the author and her husband demonstrate a shift in perspective regarding worldly achievements and trophies?

_____

_____

Application Questions

1. In what areas of your life are you currently chasing temporary recognition, success, or approval instead of focusing on eternal impact?

_____

_____

2. How can you begin to prioritize actions and decisions that store up "treasures in heaven" rather than earthly rewards?

_____

_____

Section 2 - When God Smiles

There's this verse in Hebrews 11:7 that says, "By faith, Noah built a ship in the middle of dry land. He was warned by God about things he could not yet see, and in holy fear, he built an ark to save his family." I love that it says Noah "pleased God."

Can you imagine God smiling? Like, genuinely smiling...proud of Noah's obedience even when it made no sense? I think that's the kind of life I want. Because there have been seasons where God asked me to do things that didn't make sense either...to give when I didn't have much, to forgive when it felt unfair, to risk when it looked foolish.

I've lost large sums of money, and yet I've seen God multiply what's left. I've sown in times of scarcity, and watched Him bring abundance out of nowhere.

Sometimes obedience costs you...but disobedience costs more. Noah understood that. He had never even seen rain before...at that time, the earth was watered from underground springs. And he lived nowhere near the ocean! Imagine the ridicule: *"You're building a what? For what storm?!"*

Yet Noah never complained. He didn't make excuses. He just built. Day after day. Year after year. 120 years of hammering, cutting, and trusting...with no sign of rain.

Imagine his kids: "Dad, everyone's laughing at us!" But Noah kept building, because his focus wasn't on approval...it was on obedience. And when the rain finally came, the mockers disappeared, but Noah's faith stood tall.

Every time I think of Noah, I think of that rope. That endless rope that stretches on forever, and the tiny red line that's just our time on earth.

When you remember that this life is temporary, it changes how you live. You stop clinging to possessions. You stop fearing failure. You stop wasting time on things that don't matter. Instead, you start asking, "What will last forever?" Because when you live for eternity, you'll live differently.

You'll love deeper. You'll give freer. You'll forgive faster. And you'll trust God...even when the ark still looks ridiculous.

My prayer is that one day, when I stand before God, He'll look at my life and smile...the same way He smiled at Noah...not because I was perfect, but because I trusted Him completely. When you live for eternity, you stop chasing applause and start chasing the smile of God.

Observation Questions

1. How long did Noah work on building the ark before seeing any sign of rain, and what does that illustrate about faith?

   _____

   _____

2. What lessons does the author draw from Noah's story about living for eternity rather than seeking approval or possessions?

   _____

   _____

Application Questions

1. In what areas of your life is God asking you to act in faith, even when it doesn't make sense or seems risky?

_____

_____

2. How can focusing on eternity rather than temporary approval change the way you make decisions today?

_____

_____

HEARING GOD PERSONAL REFLECTION

1. In what areas of your life are you currently chasing temporary approval or success, and how might focusing on eternity change your perspective or decisions?

2. Are there steps of obedience God is asking you to take that feel risky, confusing, or "ridiculous," and how can you trust Him like Noah did while moving forward?

Chapter 33

Barriers to Hearing God (The Real-Life Stories Behind the Static)

ICEBREAKER QUESTIONS

1. When was the last time you felt like your life was so loud inside that you could not hear God clearly at all?

2. Which feels harder for you right now, slowing down, confessing honestly, forgiving deeply, or letting go of control? Why?

3. Can you think of a time you knew God was trying to speak, but something in you kept translating it wrong? What was the barrier?

BIBLE PASSAGE

Acts 13:1–3 (NIV)

In the church at Antioch there were prophets and teachers: Barnabas, Simeon called Niger, Lucius of Cyrene, Manaen (who had been brought up with Herod the tetrarch) and Saul. While they were worshiping the Lord and fasting, the Holy Spirit said, "Set apart for me Barnabas and Saul for the work to which I have called them." So after they had fasted and prayed, they placed their

Questions

1. What practices in your life help you hear God's voice, and how ready are you to act when He calls you to something new or uncomfortable?

_____

_____

Section 1 - BUSYNESS: The Lifestyle That Becomes a Distraction

I've noticed four major barriers that keep us from hearing God. I've also discovered a simple way to overcome them. These are things I've personally lived through and had to work on deeply with the Lord, because honestly hearing God doesn't just happen because you want it. It's a natural side effect when you clear out what's blocking your spiritual ears. Do you recognize any of these?

The first barrier is busyness. And when I say busyness, I'm not talking about just having a full schedule. I'm talking about a lifestyle where you don't even know what stillness feels like. A life where your mind runs before your feet hit the floor in the morning. A life where you're doing, doing, doing…and somehow still feel behind.

Jesus said to Martha in Luke 10:41–42:

"You are worried and upset about many things… but few things are needed."

That verse hits me right in the chest because I see myself in Martha so clearly. I've been busy my entire life … not by accident, but almost by identity. I grew up in chaos, so chaos became familiar, and somehow it became comfortable. Even now, if things feel "too peaceful," I'll subconsciously add something to do. I'll volunteer for one more thing. Add one more responsibility. Squeeze in one more errand. I'll look at the clock and think, "I have seven minutes before I need to leave… I can probably organize the pantry, email two people, and switch the laundry." And then boom — now I'm late. Every. Single. Time.

And the perfectionism? That just adds fuel to the fire. If you come to my house, nothing can be out of place. I mean NOTHING. Not a pillow, not a candle, not a glass on the counter. When guests come over … and we have guests constantly... I want the house to feel like a boutique hotel lobby. Music just right, lights dimmed perfectly, candles lit, no clutter anywhere. And yes… I have a house manager. But even with that, I'm still fluttering around behind her adjusting, perfecting, making sure everything feels "just right."

And here's the part that God really had to deal with: At the end of the day, I measured my worth by my productivity. If I did twenty things, I feel good. If I did three, I felt behind. God had to show me that sometimes the noise is coming from my own pace. I cannot hear God when my entire life is turned up to a 10. After Jesus pointed out to Martha that she was distracted by all the many things, he said, "...few things are needed, indeed only one. Mary has chosen the better, and it will not be taken from her." Martha was rushing to do all the things. Mary was sitting in peace and receiving from her Savior. I have learned this too now, and boy was my busyness a huge distraction from what really mattered.

Observation Questions

1. What contrast does the author draw between Martha and Mary in Luke 10:41–42, and how does it illustrate the impact of busyness on hearing God?

    _____

    _____

2. How does the author describe the ways busyness and perfectionism acted as barriers in her own life?

    _____

    _____

Application Questions

1. In what areas of your life is busyness keeping you from spending intentional time with God, and what is one step you can take this week to create stillness?

    _____

    _____

2. How can you shift your focus from measuring your worth by productivity to valuing time spent in God's presence?

    _____

    _____

Section 2 - SIN: The Internal Static

The next barrier is sin. People hear that word and immediately think of dramatic behaviors... the "big stuff." But sin shows up in all kinds of quieter ways. Ways we almost ignore because they become part of our personality.

For me? One of my biggest early struggles was my eating disorder. I struggled with bulimia for years. It controlled my thoughts every single day. Every mirror. Every photo. Every meal. I obsessed over being thin. I obsessed over the scale. And I carried shame because of it. That wasn't just a bad habit. It was bondage. It was unforgiven sin that needed healing. And my emotional sins too. The attitude sins. The ones nobody talks about. I struggled with unforgiveness. I struggled with not being kind, especially when I was stressed. I struggled with arrogance, pride and a judgmental, unforgiving spirit. Because here's the truth about me: I am a ball-buster. Driven and passionate, I like to get things DONE and when other people didn't operate that way, perhaps they were slower or just more relaxed and less intense, it irritated me. I judged them. I assumed they weren't trying as hard or weren't committed. At the same time, I would show huge compassion for the homeless, giving and praying, seeing the humanity in their situation because nobody plans to become homeless. It's funny how we can be deeply compassionate in some areas and deeply impatient in others. We are complicated beings.

But God started working on me. Every time I snapped or spoke sharply. Every time anger flared up or some other emotion made me communicate poorly, he kept convicting me. He kept pulling me in. He kept softening me and still does to this day as sin continues to block God's voice through distraction, preoccupation, and spiritual fog. But every time God points out something I need to release, I get to unclog the flow through confession.

Observation Questions

1. How does the author describe the subtle ways sin can manifest in daily life, beyond the "big stuff"?

   _____

   _____

2. What role did God's conviction play in helping the author recognize and address her personal sins?

   _____

   _____

Application Questions

1. What areas of hidden or habitual sin in your life might be clouding your ability to hear God, and how can you bring them to Him for confession and healing?

   _____

   _____

2. How can you cultivate awareness of emotional or attitude sins, like impatience or pride, that may be affecting your relationship with God and others?

   _____

   _____

Section 3 - UNFORGIVENESS: The Heavy Barrier That Quietly Builds Walls

While confession unclogs what's stuck nothing new ever happens without forgiveness. This is why unforgiveness of sin is one of the biggest spiritual blockages there is. It's heavy. It's sticky. It's sneaky. And it sits in the heart quietly until God points His finger right at it.

I had unforgiveness toward my dad for most of my life. He was never in my life. Ever. If I combined all the hours I spent with him, maybe 20. And 20 hours in a lifetime is nothing. He was on drugs, working, gone ...whatever the reason, he wasn't there. And when a parent isn't present, your heart builds defenses whether you want it to or not.

With my mom it was different. The defenses there grew from shock. From ages 0 to 12, she and I were inseparable. Just me and her....all day, every day. I went everywhere with her. She was my world. And then one day then she remarried my stepdad Wally, an alcoholic, and everything shifted. I went from being the center of someone's life to forgotten overnight.

The closeness turned into tension. The affection turned into distance. The safety turned into instability.

And that lasted years… from age 12 all the way until about 22. Those wounds don't just disappear because you love Jesus. You have to deal with them. You have to forgive. Unforgiveness not only blocks your heart ...it blocks your hearing. At 22, I finally forgave my mom and we have had a great relationship ever since and it made me grow closer to God.

These were big things to forgive of course, but we also all get to practice releasing unforgiveness even in the mundane trappings of daily life. Like that one time we pulled into The Landings ...a shopping area near our house. My husband parked normally in a spot. Not crooked. Not stealing anyone's place. Just a normal park. Across from us was another woman who had already planned to shortcut straight through two parking spots to exit ...and because we were now blocking her ability to do that, she went OFF.

She got out of her car and started cussing my husband out so loudly and intensely that we literally looked around like, "Is she talking to us? Did we miss something?" Nope. She was yelling at us for something we didn't even do. My husband and I looked at each other. We knew we were in the right. We also knew this was not worth wasting energy on. People will offend you out of nowhere. People will misunderstand you. People will blame you for their bad day and make you doubt yourself. But unforgiveness only hurts you, and even when you know you're in the right sometimes it's best to let it go. We let the woman say what she needed to, and she soon moved on and so did we. My husband and I had a great lunch in The Landings, and felt the presence of God.

Of course, sometimes unforgiveness isn't towards people, but God. We blame Him for what happens or doesn't happen. "Why didn't You give me that spouse? Why didn't that business deal work? I did everything right." Or we pray for blessings and when they arrive we fail to praise Him and instead take all the credit.

Like that time my husband and I were driving round and round the car lot at the mall at Christmastime. It was like a war zone. So we prayed: "Lord, please help us find a parking space." A spot immediately opened up and my husband said, "never mind, Lord, I found one!" We laughed because we knew God had provided the spot but the comment was such a picture of human nature ...how we can be rescued, blessed, guided, and still take the credit and blame God two seconds later. This kind of unforgiving position creates distance. And distance makes it harder to tune in. But when I accept that God is always good, and release Him from all my expectations and timelines for how I think things should be, I get to experience His presence all the time.

Observation Questions

1. How did unforgiveness toward the author's parents affect her ability to hear and experience God's presence?

   _____

   _____

2. What examples does the author give of unforgiveness in daily life, and how did choosing to forgive change the outcome?

   _____

   _____

Application Questions

1. Are there people, situations, or even God Himself that you need to forgive in order to remove spiritual blockages in your life? How can you take a concrete step toward releasing that unforgiveness today?

   _____

   _____

2. How can you practice forgiveness in small, everyday situations—like minor offenses or misunderstandings—to train your heart to stay open to God's presence?

_____

_____

Section 4 -SELFISHNESS: The One We Don't Like to Admit

Selfishness can be subtle. For me, it still shows up with food. Now that I have overcome and transformed my adolescent bulimia I've become such a foodie. I'm also still super picky and I have a gluten allergy. And because of all that, my husband always lets me choose the restaurant. He's gracious about it, but the truth is, I'm selfish in that area. I want what I want. And sometimes I bulldoze right through what everyone else might want.

Selfishness makes you so focused on your own desires that it's hard to hear God's. God's voice always calls you beyond yourself. 100% of the time, beyond ourselves we find other people, and are so often concerned about what "they" think about us. This vanity is also selfishness. Imagine being so afraid of what others might think that you're never listening for and freely obeying the voice of God. If that's you, you might never have been to a silent disco, which is the perfect illustration of what it feels like to hear God clearly!

For my birthday at the St. Regis in Longboat Key, we did a silent disco by the pool. We had everyone bring wireless headphones. And let me tell you, if you've never been to one, it is the most hilarious experience if you are NOT wearing headphones. Everyone wearing headphones was dancing, laughing, singing, having the best time ever. And all those watching from the outside were like: "What in the WORLD are they doing?" Can you imagine it? We had all counted down, "Ready? One… two… three!" ...and pressed play and started moving, and not one of us was on the same beat! Some people were a little ahead. Some behind. Some were belting out lyrics that others weren't at yet, and to everyone without the headphones ...we looked insane! But to us? It made perfect sense, because we could hear something they couldn't hear. And that is EXACTLY what it's like to hear God's voice. When you're tuned in, you will move differently. You will respond differently. You will walk to a rhythm other people don't understand. (If you want to see what this looked like, go to TuneInGodsVoice.com/silentdisco.)

Can I release my selfishness to the point of not caring if my obedience looks weird to others? Or whether all my dietary preferences are met when my husband really wants take-out? If so, God can trust that I'll hear His voice loud and clear, and without distortions.

Observation Questions

1. How does the author illustrate the effect of selfishness on hearing God using the silent disco example?

   _____

   _____

2. What specific behaviors or attitudes does the author identify as forms of subtle selfishness that can distort spiritual listening?

   _____

   _____

Application Questions

1. In what areas of your life might selfishness or vanity be blocking you from hearing God's voice? How can you intentionally release control in those areas?

   _____

   _____

2. Are there situations where obeying God might look "weird" or go against others' expectations? How can you practice stepping out in obedience despite potential judgment?

   _____

   _____

Section 5 - Barriers Distort the Voice of God

People ask me all the time, "Chantel, can you misunderstand God? Like, can you think He's saying one thing when He's actually saying another?" YES. 100% yes. Hearing God is not a text message. It's not always perfectly clear. The voice of God is easily distorted by filters.

I saw it myself when a woman named Brenda from Bayside Community Church texted me asking if I was coming to Bible study. I sent her a voice-to-text reply: "I was planning on it, but my husband ended up taking a later flight, so I was going to come myself."

Brenda immediately called me: "ARE YOU OKAY!?"

"What are you talking about!?" I said.

"You texted me saying you wanted to kill yourself!"

I opened the text. That is exactly what it said! My voice-to-text function had completely distorted the message and created a crisis! We laughed SO hard. I mean, we could not stop laughing. What a perfect example of how easy it is to misunderstand something. A message was given, but the translation was way off, distorted by some impersonal filter between you and the other.

This is how it can feel sometimes when we're trying to hear God: We hear part of it. We fill in the rest. We interpret it through our emotions or assumptions. This is exactly why I created the W-I-I-I-D-O-H (Why-Do) principle, because when you run what you believe you heard from God through those filters, it helps prevent misinterpretation.

And honestly, the only times I've ever seen someone go through all seven filters and still get it wrong were the times when God needed them to start moving in a certain direction first ...and then He redirected them later. Which brings me to Acts 13.

Observation Questions

1. How does the voice-to-text story illustrate the concept of distortion in communication and hearing God?

   _____

   _____

2. According to the author, why do misinterpretations still happen even when using filters like W-I-I-I-D-O-H?

   _____

   _____

Application Questions

1. How might your emotions, assumptions, or personal biases be distorting what you think God is saying? How can you apply the W-I-I-I-D-O-H principle to clarify His voice?

   _____

   _____

2. Reflect on a time when you thought you heard God but later realized you misunderstood. What did that teach you about listening carefully and testing what you hear?

Section 6 - Acts 13

Acts 13 is honestly one of my favorite pictures in the whole Bible of how God speaks. And I love it because it shows something we don't talk about enough: God doesn't just lead you once. He leads you through seasons. Through shifts. Through changes. Through assignments that evolve and through every barrier that the enemy tries to build between you and the voice of God. Following his voice is not one straight line. It's not one lifetime blueprint. It's step-by-step, and God updates the directions as you go.

The leaders at Antioch were worshiping and fasting ...they weren't rushing, they weren't multitasking, they weren't trying to squeeze God into their schedule. They created space. And right there, in that spiritual quiet, the Holy Spirit spoke. It wasn't subtle, like a guess or "I kind of think God might be saying..." No. God spoke something crystal clear: "Set apart for Me Barnabas and Saul for the work I've already called them to."

This is one of those moments where you don't have to decode anything. God gives two names. He gives a direct command. And He gives a purpose. And they did exactly what God told them to do ...they prayed, laid hands on them, sent them off ...and they stepped right into God's will. There was no confusion. They absolutely heard God correctly.

But even in a moment that clear, God still didn't give them the whole plan. He didn't tell them where they were going next. He didn't tell them how long it would last. He didn't tell them which cities they'd preach in, who would join them, or who would walk away. He didn't tell them how their friendships or leadership roles would shift over time. He just gave them the next step. That's how God usually leads us ...clear assignment, but not the entire timeline.

And then comes the part everyone forgets. In the very same chapter where God calls Barnabas and Saul, the whole dynamic changes. At the beginning, it's always "Barnabas and Saul," because Barnabas was the established leader. But by verse 13, it quietly switches to "Paul and his companions." No announcement. No drama. Just a shift. Suddenly Paul is the one leading, the one speaking more, the one God is highlighting. Nothing in verse 2 predicted this. God never said, "Barnabas will start, and then Paul will take over." But that's what happened as the assignment unfolded.

More changes came. Later, in Acts 15, Paul and Barnabas actually split. They had a sharp disagreement, no small argument; the Bible specifically says it was sharp. They parted ways. Paul took Silas and Barnabas took Mark. And just like that, the team God called together earlier becomes two separate teams.

And here's the thing: the split didn't mean they missed God. It didn't mean Acts 13 was a mistake. It didn't mean they failed to hear His voice. What it meant was that God can call you into a season… and then God can call you out of that season. The original assignment was real, and the shift was real too.

This is where so many people get stuck, because we think if God really spoke once, that direction should last forever. But Acts 13 shows us that God's voice is progressive. He gives you enough clarity to obey right now, but not so much clarity that you stop depending on Him tomorrow. He leads step by step, and He'll redirect you without apologizing for it.

This is how God has always worked. Abraham heard God clearly, and still needed updates along the way. David was anointed king, but his path shifted constantly. Elijah heard God, and then got redirected to anoint Elisha. The disciples were told, "Follow Me," but had no idea what that meant long-term. And Paul heard, "Set apart," but the team, the strategy, and even his closest relationships changed later.

So if you today feel confused because a calling shifted or a relationship that used to feel God-ordained suddenly ended, or a ministry closed or a season that once felt crystal clear now feels blurry, take heart. Acts 13 shows us that this is not failure. This is actually how God guides His people. You did hear Him. And you're still hearing Him. The assignment changed because the season changed. It's not a mistake, it's maturity and obedience. And that's what it looks like to walk with God in real life.

Observation Questions

1. How did the leadership transition from Barnabas to Paul illustrate God's progressive and evolving guidance?

   _____

   _____

2. According to the passage, why is it important to recognize that God often gives clarity for the next step, but not the entire timeline of our journey?

   _____

   _____

Application Questions

1. Are there areas in your life where you're expecting God's guidance to be permanent or unchanging? How can you practice trusting Him step by step instead of needing the full plan upfront?

   _____

   _____

2. Reflect on a time when God shifted a season, calling, or relationship in your life. How can you respond with obedience and faith rather than seeing it as a failure or mistake?

   _____

   _____

Section 7 - Everyone Needs a Nathan

There's this moment in Scripture that I come back to over and over, because it shows how deeply we all need people in our lives who will courageously and lovingly tell us the truth about the barriers we have built for ourselves. It's the story of David and Bathsheba. And if you know anything about David's life, you know this was one of the darkest moments in his entire story. It goes like this:

David sees Bathsheba, a beautiful married woman, bathing. Instead of turning away, he lets his sin lead him. His lust takes over, he sends for her, sleeps with her, and she becomes pregnant. Then, instead of owning his choices, he selfishly tries to cover it up. He arranges for her husband, Uriah, to be killed so he can take Bathsheba as his wife. A web of adultery, lies, manipulation, and murder all wrapped into one dark chapter of his life, and people know about it. There are servants involved. Messengers involved. People see what was happening. But no one says a word. No one has the courage to confront their king, one who is so respected for following the voice of God.

Except Nathan. Nathan is a prophet and an old friend of David's. And God sends him straight to David, not to shame or destroy him, but to save him from himself. Nathan is brilliant. He doesn't walk in guns blazing, pointing fingers. Instead, he tells David a story.

"There were two men in a city," he says. "One rich. One poor. The rich man had many sheep. The poor man had only one little lamb and he loved it like a daughter. He fed it from his own plate. He cared for it. A traveler came to visit the rich man. And instead of taking one of his own many sheep, the rich man stole the poor man's beloved lamb, killed it, and served it for dinner."

When David hears this, he is furious. He says, "That man deserves to die. How could he do such a thing?" And Nathan looks him straight in the eyes and says, "You are the man."

That moment pierced David. The denial shattered, the pride melted, the justification evaporated, all the excuses he had told himself all broke. And instead of fighting Nathan or trying to pretend he didn't know, David repented. He turned back to God. Honestly, that moment saved him.

That's what a Nathan does. A Nathan loves you enough to tell you the truth ...not with shame, not with destruction, but with clarity. A Nathan cares more about your soul than your reaction. A Nathan shows you what you can't see in yourself.

And I can tell you from my own life… we all need people like that. I have a friend who hasn't been intimate with her husband in six years. Of course, there were good reasons like medical issues, life stress, habits that faded, but they nonetheless drifted into a place of disconnection without ever addressing it. And because we're close, I've brought it up gently. Not to judge her. Not to shame her. But because I love her, and I know what disconnection can do to a marriage. I've been honest with her, and I've stayed loving and available. That's what a Nathan does.

My husband is a Nathan to me too. We both have short fuses at times. We'll get irritated, worked up, frustrated, and the other one will say, "Hey… this is something we need to look at." Not in anger. Not in accusation. But in that, "I love you enough to call this out" way.

God uses people like that. Both to confront sin and also to confirm what He's already whispering to you. I remember going to a conference recently. For months leading up to it, God had been dealing with me on striving ...telling me to rest, to trust Him, to stop running at a hundred miles an hour trying to hold everything together myself. He kept whispering, "Let Me provide for you. Slow down. Breathe. Stop trying to earn what I've already promised." I heard Him alright, but I wasn't listening. I was still on full speed ahead.

And then at the conference, I sat next to a guy I had never met. Our conversation was rich and soon he was sharing with me everything God had been telling him. It was word for word what God had been speaking to me! He said, "God's been telling me to rest in Him. Stop working so hard. Let Him provide. Stop striving."

I listened in awe. God was saying, "See? You heard Me correctly. This is Me. I'm confirming it."

That's also what a Nathan does. They don't just correct ...they confirm. They say the thing that makes your spirit go, "Oh wow. That's exactly what God's been trying to get through to me." Sometimes God uses people to get your attention, to bring clarity, to break through confusion, or to say what you've been afraid to admit. That's why every one of us needs a Nathan.

And every one of us needs to be a Nathan when God prompts us. Sometimes the fastest way God can get through a barrier is through the courage and kindness of another person. Could you be the one to bring the voice of God to another who is misguided by their own barriers?

Observation Questions

1. How did Nathan use a story to confront David instead of directly accusing him, and why was this method effective?

_____

_____

2. According to the passage, what are the two primary ways God uses people like Nathan in our lives?

_____

_____

Application Questions

1. Who in your life could benefit from you speaking truth in love, even if it feels uncomfortable? How can you approach that conversation with both courage and compassion?

_____

_____

2. Reflect on a time someone acted as a "Nathan" in your life. How did their words help you hear God more clearly or overcome a personal barrier?

_____

_____

Section 8 - Transforming These Barriers

Remember the 15-minute challenge? If you want to transform whatever is keeping you from hearing the voice of God, you need silence. Real silence. Turn your phone off. Most of us haven't had physical silence in weeks, let alone spiritual silence. For some people it's been years.

In the silence we can ask ourselves: Am I addicted to busyness and productivity? Am I holding onto my sins and distractions? Am I choosing bitterness and unforgiveness over releasing myself, someone else or even God from past expectations? Am I so focused on my own voice that I can't hear God's? And with a renewed awareness, we can confess, forgive and refocus on His voice. This is a prayer that has helped me do this over the years:

"God, You say that Your sheep listen to Your voice.

You call us by name ...personally and intimately.

Lead me today.

Help me hear Your voice, know Your voice, and recognize Your voice.

I don't want to follow a stranger.

I want to follow You."

Pray that daily and notice how barriers fade and everything changes as your listening focuses beyond yourself, exposing distractions and barriers and helping you choose love and forgiveness in each moment because that is His Way.

Observation Questions

1. According to the passage, why is physical and spiritual silence important for hearing God?

   _____

   _____

2. What four questions does the author suggest asking oneself in silence to uncover barriers to hearing God?

   _____

   _____

Application Questions

1. What steps can you take this week to create intentional silence in your life, removing distractions so you can hear God more clearly?

   _____

   _____

2. How can daily prayer and reflection help you identify and release barriers like busyness, sin, unforgiveness, or selfishness that keep you from hearing God?

HEARING GOD - PERSONAL REFLECTION

1. Which of the four barriers... busyness, sin, unforgiveness, or selfishness... resonates most with you personally, and how has it impacted your ability to hear God clearly?

2. How might creating intentional silence and reflecting on your heart, actions, and relationships help you identify and release the barriers that are currently distorting God's voice in your life?

Week 12

Staying Anchored When Decisions Matter

This is the stage where wisdom becomes essential. Not just spiritual insight, but steady judgment. Not just passion, but restraint. Not just obedience, but alignment.

God's voice is gentle and true, but life is loud. Pressure, emotion, urgency, opportunity, fear, and ambition can all rush in at once. And if we are not anchored, even a sincere heart can drift.

This week introduces wisdom as a stabilizing force. Like a buoy in open water, it keeps you from being pulled by every wave or current. Wisdom does not rush. It listens. It tests. It waits. It asks better questions before taking bigger steps.

You may already sense that some decisions feel heavier now. The stakes are higher. The consequences longer lasting. This is not a sign of fear. It is a sign of growth. Mature faith learns to slow down, not speed up.

Wisdom does not replace hearing God. It protects it. It keeps His voice clear when emotions run high. It helps you discern peace from pressure. Conviction from impulse. Calling from escape.

This week invites you to pause before reacting. To involve Scripture, counsel, self awareness, and prayer. To recognize that God often confirms His direction through alignment, not urgency.

As you move through this chapter, ask yourself where you may be reacting instead of discerning. Where you may be forcing instead of trusting. Where you may need to let wisdom hold you steady.

Because the goal is not just to hear God.

It is to walk with Him wisely.

Chapter 34

FRIENDSHIP AND SURRENDER: THE FOUNDATION OF HEARING GOD

ICEBREAKER QUESTIONS

1. When you think about hearing God, do you naturally think about *methods* or *relationship* first?
2. What usually competes most for your attention when you try to spend time with God?
3. How comfortable are you with simply being present with God without an agenda?

BIBLE PASSAGE

John 15:15 (NIV)

[15] I no longer call you servants, because a servant does not know his master's business. Instead, I have called you friends, for everything that I learned from my Father I have made known to you.

Psalm 97:9 (NIV)

For you, LORD, are the Most High over all the earth;

　you are exalted far above all gods.

Matthew 1:23 (NIV)

"The virgin will conceive and give birth to a son, and they will call him Immanuel"[a] (which means "God with us").

Questions

1. How does knowing that God calls you a friend, is sovereign over all, and is fully present with you (Immanuel) change the way you listen for His voice and trust His direction in everyday decisions?

   _____

   _____

2. What would it look like for you to be still before God, love Him fully, and offer what's already in your hand—your time, gifts, or obedience—as an act of loving Him and others right where you are?

   _____

   _____

SECTION 1 – Hearing God Begins with Friendship, Not Formula

　One of the most common misunderstandings about hearing God is the belief that it begins with mastering spiritual techniques. Many believers assume that clearer communication with God comes from praying longer, journaling better, or following a specific spiritual process. While spiritual disciplines are valuable, Scripture consistently reveals that God's voice flows most clearly through relationship, not routine. Jesus fundamentally reframed how His followers relate to God when He declared that they were no longer servants but friends. This shift is significant because servants obey without insight, but friends are invited into understanding, trust, and shared purpose. Friendship assumes access, familiarity, and ongoing conversation. God does not simply issue instructions; He reveals His heart.

Throughout Scripture, God speaks to those who walk closely with Him. Moses spoke with God face to face, Elijah heard Him in a gentle whisper, and Abraham was called God's friend. These examples demonstrate that hearing God is not reserved for the spiritually elite but for those who cultivate intimacy. God is presented as both exalted and near—fully sovereign and yet personally present. This dual reality invites believers to approach God with reverence and closeness at the same time. When believers rush through prayer or treat time with God as a task to complete, intimacy is limited. Friendship requires presence, listening, and unhurried attention. God desires conversation, not performance. As intimacy grows, God's voice becomes more recognizable, steady, and familiar. Hearing God clearly begins not with striving to hear better, but with learning to stay close.

Observation Questions

1. What does Jesus mean when He calls His followers friends instead of servants?

   _____

   _____

2. How does friendship change the expectation of how God communicates?

   _____

   _____

Application Questions

1. How might your prayer life change if you approached God primarily as a friend?

   _____

   _____

2. What distractions most often rush your time with God?

   _____

   _____

SECTION 2 – Surrender and Rest Create the Environment for God's Voice

While friendship opens the door to hearing God, surrender creates the environment where His voice can be trusted and followed. Scripture teaches that intimacy with God cannot grow where control dominates. The story of Moses' staff provides a powerful picture of this truth. What Moses held tightly was ordinary and lifeless, but when he released it, God transformed it. This pattern reveals a spiritual principle: what we grip for control often loses life, while what we surrender becomes available for God's power. Many believers unknowingly block clarity by clinging tightly to identity, income, influence, or outcomes. Control feels safe, but it limits dependence.

Striving often disguises itself as responsibility, productivity, or faithfulness, yet Scripture repeatedly calls believers into rest and trust. Stillness is not inactivity; it is alignment. When God commands His people to "be still," He is inviting them to stop relying on their own strength and recognize His sufficiency. Striving clouds discernment because it amplifies fear, urgency, and self-reliance. Rest restores clarity because it re-centers trust in God's provision and character. Identity was never meant to be built on performance, and purpose does not emerge from hustle. Purpose grows out of intimacy. When believers cease striving and surrender control, spiritual noise quiets. God's voice becomes clearer when hearts release pressure and learn to rest in relationship. Surrender is not loss—it is the doorway to life, clarity, and deeper trust.

Observation Questions

1. What does Moses' staff illustrate about surrender and control?

   _____

   _____

2. Why does striving often feel necessary even when God calls for rest?

   _____

   _____

Application Questions

1. What is one area where you may be gripping too tightly instead of trusting God?

   _____

   _____

2. What would it look like to rest in God's provision instead of striving for control?

HEARING GOD – PERSONAL REFLECTION

1. Do you find it easier to work *for* God or to walk *with* God? Why?

2. What might God be inviting you to release so intimacy with Him can deepen?

Chapter 35

God's Voice Through People: Correction, Confirmation, and Community

ICEBREAKER QUESTIONS

1. Has someone ever spoken truth into your life that was difficult to hear but ultimately helpful?

2. Do you find it harder to lovingly confront others or to receive correction yourself?

3. How connected do you feel to spiritual community when making important decisions?

BIBLE PASSAGE

2 Samuel 12:1–7 (NIV)

12 The LORD sent Nathan to David. When he came to him, he said, "There were two men in a certain town, one rich and the other poor. ² The rich man had a very large number of sheep and cattle, ³ but the poor man had nothing except one little ewe lamb he had bought. He raised it, and it grew up with him and his children. It shared his food, drank from his cup and even slept in his arms. It was like a daughter to him.

⁴ "Now a traveler came to the rich man, but the rich man refrained from taking one of his own sheep or cattle to prepare a meal for the traveler who had come to him. Instead, he took the ewe lamb that belonged to the poor man and prepared it for the one who had come to him."

⁵ David burned with anger against the man and said to Nathan, "As surely as the LORD lives, the man who did this must die! ⁶ He must pay for that lamb four times over, because he did such a thing and had no pity."

⁷ Then Nathan said to David, "You are the man! This is what the LORD, the God of Israel, says: 'I anointed you king over Israel, and I delivered you from the hand of Saul.

John 16:12–13 (NIV)

"I have much more to say to you, more than you can now bear. ¹³ But when he, the Spirit of truth, comes, he will guide you into all the truth. He will not speak on his own; he will speak only what he hears, and he will tell you what is yet to come.

Questions

1. Why do you think David was able to see injustice so clearly in Nathan's story but struggled to recognize the same sin in his own life, and how does God still use trusted voices to reveal truth to us today?

   _____

   _____

2. How do Proverbs 27 and John 16 together show the difference between harmful criticism and loving correction, and what role do the Holy Spirit and godly relationships play in sharpening your character and guiding you into truth?

   _____

   _____

SECTION 1 – God Speaks Through Loving Correction

One of the most consistent yet resisted ways God speaks is through correction delivered by other people. While many believers desire private, unmistakable direction from God, Scripture repeatedly shows that God often chooses relationship as His primary channel of communication. Community is not optional for spiritual growth; it is essential for spiritual clarity. The story of David and Nathan illustrates this powerfully. David was a man after God's own heart, yet in a season of unchecked sin, he became spiritually blind. Despite being surrounded by people, only one person was willing to speak truth.

Nathan's approach reveals the heart of godly correction. He did not confront David with accusation or humiliation. Instead, he invited David to see truth for himself through a story, allowing conviction to rise before defense. When Nathan declared, "You are the man," the goal was not condemnation but restoration. God's correction is never meant to crush; it is meant to rescue. Blind spots grow strongest in isolation and power, but correction brings them into the light. When believers resist correction, hearts harden quietly. When correction is received humbly, alignment is restored. God speaks through correction to protect His people from paths that lead away from Him. True spiritual maturity includes the willingness to hear truth even when it challenges comfort, pride, or self-perception.

Observation Questions

1. Why was David unable to recognize his own sin without Nathan's intervention?

   _____

   _____

2. How did Nathan's method of confrontation reflect God's heart?

   _____

   _____

3. What does this story reveal about the danger of unchecked blind spots?

   _____

   _____

4. Why is correction an act of love rather than punishment?

   _____

   _____

5. How does Scripture describe the outcome of receiving godly correction?

   _____

   _____

Application Questions

1. Who has permission to speak hard truth into your life when needed?

_____

_____

2. How do you typically respond when confronted—defensiveness or reflection?

_____

_____

3. What step can you take to remain teachable and open to correction?

_____

_____

SECTION 2 – God Confirms His Voice Through Community

In addition to correction, God often speaks through confirmation. Confirmation is God's gracious way of strengthening trust when obedience feels difficult or unclear. Scripture shows that God does not rush His people into decisions without support; instead, He patiently repeats His guidance through multiple channels. Often, God first whispers direction internally... through Scripture, prayer, or peace... and later confirms it externally through people, circumstances, or provision. This repetition is not because God is unclear, but because He is compassionate.

Confirmation protects believers from doubt, fear, and self-deception. When the same message is echoed through godly voices, confidence grows and obedience becomes steadier. John's Gospel reminds us that the Holy Spirit guides believers into truth progressively, not all at once. God confirms His voice because He understands human hesitation. He reassures rather than pressures. Community becomes the environment where discernment is sharpened and faith is strengthened. Ignoring confirmation often delays obedience, while embracing it deepens trust. God never intended His people to discern alone. Through relationships, He refines direction, stabilizes hearts, and reinforces clarity.

Observation Questions

1. Why does God often repeat His guidance through different people?

_____

_____

2. How does confirmation strengthen trust and confidence in God's leading?

_____

_____

3. What role does the Holy Spirit play in guiding believers into truth over time?

_____

_____

4. Why is community essential for healthy discernment?

_____

_____

5. How does confirmation prevent impulsive or fear-driven decisions?

_____

_____

Application Questions

1. Where might God already be confirming something He has spoken to you?

_____

_____

2. How can you intentionally invite godly counsel into your decision-making?

_____

_____

3. What would obedience look like if you trusted God's confirmations fully?

_____

_____

HEARING GOD – PERSONAL REFLECTION

1. How open are you to hearing God through correction as well as encouragement?
2. Where might God be using people around you to clarify or confirm His direction?

Chapter 36

Clearing the Signal: Barriers, Discernment, and Divine Clarity

ICEBREAKER QUESTIONS

1. What tends to create the most "noise" in your life—busyness, emotions, distractions, or unresolved issues?

2. Have you ever sensed God speaking but felt unsure because of confusion or internal conflict?

3. What helps you slow down enough to become more spiritually attentive?

BIBLE PASSAGES

Luke 10:41–42 (NIV)

[41] "Martha, Martha," the Lord answered, "you are worried and upset about many things, [42] but few things are needed—or indeed only one.[a] Mary has chosen what is better, and it will not be taken away from her."

Isaiah 59:2 (NIV)

But your iniquities have separated
    you from your God;
your sins have hidden his face from you,
    so that he will not hear.

Questions

1. According to Luke 10 and Isaiah 59, what internal distractions or heart conditions can interfere with hearing God's voice, and what choices do these passages show us must come *before* clarity and direction can come?

_____

_____

SECTION 1 – Removing the Barriers That Dull Spiritual Hearing

God is always speaking, but spiritual clarity is often hindered by internal and external barriers rather than divine silence. Scripture shows that distraction, emotional turbulence, and unresolved issues can crowd the heart and dull sensitivity to God's voice. One of the most subtle yet powerful barriers is busyness. In the story of Mary and Martha, Jesus does not rebuke Martha for doing wrong things, but for being distracted by many things. Busyness often feels responsible and productive, yet it quietly replaces intimacy with activity. When worth becomes tied to productivity, stillness begins to feel uncomfortable and unnecessary.

Another major barrier is sin… not only outward behavior, but inward attitudes such as pride, anger, judgment, control, and unforgiveness. These internal postures create spiritual interference that distorts perception and clouds discernment. Scripture teaches that sin separates—not relationally from God, but experientially from His voice. Confession restores clarity by bringing what is hidden into the light. God does not call His people to confession to produce shame, but to restore alignment and peace. When barriers are named and removed, spiritual hearing sharpens. Clearing the signal often begins with honest evaluation rather than deeper effort. God's voice becomes clearer when distractions are reduced and the heart is brought back into alignment.

Observation Questions

1. Why does busyness often feel productive while quietly diminishing intimacy with God?

_____

_____

2. What does the story of Mary and Martha reveal about distraction and focus?

_____

_____

3. How do internal attitudes like pride or unforgiveness affect spiritual discernment?

_____

_____

4. Why does Scripture connect confession with clarity rather than condemnation?

_____

_____

5. What barriers most commonly interfere with hearing God clearly?

_____

_____

Application Questions

1. What distractions are currently crowding your spiritual attention?

_____

_____

2. Are there any attitudes or unresolved issues God may be inviting you to bring into the light?

_____

_____

3. What practical step could help reduce noise and restore focus this week?

_____

_____

SECTION 2 – Discernment Grows Through Stillness, Testing, and Trust

Even when barriers are addressed, discernment still requires patience and intentional slowing. Scripture reveals that hearing God is not an instant process but a relational rhythm built through waiting, testing, and trust. In Acts 13, spiritual leaders sensed the Holy Spirit speaking, yet they did not rush forward. Instead, they paused, worshiped, fasted, and prayed again. Their response demonstrates spiritual maturity—valuing clarity over speed. God is not offended by the need for confirmation; He welcomes it.

Stillness plays a critical role in this process. Habakkuk intentionally withdrew, climbed the watchtower, and waited to hear from God. Waiting requires trust and restraint. It involves quieting the body, calming the soul, and resisting the urge to fill silence with activity. Journaling and reflection become powerful tools in discernment, allowing believers to process what they sense God is saying and test it against Scripture. Over time, patterns emerge, confidence grows, and spiritual clarity deepens. God confirms His voice through Scripture, peace, timing, and godly counsel. Slowing down does not delay obedience; it strengthens it. Discernment matures when believers prioritize alignment over urgency and trust God's pace rather than forcing outcomes.

Observation Questions

1. Why did the leaders in Acts 13 choose to pause instead of act immediately?

   _____

   _____

2. How does stillness create space for clearer discernment?

   _____

   _____

3. What role does testing play in spiritual maturity?

   _____

   _____

4. Why is waiting an act of trust rather than passivity?

   _____

   _____

5. How does Scripture guide believers in confirming what they hear?

   _____

   _____

Application Questions

1. Where might God be inviting you to slow down before moving forward?

   _____

   _____

2. What practices help you test what you believe God is saying?

   _____

   _____

3. How can you create margin for stillness and reflection in your daily life?

_____

_____

HEARING GOD – PERSONAL REFLECTION
1. What internal or external noise most often interferes with your ability to hear God?

2. How might slowing down and clearing distractions help sharpen your spiritual discernment?

Week 13

Living Tuned In

This week is not about learning something new.

It is about living what you already know.

By now, you have learned how God speaks. You have practiced slowing down. You have identified barriers, tested His voice, sought wisdom, welcomed correction, and learned to recognize when striving is replacing trust. This week brings all of that together.

Week 13 is about integration.

It is the moment where hearing God moves from a study into a lifestyle. Where intimacy, surrender, community, rest, and discernment begin to work together instead of separately. You are no longer just asking, "Can I hear God?" You are learning how to stay tuned in when life gets loud, decisions get heavier, and obedience costs more.

These chapters are not meant to overwhelm you. They are meant to anchor you. They remind you that hearing God clearly is not about perfection, speed, or spiritual performance. It is about relationship. About staying close. About remaining honest. About being willing to pause, release control, and listen again.

This is also a moment of preparation.

Before moving into the bonus week, which will take everything deeper and slower, this week helps you recognize what it looks like to walk daily with God's voice guiding you. Not just in prayer time, but in relationships. In decisions. In correction. In rest. In surrender.

As you move through this final core week, notice what feels settled in you. Notice what still feels tender. Notice where God may be inviting you to trust Him more fully.

You are not finishing something here.

You are stepping into a way of living.

And the deeper journey begins next.

Bonus Chapter 1 - Judges Chapter 6

From Fear, to Calling, to Trusting God's Voice

ICEBREAKER QUESTIONS

1. Have you ever felt overlooked, underqualified, or like you were the wrong person for something important?
2. When life feels overwhelming, do you tend to face it head-on or retreat and hide?
3. Have you ever sensed God nudging you to do something that felt uncomfortable, inconvenient, or scary?

BIBLE PASSAGE

Before discussing, read Judges Chapter 6 in its entirety. This chapter shows the pattern of God speaking, people responding in fear, and God patiently leading them toward obedience and trust. Judges 6 reveals how God calls ordinary people, meets them in their insecurity, and speaks clearly even when they struggle to believe Him.

Judges Chapter 6 (NIV) Gideon

6 The Israelites did evil in the eyes of the LORD, and for seven years he gave them into the hands of the Midianites. [2] Because the power of Midian was so oppressive, the Israelites prepared shelters for themselves in mountain clefts, caves and strongholds. [3] Whenever the Israelites planted their crops, the Midianites, Amalekites and other eastern peoples invaded the country. [4] They camped on the land and ruined the crops all the way to Gaza and did not spare a living thing for Israel, neither sheep nor cattle nor donkeys. [5] They came up with their livestock and their tents like swarms of locusts. It was impossible to count them or their camels; they invaded the land to ravage it. [6] Midian so impoverished the Israelites that they cried out to the LORD for help.

[7] When the Israelites cried out to the LORD because of Midian, [8] he sent them a prophet, who said, "This is what the LORD, the God of Israel, says: I brought you up out of Egypt, out of the land of slavery. [9] I rescued you from the hand of the Egyptians. And I delivered you from the hand of all your oppressors; I drove them out before you and gave you their land. [10] I said to you, 'I am the LORD your God; do not worship the gods of the Amorites, in whose land you live.' But you have not listened to me."

[11] The angel of the LORD came and sat down under the oak in Ophrah that belonged to Joash the Abiezrite, where his son Gideon was threshing wheat in a winepress to keep it from the Midianites. [12] When the angel of the LORD appeared to Gideon, he said, "The LORD is with you, mighty warrior."

[13] "Pardon me, my lord," Gideon replied, "but if the LORD is with us, why has all this happened to us? Where are all his wonders that our ancestors told us about when they said, 'Did not the LORD bring us up out of Egypt?' But now the LORD has abandoned us and given us into the hand of Midian."

[14] The LORD turned to him and said, "Go in the strength you have and save Israel out of Midian's hand. Am I not sending you?"

[15] "Pardon me, my lord," Gideon replied, "but how can I save Israel? My clan is the weakest in Manasseh, and I am the least in my family."

[16] The LORD answered, "I will be with you, and you will strike down all the Midianites, leaving none alive."

[17] Gideon replied, "If now I have found favor in your eyes, give me a sign that it is really you talking to me. [18] Please do not go away until I come back and bring my offering and set it before you."

And the LORD said, "I will wait until you return."

¹⁹ Gideon went inside, prepared a young goat, and from an ephah[a] of flour he made bread without yeast. Putting the meat in a basket and its broth in a pot, he brought them out and offered them to him under the oak.

²⁰ The angel of God said to him, "Take the meat and the unleavened bread, place them on this rock, and pour out the broth." And Gideon did so. ²¹ Then the angel of the LORD touched the meat and the unleavened bread with the tip of the staff that was in his hand. Fire flared from the rock, consuming the meat and the bread. And the angel of the LORD disappeared. ²² When Gideon realized that it was the angel of the LORD, he exclaimed, "Alas, Sovereign LORD! I have seen the angel of the LORD face to face!"

²³ But the LORD said to him, "Peace! Do not be afraid. You are not going to die."

²⁴ So Gideon built an altar to the LORD there and called it The LORD Is Peace. To this day it stands in Ophrah of the Abiezrites.

²⁵ That same night the LORD said to him, "Take the second bull from your father's herd, the one seven years old.[b] Tear down your father's altar to Baal and cut down the Asherah pole[c] beside it. ²⁶ Then build a proper kind of[d] altar to the LORD your God on the top of this height. Using the wood of the Asherah pole that you cut down, offer the second[e] bull as a burnt offering."

²⁷ So Gideon took ten of his servants and did as the LORD told him. But because he was afraid of his family and the townspeople, he did it at night rather than in the daytime.

²⁸ In the morning when the people of the town got up, there was Baal's altar, demolished, with the Asherah pole beside it cut down and the second bull sacrificed on the newly built altar!

²⁹ They asked each other, "Who did this?"

When they carefully investigated, they were told, "Gideon son of Joash did it."

³⁰ The people of the town demanded of Joash, "Bring out your son. He must die, because he has broken down Baal's altar and cut down the Asherah pole beside it."

³¹ But Joash replied to the hostile crowd around him, "Are you going to plead Baal's cause? Are you trying to save him? Whoever fights for him shall be put to death by morning! If Baal really is a god, he can defend himself when someone breaks down his altar." ³² So because Gideon broke down Baal's altar, they gave him the name Jerub-Baal[f] that day, saying, "Let Baal contend with him."

³³ Now all the Midianites, Amalekites and other eastern peoples joined forces and crossed over the Jordan and camped in the Valley of Jezreel. ³⁴ Then the Spirit of the LORD came on Gideon, and he

blew a trumpet, summoning the Abiezrites to follow him. ³⁵ He sent messengers throughout Manasseh, calling them to arms, and also into Asher, Zebulun and Naphtali, so that they too went up to meet them.

³⁶ Gideon said to God, "If you will save Israel by my hand as you have promised— ³⁷ look, I will place a wool fleece on the threshing floor. If there is dew only on the fleece and all the ground is dry, then I will know that you will save Israel by my hand, as you said." ³⁸ And that is what happened. Gideon rose early the next day; he squeezed the fleece and wrung out the dew—a bowlful of water.

³⁹ Then Gideon said to God, "Do not be angry with me. Let me make just one more request. Allow me one more test with the fleece, but this time make the fleece dry and let the ground be covered with dew." ⁴⁰ That night God did so. Only the fleece was dry; all the ground was covered with dew.

SECTION 1 - Israel's Pattern and God's Response (Judges 6:1–10)

Judges 6 opens with a cycle that feels painfully familiar. The people of Israel once again do evil in the sight of the Lord, and as a result, they are given over to the Midianites. This oppression is not mild or occasional. It is crushing. The Midianites strip Israel of food, livestock, and security year after year. The Israelites plant crops knowing they will be destroyed. They work knowing their work will be taken from them. Fear shapes how they live, where they live, and how they survive. They hide in caves, dens, and strongholds, constantly bracing for loss.

Eventually, after years of suffering, the Israelites cry out to the Lord. And this is where the chapter slows down in an important way. God does not immediately remove the Midianites. He sends a prophet first. Through the prophet, God reminds Israel of who He is and what He has already done. He reminds them that He brought them out of Egypt, delivered them from slavery, and gave them the land they now occupy.

God identifies the real issue. It is not that He has gone silent. It is not that He has abandoned them. The issue is that they did not obey His voice. Before God deals with the external oppression, He addresses the internal condition of their hearts. God speaks truth before He brings rescue. He calls them back to remembering Him before He changes their circumstances.

Observation Questions

1. What specific hardships do the Israelites experience under Midian's control?

_____

_____

2. How does fear influence where the Israelites live and how they survive?

_____

_____

3. What does God remind Israel of through the prophet before offering deliverance?

_____

_____

4. According to verse 10, what does God identify as the real issue behind their suffering?

_____

_____

Application Questions

1. Why do you think God addresses obedience and remembrance before bringing relief?

_____

_____

2. Are there areas in your life where fear has shaped your habits, decisions, or expectations?

_____

_____

3. What might it look like to pause and listen for God's voice before asking Him to change your circumstances?

_____

_____

SECTION 2 - God Finds Gideon Hiding (Judges 6:11–24)

God's response to Israel's cry does not begin with an army or a dramatic miracle. It begins quietly with one man hiding. Gideon is threshing wheat in a winepress, an unusual and inefficient place to do that work. He is hiding because fear has taught him that visibility equals danger. He is trying to survive without being seen.

This is exactly where the angel of the Lord finds him. And the first words spoken to Gideon feel almost shocking. The Lord is with you, mighty man of valor. Gideon does not feel mighty. He does not feel brave. He feels forgotten, weak, and insignificant. He immediately points to circumstances. If the Lord is with us, why has all this happened? Where are all His miracles?

God does not rebuke Gideon for his honesty. He does not dismiss his doubts. Instead, God speaks purpose into Gideon before Gideon feels ready. God calls him based on who he will become, not who he believes himself to be in that moment. God's voice cuts through Gideon's fear and insecurity with identity and calling.

Observation Questions

1. Where is Gideon physically when God speaks to him, and what does that reveal about his fear?

   _____

   _____

2. What title does God give Gideon, and how does it contrast with Gideon's self image?

   _____

   _____

3. What doubts does Gideon express about God's presence and past faithfulness?

   _____

   _____

4. How does God respond to Gideon's insecurity and questioning?

   _____

   _____

Application Questions

1. What labels have you placed on yourself that may conflict with how God sees you?

   _____

   _____

2. What fears might be keeping you hidden instead of stepping into obedience?

   _____

   _____

3. How would your daily decisions change if you truly believed the Lord is with you?

_____

_____

SECTION 3 - Obedience Starts Privately (Judges 6:25–32)

Before Gideon is ever called to lead publicly, God gives him a private assignment. God asks Gideon to tear down his father's altar to Baal and cut down the Asherah pole beside it. This assignment is deeply personal. It affects Gideon's household, reputation, and safety. It is not a heroic public moment. It is quiet, risky obedience.

Gideon obeys, but he does so at night because he is afraid. Scripture does not hide this detail. God does not demand fearless obedience. He honors willing obedience. Gideon's obedience stirs conflict, but it also reveals God's protection. When the people demand Gideon's death, Gideon's father defends him, pointing out that if Baal is truly a god, he should be able to defend himself.

God begins dismantling false worship before delivering Israel. Gideon's first victory is not over Midian. It is over idolatry.

Observation Questions

1. What is the first task God gives Gideon after calling him?

   _____

   _____

2. Why is this assignment personally dangerous and uncomfortable for Gideon?

   _____

   _____

3. How does Gideon obey, and what does this reveal about his faith?

   _____

   _____

4. How do the people respond, and how does God protect Gideon?

   _____

   _____

Application Questions

1. Are there altars in your life competing with God for trust or devotion?

   _____

   _____

2. Is there something God has asked you to surrender privately before acting publicly?

_____

_____

3. What small act of obedience might God be asking of you right now?

_____

_____

SECTION 4 - God Empowers Gideon (Judges 6:33–35)

After Gideon obeys, the Spirit of the Lord comes upon him. This moment marks a shift. Gideon moves from hiding to leadership. The same man who was afraid to be seen now blows the trumpet and summons Israel to follow him. God does not remove fear by eliminating risk. He replaces fear with His presence.

Gideon's confidence does not come from personality or experience. It comes from empowerment. God equips those He calls.

Observation Questions

1. What happens when the Spirit of the Lord comes upon Gideon?

_____

_____

2. How does Gideon's role change compared to earlier in the chapter?

_____

_____

Application Questions

1. Where do you need God's strength instead of relying on your own abilities?

_____

_____

2. What does trusting God's timing look like in your current season?

_____

_____

SECTION 5 - The Fleece and God's Patience (Judges 6:36–40)

Even after obedience and empowerment, Gideon still seeks reassurance. He asks God for signs, not once but twice. God responds with patience. He does not shame Gideon for his questions. He meets him where he is.

This moment reminds us that faith can coexist with uncertainty. Gideon's questions do not cancel his calling. They become part of his growth process. God remains steady even when Gideon wavers.

Observation Questions

1. Why does Gideon ask God for a sign?

   _____

   _____

2. How does God respond to Gideon's requests?

   _____

   _____

3. What does this reveal about God's patience and character?

   _____

   _____

Application Questions

1. Do you wait for certainty before obeying God?

   _____

   _____

2. How can you take steps of faith even while still unsure?

   _____

   _____

HEARING GOD - PERSONAL REFLECTION

1. Where in your life might God be speaking even though you feel unready or insecure?
2. How do you personally discern and trust God's voice when fear tries to speak louder?

Bonus Chapter 2 - Judges Chapter 7

Hearing God's Voice When His Direction Doesn't Make Sense

ICEBREAKER QUESTIONS

1. Have you ever watched a plan shrink instead of grow, even though you were convinced it needed to get bigger to succeed?

2. Do you find it harder to trust God when His instructions feel illogical, uncomfortable, or risky?

3. What helps you stay grounded when you are unsure how things will turn out?

BIBLE PASSAGE

Before discussing, read Judges Chapter 7 in its entirety. This chapter continues the story of Gideon and reveals a powerful truth about hearing God's voice. Judges 7 shows us that God does not always speak in ways that feel safe, logical, or strategic by human standards. Instead, He often speaks in ways that remove our ability to rely on ourselves. This chapter teaches us how God refines trust, strips away false confidence, and confirms His voice even when obedience feels risky

Judges Chapter 7 (NIV) Gideon Defeats the Midianites

7 Early in the morning, Jerub-Baal (that is, Gideon) and all his men camped at the spring of Harod. The camp of Midian was north of them in the valley near the hill of Moreh. ² The LORD said to Gideon, "You have too many men. I cannot deliver Midian into their hands, or Israel would boast against me, 'My own strength has saved me.' ³ Now announce to the army, 'Anyone who trembles with fear may turn back and leave Mount Gilead.'" So twenty-two thousand men left, while ten thousand remained.

⁴ But the LORD said to Gideon, "There are still too many men. Take them down to the water, and I will thin them out for you there. If I say, 'This one shall go with you,' he shall go; but if I say, 'This one shall not go with you,' he shall not go."

⁵ So Gideon took the men down to the water. There the LORD told him, "Separate those who lap the water with their tongues as a dog laps from those who kneel down to drink." ⁶ Three hundred of them drank from cupped hands, lapping like dogs. All the rest got down on their knees to drink.

⁷ The LORD said to Gideon, "With the three hundred men that lapped I will save you and give the Midianites into your hands. Let all the others go home." ⁸ So Gideon sent the rest of the Israelites home but kept the three hundred, who took over the provisions and trumpets of the others.

Now the camp of Midian lay below him in the valley. ⁹ During that night the LORD said to Gideon, "Get up, go down against the camp, because I am going to give it into your hands. ¹⁰ If you are afraid to attack, go down to the camp with your servant Purah ¹¹ and listen to what they are saying. Afterward, you will be encouraged to attack the camp." So he and Purah his servant went down to the outposts of the camp. ¹² The Midianites, the Amalekites and all the other eastern peoples had settled in the valley, thick as locusts. Their camels could no more be counted than the sand on the seashore.

¹³ Gideon arrived just as a man was telling a friend his dream. "I had a dream," he was saying. "A round loaf of barley bread came tumbling into the Midianite camp. It struck the tent with such force that the tent overturned and collapsed."

¹⁴ His friend responded, "This can be nothing other than the sword of Gideon son of Joash, the Israelite. God has given the Midianites and the whole camp into his hands."

¹⁵ When Gideon heard the dream and its interpretation, he bowed down and worshiped. He returned to the camp of Israel and called out, "Get up! The LORD has given the Midianite camp into your hands." ¹⁶ Dividing the three hundred men into three companies, he placed trumpets and empty jars in the hands of all of them, with torches inside.

¹⁷ "Watch me," he told them. "Follow my lead. When I get to the edge of the camp, do exactly as I do. ¹⁸ When I and all who are with me blow our trumpets, then from all around the camp blow yours and shout, 'For the LORD and for Gideon.'"

¹⁹ Gideon and the hundred men with him reached the edge of the camp at the beginning of the middle watch, just after they had changed the guard. They blew their trumpets and broke the jars that were in their hands. ²⁰ The three companies blew the trumpets and smashed the jars. Grasping the torches in their left hands and holding in their right hands the trumpets they were to blow, they shouted, "A sword for the LORD and for Gideon!" ²¹ While each man held his position around the camp, all the Midianites ran, crying out as they fled.

²² When the three hundred trumpets sounded, the LORD caused the men throughout the camp to turn on each other with their swords. The army fled to Beth Shittah toward Zererah as far as the border of Abel Meholah near Tabbath. ²³ Israelites from Naphtali, Asher and all Manasseh were called out, and they pursued the Midianites. ²⁴ Gideon sent messengers throughout the hill country of Ephraim, saying, "Come down against the Midianites and seize the waters of the Jordan ahead of them as far as Beth Barah."

So all the men of Ephraim were called out and they seized the waters of the Jordan as far as Beth Barah. ²⁵ They also captured two of the Midianite leaders, Oreb and Zeeb. They killed Oreb at the rock of Oreb, and Zeeb at the winepress of Zeeb. They pursued the Midianites and brought the heads of Oreb and Zeeb to Gideon, who was by the Jordan.

SECTION 1 - God Reduces the Army (Judges 7:1–3)

Judges 7 opens with Gideon finally positioned for battle. From the outside, it looks like progress. The army has gathered. The enemy is visible. Momentum is building. But God speaks again, and His voice immediately challenges what feels logical.

God tells Gideon that the army is too large. Not because Midian is small, but because Israel's hearts are vulnerable. God knows that if the people win with overwhelming numbers, they will claim the victory for themselves. He says plainly that Israel would boast, saying their own hand saved them.

God's solution is not strategy. It is exposure. He instructs Gideon to release anyone who is fearful. Fear is acknowledged, not shamed, but it cannot remain. Twenty two thousand men leave. In one moment, what felt strong becomes small.

This is often how God speaks. He removes what we think we need so we can learn to trust what He has already promised.

Observation Questions

1. Why does God say the army is too large?

_____

_____

2. What does God identify as the real danger in winning with many people?

_____

_____

3. How many men leave when fear is addressed?

_____

_____

4. What does this reveal about fear and obedience?

_____

_____

Application Questions

1. Where might God be removing something you depend on too heavily?

_____

_____

2. How do you respond when God's direction feels like loss instead of progress?

_____

_____

3. What fears might God be inviting you to release before moving forward?

_____

_____

SECTION 2 - God Reduces the Army Again (Judges 7:4–8)

Even after the massive reduction, God speaks again and says the army is still too large. This time, there is no explanation, only instruction. Gideon is told to bring the men to the water. God will choose who stays and who goes.

The method makes no sense militarily. Men are separated based on how they drink water. No battle readiness test. No strength assessment. Only obedience. When the process is finished, only three hundred men remain.

At this point, Gideon has no option but to trust God fully. There is no room left for confidence in numbers or planning. God has intentionally reduced Gideon to total dependence.

This section reminds us that God does not always explain His reasoning when He speaks. Hearing God's voice often requires obedience before understanding.

Observation Questions

1. What instruction does God give Gideon at the water?

   _____

   _____

2. How many men remain after the second reduction?

   _____

   _____

3. What explanations does God give, and what does He withhold?

   _____

   _____

4. What does this teach us about trusting God without clarity?

   _____

   _____

Application Questions

1. How do you respond when God gives direction without explanation?

   _____

   _____

2. What security might God be asking you to surrender?

   _____

   _____

3. What would obedience look like even without understanding?

   _____

   _____

SECTION 3 - God Reassures Gideon (Judges 7:9–15)

Even after Gideon obeys everything God has said, fear still lingers. God does not rebuke him. Instead, God reassures him. He invites Gideon to go down to the enemy camp and listen.

What Gideon hears is unexpected. An enemy soldier shares a dream, and its meaning is clear. God has already delivered Midian into Gideon's hands. The enemy knows it. Fear has shifted.

This confirmation does not come through instruction, but through reassurance. When Gideon hears it, his response is worship. God meets Gideon right where his fear still lives.

Observation Questions

1. What does God offer Gideon when fear remains?

   _____

   _____

2. What does the dream reveal about the enemy's mindset?

   _____

   _____

3. How does this confirm what God has already spoken?

   _____

   _____

4. Why does Gideon respond with worship?

   _____

   _____

Application Questions

1. How has God reassured you in moments of fear?

   _____

   _____

2. What does worship communicate about trust?

   _____

   _____

3. Where might God be quietly confirming His word to you?

   _____

   _____

SECTION 4 - Victory Through Obedience (Judges 7:16–22)

The battle plan is simple and strange. Trumpets. Pitchers. Torches. No swords. Gideon tells the men to watch him and do exactly what he does.

When they obey, God moves. Confusion breaks out in the enemy camp. The Midianites turn on one another and flee. Israel does not fight. God does.

This victory belongs fully to the Lord. Obedience activates God's power. Gideon's role was to listen and respond.

Observation Questions

1. What instructions does Gideon give the three hundred men?

_____

_____

2. What weapons do they carry, and what do they lack?

_____

_____

3. How does God bring victory without direct combat?

_____

_____

4. What does this show about obedience and power?

_____

_____

Application Questions

1. Where might God be asking you to obey without full understanding?

_____

_____

2. How does obedience clarify God's voice over time?

_____

_____

3. What step of obedience might unlock breakthrough for you?

_____

_____

SECTION 5 - The Aftermath and God's Faithfulness (Judges 7:23–25)

After the victory, the rest of Israel joins the pursuit. What began with reduction ends with unity. God proves faithful not only in victory, but in the process that led there.

Judges 7 reminds us that God often speaks through reduction before restoration. Through surrender before celebration. Through trust before triumph.

Observation Questions

1. How does Israel respond after the victory?

    _____

    _____

2. What does this reveal about God's faithfulness?

    _____

    _____

3. How does Judges 7 complete the preparation begun in Judges 6?

    _____

    _____

Application Questions

1. What past victories remind you that God is faithful?

    _____

    _____

2. How does remembering God's faithfulness strengthen trust today?

    _____

    _____

3. Where might God be preparing you for something ahead?

    _____

    _____

HEARING GOD - PERSONAL REFLECTION

1. Where in your life does God's direction feel illogical right now?
2. What would it look like to trust God fully, even if the plan keeps getting smaller?

Bonus Chapter 3 - 2 Samuel 12:1–25

Hearing God's Voice When It Confronts, Convicts, and Calls Us Back

BIBLE PASSAGE

Before discussing, read 2 Samuel 12:1–25 in its entirety. This passage shows how God speaks through confrontation, truth, consequence, and restoration. God does not remain silent in David's sin. He sends a messenger, speaks clearly, exposes the heart, disciplines with justice, and still offers mercy. This chapter reveals that hearing God's voice is not only about comfort and direction, but also about correction, repentance, and transformation.

2 Samuel 12:1–25 (NIV) Nathan Rebukes David

12 The LORD sent Nathan to David. When he came to him, he said, "There were two men in a certain town, one rich and the other poor. ²The rich man had a very large number of sheep and cattle, ³but the poor man had nothing except one little ewe lamb he had bought. He raised it, and it grew up with him and his children. It shared his food, drank from his cup and even slept in his arms. It was like a daughter to him.

⁴"Now a traveler came to the rich man, but the rich man refrained from taking one of his own sheep or cattle to prepare a meal for the traveler who had come to him. Instead, he took the ewe lamb that belonged to the poor man and prepared it for the one who had come to him."

⁵David burned with anger against the man and said to Nathan, "As surely as the LORD lives, the man who did this must die! ⁶He must pay for that lamb four times over, because he did such a thing and had no pity."

⁷ Then Nathan said to David, "You are the man! This is what the LORD, the God of Israel, says: 'I anointed you king over Israel, and I delivered you from the hand of Saul. ⁸ I gave your master's house to you, and your master's wives into your arms. I gave you all Israel and Judah. And if all this had been too little, I would have given you even more. ⁹ Why did you despise the word of the LORD by doing what is evil in his eyes? You struck down Uriah the Hittite with the sword and took his wife to be your own. You killed him with the sword of the Ammonites. ¹⁰ Now, therefore, the sword will never depart from your house, because you despised me and took the wife of Uriah the Hittite to be your own.'

¹¹ "This is what the LORD says: 'Out of your own household I am going to bring calamity on you. Before your very eyes I will take your wives and give them to one who is close to you, and he will sleep with your wives in broad daylight. ¹² You did it in secret, but I will do this thing in broad daylight before all Israel.'"

¹³ Then David said to Nathan, "I have sinned against the LORD."

Nathan replied, "The LORD has taken away your sin. You are not going to die. ¹⁴ But because by doing this you have shown utter contempt for[a] the LORD, the son born to you will die."

¹⁵ After Nathan had gone home, the LORD struck the child that Uriah's wife had borne to David, and he became ill. ¹⁶ David pleaded with God for the child. He fasted and spent the nights lying in sackcloth[b] on the ground. ¹⁷ The elders of his household stood beside him to get him up from the ground, but he refused, and he would not eat any food with them.

¹⁸ On the seventh day the child died. David's attendants were afraid to tell him that the child was dead, for they thought, "While the child was still living, he wouldn't listen to us when we spoke to him. How can we now tell him the child is dead? He may do something desperate."

¹⁹ David noticed that his attendants were whispering among themselves, and he realized the child was dead. "Is the child dead?" he asked.

"Yes," they replied, "he is dead."

²⁰ Then David got up from the ground. After he had washed, put on lotions and changed his clothes, he went into the house of the LORD and worshiped. Then he went to his own house, and at his request they served him food, and he ate.

²¹ His attendants asked him, "Why are you acting this way? While the child was alive, you fasted and wept, but now that the child is dead, you get up and eat!"

²² He answered, "While the child was still alive, I fasted and wept. I thought, 'Who knows? The LORD may be gracious to me and let the child live.' ²³ But now that he is dead, why should I go on fasting? Can I bring him back again? I will go to him, but he will not return to me."

²⁴ Then David comforted his wife Bathsheba, and he went to her and made love to her. She gave birth to a son, and they named him Solomon. The LORD loved him; ²⁵ and because the LORD loved him, he sent word through Nathan the prophet to name him Jedidiah.

SECTION 1 - God Speaks Through Loving Confrontation (2 Samuel 12:1–7)

This chapter begins with a sentence that should stop us. The Lord sent Nathan unto David. God does not stay silent. He does not look away. He does not excuse David's position, influence, or past faithfulness. God sends a voice.

Nathan does not begin with accusation. He begins with a story. A story that draws David in emotionally. A rich man. A poor man. One little lamb. Something precious, personal, and deeply loved. David listens. He feels anger. He calls for justice. He is confident in his judgment.

And then Nathan speaks one of the most piercing sentences in Scripture. Thou art the man.

This is what it looks like when God speaks in truth. Not to shame, but to expose. David could see sin clearly when it belonged to someone else. But God lovingly turns the mirror toward him. God's voice in this moment is direct, unmistakable, and personal.

God reminds David of everything He has given him. Protection. Position. Provision. Favor. God's voice is not harsh, but it is honest. He names the sin. He calls it what it is. He makes it clear that this is not a misunderstanding. This is disobedience.

This section shows us something we often resist. God's voice does not only comfort. Sometimes it confronts. And when it does, it is an invitation back, not a sentence of rejection.

Observation Questions

1. Who does God send to speak to David, and why is that significant?

   _____

   _____

2. Why do you think Nathan begins with a story instead of an accusation?

   _____

   _____

3. How does David initially respond to the story, and what does that reveal about his heart?

_____

_____

4. What is the impact of Nathan saying, Thou art the man?

_____

_____

5. What does God remind David of before naming the sin?

_____

_____

Application Questions

1. How do you typically respond when God's voice confronts something in your life?

_____

_____

2. Are there areas where you recognize sin more easily in others than in yourself?

_____

_____

3. What would it look like to receive God's correction as an act of love instead of rejection?

_____

_____

SECTION 2 - Conviction, Consequences, and a Repentant Heart (2 Samuel 12:8–14)

After Nathan says, Thou art the man, God continues speaking with clarity and weight. He reminds David of what He has already done. God says, I anointed thee king. I delivered thee. I gave thee. I protected thee. I provided for thee. And then He says something that is easy to miss if we rush past it. If that had been too little, I would moreover have given unto thee such and such things. God is not just pointing out David's sin. He is revealing David's distrust.

David did not take because God withheld. He took because he stopped listening. He despised the commandment of the Lord. That word despised is strong. It shows us that sin is not accidental ignorance. It is a moment when we decide our desire matters more than God's voice.

God then names the consequences. The sword shall never depart from thine house. What David did in secret will be exposed. This is not God being cruel. This is God being just. His voice does not only forgive. It also corrects. Love does not ignore the damage sin causes.

And then David speaks. There are no excuses. No explanations. No shifting blame. He simply says, I have sinned against the Lord. That sentence matters. It is short. It is honest. It is surrendered.

Immediately, God responds. The Lord also hath put away thy sin. Thou shalt not die. Forgiveness is real. Restoration is possible. But consequence still remains. The child will die. This is one of the hardest truths about hearing God's voice. Repentance restores relationship, but it does not always remove earthly consequences.

This section shows us the full weight of conviction. God speaks truth. David responds in humility. God forgives. And God still allows the cost of disobedience to be felt. Hearing God's voice means trusting Him even when obedience is painful.

Observation Questions

1. What does God remind David of before explaining the consequences of his sin?

   _____

   _____

2. What does the phrase despised the commandment of the Lord reveal about the nature of David's sin?

   _____

   _____

3. How does God describe the consequences that will follow David's actions?

   _____

   _____

4. How does David respond when confronted directly with his sin?

   _____

   _____

5. What does God immediately say after David confesses?

   _____

   _____

Application Questions

1. How do you typically respond when God exposes something uncomfortable in your life?

2. Do you trust God's forgiveness even when consequences remain?

_____

_____

3. What does true repentance look like in your own words and actions right now?

_____

_____

SECTION 3 - Seeking God in the Middle of Pain (2 Samuel 12:15–18)

After Nathan leaves, the weight of God's words settles into David's life in a very real way. The child becomes sick. This is where the story moves from confrontation to suffering. David does not argue with God. He does not harden his heart. Instead, he turns fully toward Him.

David besought God for the child. He fasted. He lay all night upon the earth. This is not performance. This is desperation. David is not trying to manipulate God. He is throwing himself completely on God's mercy. He knows God's character. He knows God can still move. And so he prays with everything he has.

The elders try to lift him up, but David refuses. He will not eat. He will not be comforted by people. He stays in that place of surrender. This section shows us that hearing God's voice does not mean we stop praying when the outcome feels uncertain. David already knows what God said, but he still prays. He still fasts. He still hopes.

This is an important tension to sit with. God has spoken. The consequence has been named. And yet David continues to seek Him. That tells us something about David's relationship with God. God's voice did not push David away. It drew him closer.

When the child dies on the seventh day, the servants are afraid to tell David. They watched his grief while the child was alive. They assume the pain will only deepen. This moment captures the fear we often have when we imagine facing the finality of loss. But David's response surprises everyone.

This section reminds us that God's voice is not only heard in instruction or discipline. It is also heard in grief, waiting, and unanswered prayers. David stays connected to God even when the outcome is not what he hoped for.

Observation Questions

1. How does David respond when the child becomes sick?

   _____

   _____

2. What actions show David's posture of humility and dependence on God?

   _____

   _____

3. Why do you think David continues to pray even after hearing God's judgment?

   _____

   _____

4. How do the elders and servants respond to David's grief?

   _____

   _____

5. What does this section reveal about David's relationship with God during suffering?

   _____

   _____

Application Questions

1. How do you respond when God's answer does not align with your hope?

   _____

   _____

2. Are there situations where you stop praying because you assume the outcome is fixed?

   _____

   _____

3. What does it look like for you to seek God fully even when the situation feels painful or uncertain?

   _____

   _____

SECTION 4 - Accepting God's Will and Returning to Worship

When David sees that his servants are whispering, he knows the child is dead. He asks them directly, and they tell him the truth. What happens next is one of the most striking moments in this chapter. David rises from the earth. He washes himself. He anoints himself. He changes his clothes. Then he goes into the house of the Lord and worships.

This is not emotional detachment. This is surrender. David's actions show a clear shift. While the child was alive, David fasted and pleaded for mercy. Once God's decision was clear, David accepted it. He did not turn away from God. He turned toward Him.

This moment teaches us something profound about hearing God's voice. Sometimes God speaks through discipline. Sometimes He speaks through loss. And sometimes the clearest evidence that we have heard Him is our willingness to worship even when the outcome hurts.

David's worship does not mean the pain disappeared. It means he trusted God's character more than his circumstances. He knew who God was before the blessing, during the waiting, and after the loss. His relationship with God was not conditional on getting the answer he wanted.

The servants are confused by David's behavior. To them, it does not make sense. They expected grief to increase, not soften. But David explains something that reveals deep spiritual maturity. While the child was alive, there was still hope. Now that the child is gone, David accepts the reality of God's will. He cannot bring the child back, but he knows that one day he will go to the child.

This section shows us that hearing God's voice includes knowing when to plead and knowing when to rest. It includes discerning the difference between fighting for mercy and accepting God's final word. David models both.

Observation Questions

1. How does David respond when he learns that the child has died?

   _____

   _____

2. What actions show David's return to normal life and worship?

   _____

   _____

3. Why do the servants struggle to understand David's response?

4. What does David's explanation reveal about his faith and perspective on life and death?

_____

_____

5. How does worship play a role in David's healing process?

_____

_____

Application Questions

1. How do you typically respond when an outcome is final and painful?

_____

_____

2. What does worship look like for you when God's will is hard to accept?

_____

_____

3. Are there areas in your life where God may be inviting you to move from striving into surrender?

_____

_____

SECTION 5 - Restoration, Hope, and God's Continued Purposes (2 Samuel 12:21–25)

After David worships, he returns to his house and asks for food. His servants are still trying to understand the shift they are witnessing. David explains that while the child was alive, he fasted and wept because there was still a possibility of mercy. But now that the child is gone, David accepts that God's word has been spoken. He acknowledges a truth that is both sobering and hopeful. The child will not return to him, but one day David will go to the child. This statement reveals David's eternal perspective. His grief is real, but it is not without hope.

The chapter does not end with loss. It moves toward restoration. David comforts Bathsheba, his wife. She conceives again and gives birth to a son. They name him Solomon. Scripture tells us that the

Lord loved him. God sends word through Nathan the prophet and gives Solomon another name, Jedidiah, which means beloved of the Lord.

This is one of the most powerful truths in the entire passage. Even after sin, confrontation, consequence, and loss, God is still present. God is still speaking. God is still loving. God is still writing the story. David's failure did not cancel God's purposes. Discipline did not mean abandonment. Loss did not mean rejection.

This section teaches us that hearing God's voice is not only about conviction and correction. It is also about restoration and future hope. God does not leave David in shame. He leads him forward. The same God who spoke through Nathan in confrontation now speaks blessing over the next generation.

God's love for Solomon is not a reward for David's perfection. It is a reflection of God's grace. The chapter closes with the reminder that God's voice does not stop speaking after discipline. It continues to guide, restore, and affirm His purposes.

Observation Questions

1. How does David explain his actions to his servants after the child's death?

   _____

   _____

2. What does David mean when he says he will go to the child one day?

   _____

   _____

3. How does God show continued involvement in David and Bathsheba's lives?

   _____

   _____

4. What is significant about God loving Solomon and giving him a name through Nathan?

   _____

   _____

5. What does this ending reveal about God's character after judgment has taken place?

   _____

   _____

Application Questions

1. How does this passage reshape the way you view God after failure or loss?

_____

_____

2. Are there places in your life where God may be inviting you to move forward instead of staying stuck in shame?

_____

_____

3. What does it look like to trust that God is still writing your story even after painful consequences?

_____

_____

HEARING GOD – PERSONAL REFLECTION

1. Is there an area of your life where God has already spoken clearly, but you have been resisting, justifying, or minimizing what He is saying? Take a quiet moment and ask God to show you what honest repentance and surrender would look like there.

2. When you think about God's voice, do you associate it more with fear and punishment or with truth that leads to restoration? Ask God to help you listen without hiding and to trust that His correction is always rooted in love.

Bonus Chapter 5 - Luke 14:15–23

Hearing God's Invitation and Responding Without Excuses

ICEBREAKER QUESTIONS

1. Have you ever felt invited into something meaningful but hesitated because of timing, comfort, or fear?

2. What kinds of responsibilities or distractions most often compete for your attention?

3. How do you usually respond when God's invitation stretches you beyond what feels convenient?

BIBLE PASSAGE

Before discussing, read Luke 14:15–23 in its entirety. This passage captures Jesus teaching about God's invitation to His kingdom and the subtle ways people decline that invitation through excuses, distractions, and misplaced priorities. It reveals how hearing God's voice is not just about listening, but about responding.

Luke 14:15–23 (NIV) The Parable of the Great Banquet

¹⁵ When one of those at the table with him heard this, he said to Jesus, "Blessed is the one who will eat at the feast in the kingdom of God."

¹⁶ Jesus replied: "A certain man was preparing a great banquet and invited many guests. ¹⁷ At the time of the banquet he sent his servant to tell those who had been invited, 'Come, for everything is now ready.'

¹⁸ "But they all alike began to make excuses. The first said, 'I have just bought a field, and I must go and see it. Please excuse me.'

¹⁹ "Another said, 'I have just bought five yoke of oxen, and I'm on my way to try them out. Please excuse me.'

²⁰ "Still another said, 'I just got married, so I can't come.'

²¹ "The servant came back and reported this to his master. Then the owner of the house became angry and ordered his servant, 'Go out quickly into the streets and alleys of the town and bring in the poor, the crippled, the blind and the lame.'

²² "'Sir,' the servant said, 'what you ordered has been done, but there is still room.'

²³ "Then the master told his servant, 'Go out to the roads and country lanes and compel them to come in, so that my house will be full.

SECTION 1 - The Invitation Is Clear (Luke 14:15–17)

This passage begins with someone making a well meaning spiritual statement. "Blessed is he that shall eat bread in the kingdom of God." In response, Jesus tells a story that shifts the focus from admiration to action. The man in the parable prepares a great supper and invites many guests. Everything is ready. Nothing is missing. The invitation is clear and direct. "Come; for all things are now ready."

What stands out immediately is that the invitation is not rushed or incomplete. The meal is prepared. The table is set. The timing is intentional. This reflects the heart of God. When He speaks and invites, He does not do it impulsively or carelessly. God prepares. God plans. God makes room. His invitation is rooted in readiness and generosity.

Hearing God's voice often begins this way. It is not dramatic or confusing. It is an invitation to step into what He has already prepared. The problem in this story is not a lack of clarity. The problem is not that God failed to communicate. The invitation was clear. The issue comes in how people respond to it.

This section reminds us that God's voice is often heard through an open door rather than a command. It is an invitation to participate in His purposes. When God says "Come," He is not asking us to create something on our own. He is inviting us into something He has already made ready.

Observation Questions

1. What prompted Jesus to tell this parable?

   _____

   _____

2. How is the invitation described in verses 16 and 17?

_____

_____

3. What does the phrase "all things are now ready" reveal about the host?

   _____

   _____

4. Who is responsible for delivering the invitation in the story?

   _____

   _____

5. What does this tell us about how God communicates His invitations?

   _____

   _____

Application Questions

1. How do you usually respond when God's invitation feels clear but disruptive to your plans?

   _____

   _____

2. Are there areas in your life where God may be saying "Come," but you are hesitating?

   _____

   _____

3. What would it look like to trust that God has already prepared what He is inviting you into?

   _____

   _____

SECTION 2 - Excuses Reveal Priorities (Luke 14:18–20)

After the invitation is delivered, the response is striking. "They all with one consent began to make excuse." There is unity here, but not the good kind. Every invited guest responds with a reason why they cannot come. None of the excuses sound sinful or rebellious on the surface. They sound reasonable. They sound responsible. They sound like everyday life.

One person has purchased land and wants to inspect it. Another has invested in oxen and needs to test them. Another has just gotten married. Each excuse represents something legitimate, yet each one becomes a barrier to responding to the invitation. This is where the parable becomes deeply personal. These people did not reject the invitation because they were hostile. They rejected it because they were distracted.

Jesus is revealing something important about how people miss God's voice. It is rarely because they do not believe in Him. It is often because other voices are louder. Responsibilities, investments, relationships, and personal priorities slowly take precedence. None of these things are evil, but when they outrank obedience, they become excuses.

What is also significant is that the invitation had already been accepted earlier. These guests were "bidden" before the meal was ready. They had already said yes in theory. When the moment came to act, their lives were too full. This reflects how easy it is to admire God's kingdom while resisting the cost of participation.

Hearing God's voice requires more than agreement. It requires availability. This section exposes how quickly convenience can silence obedience and how easily good things can crowd out the best thing.

Observation Questions

1. What phrase describes how the guests responded to the invitation?

   _____

   _____

2. What reasons do the guests give for declining?

   _____

   _____

3. What do these excuses have in common?

   _____

   _____

4. Why do you think Jesus chose ordinary responsibilities as the excuses in this story?

   _____

   _____

5. What does this reveal about how people often miss God's invitation?

   _____

   _____

Application Questions

1. What kinds of excuses are most tempting for you when God invites you to step out in faith?

   _____

   _____

2. Are there good things in your life that may be crowding out obedience?

   _____

   _____

3. How can you begin to recognize when responsibility turns into resistance?

   _____

   _____

SECTION 3 - The Invitation Expands (Luke 14:21)

When the servant returns and reports the excuses, the response of the master is immediate and emotional. Scripture says the master of the house was angry. This is not petty anger. This is the grief and righteous frustration of a host whose generosity has been dismissed. The table is set. The food is ready. The invitation was sincere. And yet those who were first invited chose other things.

Instead of canceling the banquet, the master expands the invitation. He instructs the servant to go quickly into the streets and lanes of the city and bring in the poor, the maimed, the halt, and the blind. This moment reveals the heart of God. Rejection does not stop His plan. It redirects it.

The people now being invited are the ones society overlooks. They are not powerful, impressive, or self sufficient. They are aware of their need. They are not distracted by possessions or status. They are ready because they know they have nothing to lose. This is often who hears God most clearly. Those who are empty tend to recognize an invitation as grace, not inconvenience.

This section confronts the idea that proximity or familiarity with God guarantees responsiveness. The first invited guests were close enough to receive the invitation, yet far too busy to accept it. Meanwhile, those on the margins respond with humility and openness. God's voice is not reserved for the qualified. It is received by the willing.

Observation Questions

1. How does the master respond emotionally to the excuses?

   _____

   _____

2. Who does the master instruct the servant to invite next?

   _____

   _____

3. What do these newly invited people have in common?

   _____

   _____

4. Why do you think Jesus highlights physical and social limitations in this group?

   _____

   _____

5. What does this reveal about who is often most receptive to God's voice?

   _____

   _____

Application Questions

1. Do you see yourself more in the original invitees or the ones brought in from the streets?

   _____

   _____

2. How does awareness of need affect your openness to God?

   _____

   _____

3. What might God be inviting you into that requires humility rather than readiness?

   _____

   _____

SECTION 4 - Compelled to Come In (Luke 14:22–23)

After gathering people from the streets and lanes, the servant returns again and says something important. He tells the master, "Lord, it is done as thou hast commanded, and yet there is room."

This sentence reveals the abundance of God's grace. Even after rejection and redirection, the table is still not full. God's invitation is generous, expansive, and intentional. There is still room.

The master's response is striking. He does not say to wait. He does not say the effort is good enough. Instead, he sends the servant even farther out, into the highways and hedges, and tells him to compel them to come in, so that his house may be filled. This is not force or coercion. It is urgency born out of desire. God wants His house filled. He wants people to experience fellowship, provision, and belonging.

Those in the highways and hedges represent outsiders even farther removed. These are people who likely assume the invitation is not for them. They may hesitate. They may doubt. They may feel unworthy or suspicious of generosity that feels too good to be true. That is why they must be compelled. Not pressured, but persuaded. Not shamed, but reassured.

This moment reflects how God often speaks. His voice does not just invite once and walk away. He pursues. He repeats. He reassures. He sends confirmation after confirmation because He knows how quickly insecurity and fear talk us out of obedience. God's desire is not partial participation. He wants fullness. He wants response. He wants hearts that say yes, even when they feel undeserving.

Observation Questions

1. What does the servant report after inviting people from the streets and lanes?

   _____

   _____

2. What does the phrase "yet there is room" reveal about the master's heart?

   _____

   _____

3. Where does the master send the servant next?

   _____

   _____

4. Why might those in the highways and hedges hesitate to accept the invitation?

   _____

   _____

5. What does this section teach about God's persistence?

   _____

   _____

Application Questions

1. Have you ever assumed God's invitation was not meant for you?

_____

_____

2. How do doubt or insecurity keep you from fully responding to God's voice?

_____

_____

3. What might it look like to say yes without needing further reassurance?

_____

_____

SECTION 5 - The Cost of Refusal (Luke 14:24)

Jesus ends this parable with a sobering statement. "For I say unto you, That none of those men which were bidden shall taste of my supper." These words are not angry, but they are firm. The original invitation was real. The opportunity was genuine. But excuses revealed hearts that were unwilling to respond. The issue was never logistics. It was priority.

Those first invited were not excluded because they were busy. They were excluded because they chose other things over the invitation. They valued possessions, productivity, and relationships more than presence. And once the invitation passed, it did not return. This verse reminds us that delayed obedience is still disobedience. A postponed yes is often a quiet no.

God's voice is patient, but it is also purposeful. When He speaks, it is an invitation into relationship, alignment, and transformation. Ignoring that voice has consequences. Not because God is harsh, but because refusing His invitation hardens the heart. Over time, excuses turn into distance. Familiarity turns into indifference. And opportunities to respond become easier to dismiss.

This final verse forces an honest question. How often do we hear God speak and think, later? How often do we sense Him inviting us into something deeper and respond with delay instead of devotion? God's invitation is generous, but it is not casual. It asks for response. It asks for trust. It asks for surrender now, not someday.

Observation Questions

1. What does Jesus say about those who were originally invited?

   _____

   _____

2. Why do you think Jesus ends the parable with such a firm conclusion?

   _____

   _____

3. What does this verse reveal about the seriousness of responding to God's invitation?

   _____

   _____

4. How does this verse contrast with the generosity shown earlier in the parable?

   _____

   _____

Application Questions

1. Are there invitations from God you have delayed instead of declined outright?

   _____

   _____

2. What excuses tend to surface when God asks for obedience?

   _____

   _____

3. What would immediate obedience look like in your life right now?

   _____

   _____

HEARING GOD – PERSONAL REFLECTION

1. Where might God be inviting you deeper, even now, and what excuses are competing for your attention? Sit quietly and ask God to show you what needs to be reordered.

2. When you sense God speaking, do you respond quickly or do you negotiate with Him? Ask God to help you trust His invitation enough to say yes without delay.

Bonus Chapter 6 – Exodus 20:18-21

Hearing God through other people instead of god himself

One of the things I've shared before is how we handle hand-me-downs in our family.

Every year, as my son Kyle grows, we give his clothes to my sister for her son, Calen, who is only two years younger.

And there is absolutely nothing wrong with hand-me-downs.

But someone once shared an analogy with me that completely changed the way I hear God's voice.

They said listening to a sermon to hear from God can be like wearing hand-me-downs. They're good. They work. They've helped someone else grow. But when you receive a brand-new revelation directly from God, it carries a different kind of power. It fits you. It's personal. It's fresh.

That analogy hit me deeply… because for the longest time, that was exactly how I was engaging with Scripture.

For nearly twenty years, I never truly read the Bible for myself.

I listened to sermons every single day. I heard pastors explain Scripture. I learned the Bible through other people's revelation. I told myself I was "reading the Bible," but in reality, I was listening to someone else tell me what it said.

And if I'm being honest, I hated reading the Bible myself.

But because of this analogy, I forced myself to do it anyway.

I realized I didn't want to live on spiritual hand-me-downs anymore. I wanted to hear God's voice directly. I wanted fresh revelation… not just borrowed insight.

So I began reading the Bible myself, even when I didn't feel like it. Even when it was uncomfortable. Even when it felt slower than listening to a sermon.

And what I discovered changed everything.

The passage you're about to read speaks directly to this truth—the importance of not discarding a single word, of holding onto what God speaks personally to you. It's about valuing fresh revelation, not replacing it, not shortcutting it, and not settling for secondhand insight when God is inviting you into firsthand relationship.

Read this passage slowly. Don't rush it. Don't outsource it. Because what God speaks directly to you will always carry a power no hand-me-down ever could.

BIBLE PASSAGE

This study explores why the Israelites chose to hear God **through Moses** instead of hearing God **for themselves**, and how that decision affects our ability to hear God's voice today.

Exodus 20:18–21 (NIV)

[18] When the people saw the thunder and lightning and heard the trumpet and saw the mountain in smoke, they trembled with fear. They stayed at a distance [19] and said to Moses, "Speak to us yourself and we will listen. But do not have God speak to us or we will die."

[20] Moses said to the people, "Do not be afraid. God has come to test you, so that the fear of God will be with you to keep you from sinning."

[21] The people remained at a distance, while Moses approached the thick darkness where God was.

SECTION 1 - Why Some People See God Move but Never Hear Him Speak

When God finished giving the Ten Commandments, something revealing happened…not in the words God spoke, but in how the people responded to His presence. This moment explains why so many people struggle to hear God's voice for themselves.

Exodus 20:18–21 shows us a spiritual fork in the road.

The passage begins by describing the scene: thunder, lightning, the sound of a trumpet, smoke covering the mountain. This was not chaos. This was revelation. God was making His presence unmistakably clear. He was not hiding. He was drawing near.

But instead of responding with trust, the people responded with fear.

Scripture says *they trembled*. Fear was not just an emotion… it became a filter. When fear takes over, people misinterpret God. What was meant to invite them closer felt threatening instead.

Then comes the first critical decision: *they stood at a distance.*

This was not accidental. Distance is always a choice. Spiritually, distance reduces clarity. When you stay far back, you can still see movement, but you lose intimacy. You hear noise, but you miss nuance. That is exactly what happens when people keep God at arm's length. They still believe in Him. They still acknowledge His power. But they don't let Him get close enough to speak personally.

Next, they turn to Moses.

They don't say they don't want God. They say, *"You speak to us, and we will listen."*

In other words: "Moses, you go be close to God. You hear Him. You carry the weight of His presence. Then come back and tell us what He said."

This is the birth of secondhand faith.

They were willing to obey instructions that came through Moses, but they were unwilling to experience God directly themselves. They wanted the benefit of God's voice without the vulnerability of God's presence.

This is where the hand-me-down analogy fits perfectly.

They were choosing spiritual hand-me-downs. Revelation that didn't come from their own encounter. Faith that wasn't tailored to them. It might cover them for a season, but it would never truly fit. And eventually, they would outgrow it… or resent it.

Then they say the line that reveals their deepest fear:

"Do not let God speak to us, lest we die."

They believed God's closeness would destroy them.

And here's the truth: **something does die in the presence of God—but it's not what they thought.**

Flesh dies. Control dies. Pride dies. Self-reliance dies.

And that's not a loss… that's freedom.

They weren't afraid of death. They were afraid of surrender.

Moses immediately corrects their misunderstanding. He tells them not to be afraid. God was not trying to destroy them. God was testing them… not to expose weakness, but to refine them. God's presence was meant to free them from sin, not trap them in fear.

Then comes the verse that defines everything.

"The people remained at a distance, but Moses drew near into the thick darkness where God was."

God was not in the noise. God was not in the spectacle. God was in the thick darkness… the place where control ends. The place where certainty fades. The place where trust is required.

The people chose distance because distance felt safer.

Moses chose closeness because closeness leads to relationship.

The people decided they wanted a relationship with God **through Moses**.

Moses decided he wanted a relationship with God **himself**.

That single decision determined the depth of relationship.

This is why Psalm 103 later says, *"He made known His ways to Moses, but His acts to the children of Israel."*

The people saw what God did.

Moses understood why God did it.

The people witnessed miracles.

Moses knew God's heart.

You can see God move and still not hear His voice clearly. But when you know God personally, His voice becomes familiar.

That's the danger of spiritual outsourcing. When you rely on someone else to hear God for you, you may learn what God does—but you will miss how He thinks.

God never intended for relationship to be mediated like that. You were redeemed for direct access.

Not hand-me-down faith. Not borrowed revelation. Not Moses standing in your place.

Hearing God's voice does not come from staying at a distance.

It comes from drawing near.

Even when it feels uncomfortable.

Even when it feels quiet.

Even when it feels like thick darkness.

Because God is there.

And when you choose closeness over distance, relationship over rules, and surrender over control, His voice becomes familiar.

That's how you hear God.

Observation Questions

1. What physical signs of God's presence are described in Exodus 20:18?

   _____

   _____

2. How did the people respond to God's presence physically and emotionally?

   _____

   _____

3. What specific request did the people make of Moses?

_____

_____

4. What contrast does verse 21 make between the people and Moses?

_____

_____

Application Questions

1. In what ways might you be relying on "spiritual hand-me-downs" instead of personal relationship?

_____

_____

2. Where have you chosen distance from God because closeness felt uncomfortable or costly?

_____

_____

3. What part of your "flesh" might God be inviting to die so new life can rise?

_____

_____

4. What would drawing nearer to God look like in your daily life right now?

_____

_____

HEARING GOD – PERSONAL REFLECTION

1. Do you want a relationship with God that stays safe and distant, or one that goes deep and personal?

2. What is one step you can take this week to stop outsourcing your relationship with God and begin hearing Him for yourself?

About the Author

Chantel Ray Finch is an author, speaker, and entrepreneur who is passionate about helping people recognize God's voice and live out their divine calling.

She founded one of the fastest-growing real estate companies in the nation before merging with a $2 billion organization. Through that journey, Chantel discovered that true success is not about striving, but about surrendering — learning to tune in to God's voice and trust His guidance in every season.

Chantel leads Bible studies, workshops, and mentoring groups that empower others to grow in faith, hear God clearly, and find freedom in every area of life. She is also the author of *Waist Away: The Chantel Ray Way*, *Fasting to Freedom*, and *Delegate Everything But Sex*.

Her work has inspired thousands through books, podcasts, and live events, helping people experience a deeper, more intimate relationship with God. Chantel lives in Sarasota, Florida, with her husband, Rhyan, where their mornings begin with prayer, Scripture, and coffee by the water.

Visit **TuneInGodsVoice.com** to learn more or join a Bible study.

Made in United States
Orlando, FL
02 February 2026

77698148R00223